THE HOOKED X

Key to the Secret History of North America

T0312896

THE HOOKED X
Key to the Secret History of North America

Scott F. Wolter, P.G.

NORTH STAR PRESS OF ST. CLOUD, INC.
St. Cloud, Minnesota

Dedication

To Darwin Ohman and Niven Sinclair
Two men who have defended their families'
legacies with dignity, honor, and, above all else, the truth.

. . . And to my Goddess, Janet

Cover Design: Andy Awes

All photographs were taken by the author unless otherwise noted.

Copyright © 2009 Scott Wolter
www.hookedx.com

ISBN: 0-87839-312-9
ISBN-13: 978-0-87839-312-1

Printed in the United States of America

Published by
North Star Press of St. Cloud, Inc.
St. Cloud, Minnesota

www.northstarpress.com

Table of Contents

Foreword

History needs to be rewritten.

The North American Continent is awash with evidence of pre-Columbian visitors who left their imprint on the landscape and their writing on stones and boulders as markers for those who followed. Ogham and Runic inscriptions tell a story of Celtic and Viking penetration into the very hinterland of the New World.

These early seafarers must have felt very much at home as they found one watercourse leading into another with a never-ending string of lakes replete with fish and waterfowl to meet their inner needs. They had found a Paradise—a garden of Eden.

Historians have been singularly slow in explaining the presence of runic inscriptions; they describe them as "fakes" which is a convenient excuse to hide their own ignorance. Fortunately, there are those who have been prepared to challenge such arbitrary findings so that we might have a better understanding of those who left their imprint on the land. One such man is Scott Wolter whose new book, *The Hooked X: Key to the Secret History of North America,* is a masterful combination of science and logic as well as being a gripping detective story that leaves no stone un-turned (literally as well as figuratively).

Scott's book is guaranteed to make us take a fresh look at the rich evidence that lies beneath our feet and which, even when discovered, has been brutally pushed aside by the academic establishment for no better reason than to protect the "status quo." We all owe him a debt of grati-tude for the perseverance and determination he has shown in bringing an important part of America's early history to light. In his book, he quotes an inscription found in the Sinclair family chapel at Rosslyn in Scotland. It ends with the words: "The truth conquers all." There can be no better summary to describe Scott's richly revealing and rewarding manuscript. It deserves to be read.

—Niven Sinclair

Introduction

This book is the culmination of a nine-year odyssey to understand the origin of a mysterious symbol that first appeared on a highly controversial century-old artifact called the Kensington Rune Stone. The discovery of the meaning of the Hooked X was stunning, as was the secret history behind it that gradually unfolded as I continued my quest to learn more about that history through research. This journey has been nothing short of amazing. To avoid confusion I should explain a couple of things. The first is that this book is in part a continuation of the narrative I wrote in the 2005 book, co-authored with Richard Nielsen, entitled, *The Kensington Rune Stone: Compelling New Evidence*. In addition to the presentation of factual evidence that was consistent with the Kensington Rune Stone having a medieval origin, I also wrote about the amazing experiences that happened from the day I was first hired to study the artifact in July of 2000.

As research continued, I wanted to write about the discoveries that came after the publication of the first book. Important aspects of the Kensington Rune Stone inscription presented in the first book, such as the dotted R, the "Grail" prayer, and certainly the Hooked X, along with the sacred geometry at the discovery site needed additional clarity. Never-before published discoveries provide additional support for the authenticity of the Kensington Rune Stone. This new evidence serves as the foundation upon which the case for the medieval origin of the Spirit Pond and Narragansett Rune Stones, as well as the Newport Tower in Rhode Island rests. Anything that helps validate the Kensington Rune Stone also validates the Hooked X, which also appears on the other four North American rune stones and ties them all together.

The Hooked X is also found in two other unexpected places: The Larsson Papers found in Sweden in 2004, and in Christopher Columbus's mysterious sigla. The evidence and analysis presented here suggests the origin of the symbol lies within the coded alphabet of secret societies that have been in existence since at least the early part of the twelfth century right through today.

My research traces the Hooked X along a path that begins in Minnesota and makes its first stop along the Atlantic Coast, where it is found on the three Spirit Pond Rune Stones discovered at Popham Beach, Maine, in 1971. All three runic inscriptions, believed by many scholars to be fakes, are carved with the Hooked X symbol being used for the letter "a." The Spirit Pond Map Stone has inscribed on it the words, "Vinland 1402, takes two days" with an arrow pointing south.

This took me to my next stop on the Hooked X journey. If a ship sailed two days south of the area depicted on the Map Stone at Popham Beach, Maine, it would be in the vicinity of Cape Cod, Massachusetts, and Narragansett Bay, Rhode Island. Curiously, another runic inscription was found carved on a large boulder in shallow water near the shore in Narragansett Bay. It also contains the Hooked X. This suggests that those who carved all five North American rune stones are somehow connected, considering that the Hooked X is not found on any of the thousands of known runic inscriptions that occur throughout Scandinavia.

On the other side of Narragansett Bay, in Newport, Rhode Island, stands a mysterious two-story stone structure called the Newport Tower. To this day, scholars debate its origin. I present my evidence, consistent with a medieval origin for the tower and its likely connection to the same parties who carved the runic inscriptions with the mysterious Hooked X. Amazingly, the final stop on the Hooked X journey in North America was discovered from evidence constructed within the Newport Tower and brings the story full-circle back to Kensington, Minnesota.

Another important discovery came from the dates of 1401 to 1402 A.D. on the Spirit Pond Rune Stones. These dates provide an important clue to the historical figure most likely connected to these rune stones and who is possibly the person responsible for construction of the Newport Tower. Prince Henry Sinclair, the first Earl of Orkney, Scotland, reportedly sailed with several ships to the New World in 1398. There is no known tomb or gravestone for him in his homeland, and his fate after this voyage is unknown. Since most current historians avow that there are no other known candidates who can be connected to Spirit Pond at that time, he became the logical focus.

In the case of the rune stones, Dick Nielsen's and my research on the Kensington Rune Stone indicates that the authors of these inscriptions were medieval Cistercian monks using the runic practice found on Gotland in the middle of the fourteenth century. I've made a concerted effort to try to understand the mindset of the Cistercians, as well as the military Order of the Knights Templar they formally established in 1128, who shared the same religious beliefs. I believe the Hooked X is a symbolic representation of those beliefs. Understanding their beliefs was paramount to the discoveries I've made, which included the realization that the continuation of that ideology thrives today.

Keep in mind the human toll the Kensington Rune Stone controversy had on the family of its discoverer, Olof Ohman. Not only did he endure decades of accusations, scorn, and ridicule, but his wife, Karin, and their nine children suffered as well. Two of their children committed suicide—David in 1929, and their oldest daughter, Amanda, in 1951, who took her own life, it appears, at least in part because of harassment by sometimes fanatical opponents. The grandchildren and great-grandchildren of Karin and Olof were shielded by the parents, aunts, and uncles, yet are still well aware of the hardships their family endured. The factual evidence we presented in our first book fully exonerated Olof, but whenever something new surfaces that further solidifies the case, I want to ensure it is published. This includes a previously unknown letter written by Olof Ohman that came to light after I gave a presentation to a Sons of Norway group in September of 2006. Olof wrote candidly in this letter about his most direct statement concerning his involvement in the controversy.

Several people have made important contributions to this research. Some figured prominently in the first book and continue to be involved, such as Darwin Ohman and Russell Fridley. However, over the past three years, I've met many new people as my investigation switched to the coast of New England. Their tremendous friendship and support have made this a profound personal experience.

The story for me began in July 2000, when I received a phone call from a representative of the Runestone Museum in Alexandria, Minnesota. They wanted to hire me for a forensic study of the artifact. The representative spoke about it as though I already knew what it was. In reality, I'd never heard of the Kensington Rune Stone. As a licensed geologist and operator of an independent material forensics laboratory called American Petrographic Services, Inc., in St. Paul, Minnesota, I typically tell people, "We perform autopsies on concrete and rock."

During that initial phone call, I told the representative this. "I'll be happy to perform this work for you." I further said, "But you need to understand that, after I complete the work, I may come back and give you news you're not going to like."

I can honestly say that, when I started the work that summer, I didn't know what the Kensington Rune Stone was and didn't care. I definitely care now, in part because of the strong negative backlash I received about my conclusion that the stone is a genuine medieval artifact by individuals from disciplines outside geology. I encountered blatant disrespect of my work by individuals who thought archaeology was the only discipline worthy of addressing the matter. The arguments against the Kensington Rune Stone made by these archaeologists were based on a supposed lack of evidence. I've concluded that, when anything that indicates European contact in North America prior to Columbus is found, some archaeologists are going to dismiss it as a hoax or simply ignore it. It's time this came to an end. However, I do thank these opponents. Their denials and dismissals fueled my passion to compile an irrefutable body of evidence they can not ignore.

In *The Kensington Rune Stone: Compelling New Evidence*, we touched briefly on the likely connections of the Kensington Rune Stone to the military orders like the Teutonic Knights and the Knights Templar. For the purposes of this book, the word "Templar" refers to all military orders aligned with the Cistercians both before and after the Knights Templar Order was put down in 1307. The Templars did not disappear after being suppressed; they simply went underground and continued on. Once I started going down what I like to call "the Templar Road," a dam of new information burst open. Perhaps the most illuminating event occurred after reading the works of historian, astronomer, and researcher Alan Butler.

Butler wrote *The Knights Templar Revealed*. It was an epiphany for me. I had finally found a source that helped clarify the alternate history of the Cistercians and the Knights Templar about which most academics are unaware of or chose not to address. I felt a strong connection to Butler's writing and immediately ordered four more books written by, or co-authored by, Butler, and I devoured them. Then Alan and John Ritchie's summary of the history of the survival of Judaic Christianity conveyed the essence of the motivation for the ideology that appears to have created the five rune stones with the Hooked X, the Newport Tower, and very likely a host of other sites and artifacts in North America yet to be properly investigated.

I was not the first to contemplate a possible Templar connection to the early exploration of North America. Writers such as William Mann, Steven Sora, Tim Wallace-Murphy, and Gérard Leduc were just a few. However, this was the first time the connection included so much tangible evidence that fit together in a logical and cohesive way. A lot more research needs to be performed and more artifacts studied to prove a connection. The big difference is that a sound hypothesis has now been formulated that exhibits strong plausibility and is consistent with historical facts. My ideas merit further study by scholars in relevant disciplines, such as archaeology, history, language, runology, and anthropology. The anchor of my research, the Kensington Rune Stone, has finally been established as a genuine medieval artifact. This fact demands that everything that related to it in North America also receive a complete re-examination.

Before I begin the story, I feel it is important to give the reader a summary of the Kensington Rune Stone evidence from the first book. This artifact serves as the foundation for my pursuit of additional evidence to explain who carved and buried the inscription in 1362 in what is now Minnesota, and most importantly, why.

Part I

Kensington Rune Stone Summary and New Evidence

1

The Kensington Rune Stone

The evidence presented in *The Kensington Rune Stone: Compelling New Evidence* consistent with the Kensington Rune Stone being a medieval artifact, was derived from multiple disciplines, including geology, runology, linguistics, history, religion, and above all else, logic. Employing basic logic to the vexing question of the stone's authenticity helped narrow the focus and simplify the objectives of our investigation. That logic is very simple. The Kensington Rune Stone is either a late nineteenth century hoax, or it's not. If it's not a hoax, it must be genuine. Since it is dated to 1362 A.D., the language, runes, grammar, dialect, and weathering of the inscription must be consistent with the fourteenth century and, therefore, authentic. The evidence presented in our book demonstrated that this is true.

Olof Ohman

The discoverer of the Kensington Rune Stone was Olof Ohman (1854 to 1935), a carpenter and farmer who immigrated to America from the town of Forsa in Hälsinglands, Sweden, in 1879. He married Karin Danielson (1862 to 1947) in 1886, who also emigrated from Forsa in 1885. They had nine children: seven sons and two daughters.

Ohman purchased land a mile and a half from the town of Kensington, Minnesota, where he would eventually discover the Kensington Rune Stone, in April of 1890.

The Discovery

In September of 1898, Olof and his two oldest sons, Olof, Jr., and Edward, were clearing trees on the easternmost end of their property. After they had cut the roots around the base of a twenty-five- to thirty-year-old aspen, they felled the tree with a winch. When the base of the tree was exposed, a 202-pound, rectangular stone was found tightly wrapped within the roots. According to twelve eye-witnesses who signed written affidavits, including Olof and his son, Edward, the roots were three and one-half inches wide and flattened from prolonged contact with the stone as they meandered across the back side of the stone and down into the ground. It was the younger son, Edward, who first noticed the inscriptions.

Their neighbor, Nils Flaaten (1845 to 1919), an immigrant from Tinn, Telemarken, Norway, was also clearing land adjacent to Ohman's on the day of the discovery and was called over moments later to see the find. Olof and his sons initially thought they had found an "Indian almanac," but soon realized the mysterious characters were runes. There was quite a commotion over the discovery. A few days later the stone was brought into Kensington where it was displayed in the jewelry store for a couple of months. Sometime in early December, the stone was returned to the Ohman farm where Olof made an attempt to figure out what the inscription said.

Based on his book collection and personal letters, it was clear Ohman was intelligent in spite of his lack of a formal education. He decided to seek help with the stone and made a hand-written copy of the inscription. His

The three Ohman family members who were present at the discovery of the Kensington Rune Stone were Olof Ohman (left), Olof, Jr. (middle), and Edward (right). (Photos courtesy of the Ohman family)

neighbor, John Hedberg, wrote a letter on January 1, 1899, for Ohman, explaining the situation in English. This was sent to Swan Turnblad, in Minneapolis, Minnesota, then publisher of the *Svenska Americanska Posten* newspaper. Turnblad took the inscription included with the letter to University of Minnesota professor of Scandinavian Languages, Olaus Breda.

Breda thought he saw some modern Swedish words and what he thought were a few English words. He didn't know what the pentadic numbers were (a numbering system analogous to finger counting using a vertical line called a stave, with horizontal bars and loops), and quickly concluded the Kensington Rune Stone was a "clumsy" hoax. Breda then sent a copy of Ohman's inscription to runic expert Professor Oluf Rygh in Oslo, Norway, who shared the copy with colleagues Sophus Bugge and Gustav Storm. These scholars sent a telegram to the *Minneapolis Tribune* on April 16, 1899, claiming that the inscription was a modern hoax.

These four runic experts proclaimed the Kensington Rune Stone a hoax solely after examining Ohman's copy of the inscription. They never examined the actual artifact. They saw as one of the most damning points against the inscription that the first word on the split side of the

Aerial view of the Ohman Farm taken in about 1995 indicates the approximate discovery site of the Kensington Rune Stone in 1898. (Photograph courtesy of the Douglas County, Minnesota, Parks Division)

stone, "har" (Have . . .), a modern Swedish word. The runic experts were right about that point because that is what was in the copy. However, that was not what was on the stone. There are two dots above the "a" making the word "här" (There are . . .), an *Old* Swedish word!

The word "här" suddenly became one of the strongest pieces of evidence to *support* a medieval origin. In October of 2003, Henrik Williams, runologist and professor of Scandinavian language in Uppsala, Sweden, wrote the following, ". . . therefore the origin of the Kensington Rune Stone in the 1300s should not be regarded as impossible as far as this point is concerned."

It is important to note that, if Ohman was the forger of the Kensington Rune Stone, why didn't he put the umlaut over the "a" in his copy? The reason he didn't is that he didn't see them, that he didn't know they were there, which is another reason to believe he did not carve the stone. Ironically, while innocently trying to find out more information, Ohman inadvertently created his own nightmare.

The events that followed in the days after the discovery have been blurred by time and a relative lack of documentation. However, the veracity of the discovery is supported by physical evidence that was documented during my geological examination of the artifact in 2000.

Geological Evidence

The Kensington Rune Stone was first brought to my laboratory at American Petrographic Services, Inc., by the Runestone Museum in

The first four runic experts to study the inscription examined a copy made by Olof Ohman in 1899. The first word on the split side of the stone in the copy (left) is "har," a modern Swedish word meaning "have." The actual word on the stone (right) is "här," an Old Swedish word for "there are." (Left photo courtesy of the American Swedish Institute; right courtesy Wolter, 2003)

Alexandria, Minnesota, on July 14, 2000. In addition to an overall examination of both the inscription and the stone itself, a 1.5-inch-diameter by two-inch core sample was obtained from the back side of the stone, along with a small chip sample taken from the split, or dressed side. The following statements represent my conclusions about the most important physical aspects of the stone.

Rock Type and Origin—The Kensington Rune Stone is a tabular-shaped, dark-gray, meta-graywacke glacial erratic boulder approximately thirty-one by sixteen by five inches. Based upon the mineralogy and geological textures, the stone likely originated from the Paleoproterozoic (roughly 1.8 to 2.1 billion years before present) Animikie Basin of East-Central Minnesota.

Root leaching—The two white lineations on the back side of the stone are consistent with prolonged contact with young tree roots. Because of the striking similarity of the root leaching pattern on the stone and the sketches made by three first-hand witnesses (Olof Ohman in July 1901, Olof Ohman, Jr., in April 1957, and Sam Olson in March 1910), who all saw the roots around the stone, I concluded with reasonable certainty that the root leaching was made by the tree under which the stone was found.

Retooling—The scratching out of the runes with a nail (retooling), reportedly by Olof Ohman shortly after the discovery, led to confusion and bias. The scratches give the inscription a distinct, fresh-looking, recently carved appearance. However, close inspection of the characters reveals weathering along the unscratched sides or walls of the grooves.

Split side—The flat side of the stone that contains the last three lines of the inscription has a different color, texture, and weathering profile than the rest of the glacial-aged surfaces. The edges around the perimeter of this side of the stone contain several rounded fractures produced by purposeful impact. These impacts are consistent with a part of the original larger stone being intentionally broken off prior to carving the last three lines of the inscription. The entire split side exhibits the same color, texture and weathering profile as the flaked areas adjacent to the retooled characters on the face side and the non-retooled characters, indicating that they were made at the same time as the original inscription.

Pyrite Evidence – Fortunately, Ohman did not scratch out the entire inscription. Several characters on the split side were not scratched and exhibit significant weathering. Most notable are iron oxide-coated pits within the grooves, produced by pyrite crystals that had completely weathered away. The Kensington Rune Stone has not been in a weathering environment since its discovery, as evidenced by the lack of pyrite weathering in the bottom of the scratched out runes. When these pits are compared with the still actively weathering pyrite crystals in the characters of the AVM Stone, a false artifact found near the discovery site and admittedly carved by University of Minnesota graduate-level language student pranksters in June 1985, it means the pyrite in the Kensington Rune Stone inscription, as of June 2008, would have taken more than twenty-three years to weather away.

Twenty-three years prior to the discovery of the Kensington Rune Stone, Olof Ohman was twenty-one years old and still in Sweden (Ohman immigrated to the United States in 1879 at the age of twenty-five). This means Olof Ohman could not have been involved with carving the Stone, making a nineteenth century hoax by Ohman impossible.

Mica Weathering – Based on comparison of the weathering rate of biotite mica in slate tombstones with the weathering of biotite in the Kensington Rune Stone, the inscription has been weathering for longer than approximately two hundred years. On slate tombstones studied in Hallowell, Maine, highly weathered mica minerals on man-made surfaces of two-hundred-year-old tombstones had begun to fall off the surface. Since all the mica minerals (including biotite) on the original man-made surfaces of the Kensington Rune Stone have weathered away, the inscription must be at least two hundred years old. Since the arrival of the first immigrants into the Kensington area was around 1860 and the weathering of the inscription is older than 200 years from the day it was pulled from the ground in 1898, this puts the origin of the inscription back to at least the late seventeenth century. Therefore, the inscription cannot be a modern hoax.

While the geological findings I was able to document are consistent and compelling, I was not the first geologist to perform extensive geological work on the Kensington Rune Stone. Professor Newton H. Winchell was Minnesota's first state geologist from 1877 to 1900. He performed an exhaustive investigation into the stone from 1909 to 1910. In addition to obtaining a sample from the stone and examining a thin section just as I did, he also performed relative age dating analysis and determined that the weathering of the inscription was very old. He also did something that I could never have done. He made three trips to Kensington, Minnesota, between December of 1909 and March of 1910, and conducted numerous personal interviews. Winchell interviewed Olof Ohman, his wife, Karin, his children, and his neighbors. He also interviewed people who didn't believe the inscription was genuine and recorded fifty pages of hand-written notes in his geologic notebook. On December 15, 1909, Professor Winchell wrote his definitive opinion that the inscription was genuine.

There is another important person who played a key role in the history of the Kensington Rune Stone. Professor Theodore Blegen, who many call "Mr. Minnesota History," wrote a book published in 1968 entitled, *The Kensington Rune Stone: New Light on an Old Riddle*. Mr. Blegen performed exhaustive research into the artifact during the 1960s, a time when there weren't any reasonable voices arguing in favor of the inscription. Blegen heard almost exclusively from opponents who, not surprisingly, influenced his opinion. He wrote the following: "What matters is the sum total of the historical, runological and archaeological evidence. The runological and historical side is, in my judgment, conclusive. The inscription is a fake." What is notably missing from Professor Blegen's conclusions is any mention of Winchell's geologic findings. He ignored Winchell's scientific work.

Winchell deserves tremendous credit for the work he performed during an era without scanning electron microscopes, x-ray diffraction analysis or elemental mapping technology. In fact, all I've done is replicate the geological work he already did. That's the way it works in science. Any sound theory has to be able to be duplicated if it is valid. The Kensington Rune Stone has stood up to scientific scrutiny.

The Inscription

Richard Nielsen, Doctor of Technology, made exhaustive research into Swedish medieval diplomas and books of runic inscriptions. Our joint research led to the discovery that the language on the stone was consistent with the medieval language and runic practice on the Swedish island of Gotland. Perhaps the most important discovery is the realization that the longest word in the inscription on line two is not what it was long thought to be. "Journey of discovery" has changed to "journey of acquisition, or taking up land." This is due to the fact that on medieval Gotlandic inscriptions, the "Þ"-rune in the initial position of a word stood for "t," not "d" as was long believed. This is an important discovery that fundamentally changes the context of the message.

The inscription, translated from Old Swedish becomes:

> *Eight Götalanders and 22 Norwegians on (this) reclaiming /acquisition journey far to the west from Vinland. We had a camp by two (shelters?) one day's journey north from this stone. We were fishing one day. After we came home we found 10 men red with blood and death. Ave Maria. Save from evil. There are 10 men by the sea to look after our ships fourteen days journey from this island. Year 1362.*

Microscopic study of the inscription in 2001 revealed numerous, previously unseen punch marks and short strokes on several characters. These clearly intentional markings appear to have been made by the carver after the original message was carved. When the singled out characters are placed in sequence they spell out a message in words and symbols that appears to be a prayer, likely for the ten dead men. Since all ninety-two churches on Gotland were Cistercian in 1362, it would be consistent for a Cistercian monk, who after writing about the death of ten people, to also include a prayer for their souls. We don't know if the ten dead men were members of their party. They could just as well have been ten dead Native Americans. Regardless, the word "Grail" is also consistent with the Cistercians since they wrote the Grail legends during medieval times.

> *Grail; these 10 (men have) Wisdom, (the) 10 (men are with the) Holy Spirit*

The Dating Code

There are three other characters that the carver singled out for what appears to be a very important reason. The very first character in the inscription is the pentadic number eight. At the end of the second horizontal bar, the carver made a relatively deep punch mark. On line four the carver made a short horizontal bar across the "L" rune in the word "sklar" (shelters?). This rune has puzzled scholars and appears to be a code calling attention to the "L" rune. On the eighth line the unique "U" rune in the word "illu" (evils) also has a curious horizontal bar singling it out. If the carver was trying to create a date using the medieval Easter Table then these three characters become very important.

The medieval Easter Table was comprised of nineteen columns and twenty-eight rows which displays the 532-year period in runes for the perpetual calendar. On medieval Gotland, Cistercian monks used the Easter Table to calculate important religious dates. To make a date using the Easter Table, three things are needed. The first is a Sunday Letter that is derived

The first nine lines of the inscription are on the "face" side of the Kensington Rune Stone. (Wolter, 2003)

The last three lines of the inscription are on the "split" side of the Kensington Rune Stone. (Wolter, 2003)

from the first seven letters of the runic alphabet called the Futhork. The crossed "U" is the second rune in the Futhork and works perfectly as the Sunday Letter. The second item needed is a Golden Year. The "L" is the fourteenth rune in the Futhork and also works nicely. The third item needed is a column number. Of the twelve individual numbers on the Rune Stone, the pentadic number eight is the only one that has a punch on the line. When the eighth column is plotted on the Easter Dating Table (See page 78), along with the crossed "U" and "L" runes, the date derived is 1362.

Since I believe the Kensington Rune Stone was carved as a land claim, then the second coded date makes a lot of sense. The date carved in pentadic numbers using Arabic placement could easily be altered by taking a chisel and adding another bar to one of the numbers. For example, adding another horizontal bar to the pentadic number three, would add a hundred years. The encoded date within the inscription protects the date from alteration, which is the most important thing on a land claim which is who was there first.

Language, Grammar, Runes, and Dialect

We now know that all the words on the Kensington Rune Stone that were not known to be Old Swedish in 1898 have since been found to be so. This is due to the significant advancement in the understanding of medieval language and runes. The anomalies within the stone inscription that confounded both Scandinavian and American scholars for many decades have recently been explained within the rich trove of medieval runic inscriptions on Gotland. These inscriptions were the last to be studied by scholars in Scandinavia and are still being published as of 2009. This explains why the Kensington Rune Stone inscription puzzled investigators for so long. They simply didn't have the information available to them. The following points discovered by Richard Nielsen, support the inscription's medieval origin:

1. The primary proof of the inscription's medieval origin is the presence of the dotted R for the palatal R sound. The discovery of the Kensington Rune Stone in 1898 predates the discovery in 1935 of two runic inscriptions in Sweden (Ukna, Sm 145 and the Lund Bone 4) with dotted R's. The palatal R was still in use on the island of Gotland during the last half of the 1300s.

2. There are numerous small points of runic usage that tie the Kensington Rune Stone runes to Gotlandic practice. These include the dotted "L," double "r," double "l," use of Þ for "t" in the initial position, "t" for "d," and the Latin K for the k-rune.

3. The double dotted runes for ä (X̆), ö (ⴶ), and ü (ᛁ) appear to have been adopted from German manuscript practice. The Germans had a heavy influence on Gotland throughout medieval times.

4. All of the troublesome traits on the Kensington Rune Stone, such as the word forms "g" in og (and), "h" in ahr (year), öh (island) and här (are), from (from), hafÞe (had), and vaR (were) are explained by the runic practice of Gotland.

5. The continued presence of both "Þ" and "t" in medial and final position even after 1400, rather than "d" in Gotlandic inscriptions confirms the origin of the Kensington Rune Stone in Gotland almost on this point alone. These words on the Kensington Rune Stone are farÞ (journey), hafÞe (had), veÞ (by), röÞe (red), bloÞ (blood) and ÞeÞ (death).

6. The continued presence of "Þ" and "t" in the initial position helps validate optagelse (taking up) and teno (this). In 1362, opÞagelse

(taking up) could never be considered to be opdagelse (discovery) since "Þ = t" in the 1300's in Gotland.

7. The use of the gh-digraph on the Kensington Rune Stone is found on two Gotlandic inscriptions (Othem Church G 282 and Lärbro Church G 294).

8. The use of an initial word divider after the first letter of the first word as in g : öter (Götalanders) is also found on two inscriptions (Othem Church G 282 and G 283) on Gotland.

9. The use of the Easter table for dating was unique to Gotland in medieval times making it a clear indicator that the Kensington Rune Stone inscription traits have their primary origin in Gotland.

10. Gotland is a recognized e-dialect region. The word endings on the Kensington Rune Stone such as fiske (fish) rather than fiska (fish) indicate an e-dialect. Andrew Anderson, Nils Flaaten, Sven Fogelblad, Olof Ohman and even John Gran, immigrated to the United States from regions that spoke an "a"-dialect.

Points to Ponder

There are several reasons the Kensington Rune Stone has been such a vexing mystery for over a century. One of the most important is that, since the Kensington Rune Stone was found, there have been amazing advances in research science and information technology. By leaning more on the scientific evidence, subjectivity is reduced and the question is considered more objectively based on the facts. The research of past investigations we presented in *Compelling New Evidence* showed that those who found the stone to be a hoax employed improper method. They started off with a conclusion and then went looking for evidence to support it. This approach leads to incomplete, incorrect and unsupported conclusions. These investigators failed to employ the scientific method, which dictates that facts are documented first, then a hypothesis or theory is formulated that best fits those facts. The next step is to test the theory, and re-test it. If the results are consistent and repeatable, then the theory has validity. This process was employed by Professor Newton Winchell in 1909 and 1910 and then repeated by me and other geologists. Our conclusions are consistent.

The controversy over the Kensington Rune Stone often brought out the worst in people. Many exhibited bias and personal pique, rather than objectivity. Time and again problems of the human condition got in the way, further clouding the controversy.

It is important to realize that standing at the center of the controversy is the credibility of the stone's discoverer. Olof Ohman has been described by researchers, family, and friends as a serious and honest man. There is no evidence to suggest that Ohman was a prankster or practical joker as many opponents have claimed. It is well-documented that he repeatedly denied being involved in the creation of the inscription.

Another important point to remember is that any forensic investigation boils down to a problem of logic. As I stated earlier, the logic behind the Kensington Rune Stone is simple: it's either a modern hoax or it's not. In spite of what many might argue, there are not two sides to the story in a forensic investigation. There's only one correct answer. Therefore, factual evidence cannot exist to support a conclusion that's not valid. When all the second-hand sources, rumor, speculation, unsupported opinions and politics are stripped away, and only factual evidence is considered, the conclusion becomes obvious. The date carved on the stone (1362 A.D.) is the only reference that places the artifact to a specific period in time. The factual evidence that supports the Kensington Rune Stone being a medieval artifact is voluminous and derived from multiple disciplines. I have yet to see one piece of factual evidence consistent with a late nineteenth-century hoax. Logic dictates that it doesn't exist.

2

The Ohman Family Gift

It was a clear and cold evening on November 27, 2004. My wife, Janet, and I arrived for a holiday party with the Ohman family at Tom and Kim Kolberg's home in Forest Lake, Minnesota. Darwin Ohman had invited us to celebrate an amazing year of many positive experiences and discoveries. Tom and his sister Joanne, and their cousin Scott Ohman, are great-grandchildren of Karin and Olof Ohman. Darwin, a grandson and patriarch of the Ohman family, and all of Olof's descendents had been incredibly supportive of our research. They openly shared everything they had, which included all of Karin and Olof's personal letters, legal documents, photographs and their entire book collection. We went through everything together and, with each other's help, put together a complete record of the Ohman family history.

The first time I met with Darwin, I said to him, "Mr. Ohman, if I find a smoking gun of any kind, I have to report it."

Without hesitation, he looked me in the eye and said, "Scott, there has never been a doubt about the rune stone in this family. You can look at anything you want. We have nothing to hide." He was right, of course, but we still had to go through everything, and I'm so glad we did.

Everyone agreed that the dozens of letters their relatives in Sweden had found during our second and third trips to Sweden were surprising and important, as well as emotional. I'll never forget when Britta Blank, the patriarch of the Swedish relatives, introduced me to Sven-Erik Johansson. "Scott, Sven-Erik has letters written by Olof Ohman." Sven-Erik, who spoke very little English, was holding a large envelop containing several letters, which he offered to me. The two letters I first withdrew were written in Swedish but had different hand-writing. I handed the letters to our two guides with the Hälsingland's Museum, who read them aloud in English. As the first letter was read, tears slowly welled in everyone's eyes, including Scott Ohman, visiting from Minnesota. Olof's wife, Karin, had written to his family telling them of her husband's death in 1935.

In the second letter, Olof wrote to his family about being happy and proud that things with the Rune Stone were going well. He wrote, "This summer, June 1st [1927] there was a meeting in Oscar Lake [about three miles from Kensington]. There were about 10,000 people there, there were also 3,000 automobiles. It was a record at the scene." We'd found another letter later where he talked about the rally at Fahlin's Point on Oscar Lake, but never once did he complain about all the negativity toward the Kensington Rune Stone to his family in Sweden. In fact, he only mentioned the Kensington Rune Stone in these two letters.

Darwin Ohman found that the bulk of the family documents were in five large plastic tubs that his niece and nephew, Joanne Kolberg-Streeter and Tom Kolberg, had in their storage shed. Joanne, and her late husband, Bill Streeter, lived next door to her brother Tom and his wife, Kim, on property overlooking Comfort Lake, that was owned by their great aunt, Olof and Karin's oldest daughter, Amanda Ohman-Carlson. They had

Olof Ohman posing with the Rune Stone during a rally at Oscar Lake, Minnesota, June 1, 1927. Left to Right: Gilbert Hanson, Olof Ohman, and John Ecklund. (Photo courtesy the Ohman Family)

never gotten around to going through the material previously because they knew there would be some painful memories.

We had already rummaged through one of the plastic bins when Britta Blank showed me a piece of paper that had a sketch of a familiar scene. The sketch was the roots of a tree growing over the Rune Stone that I had never seen before. It was part of a letter, dated April 2, 1957, written by Olof Ohman, Jr., to his brothers Arthur and John, who were still living on the family farm in Kensington. The brothers had sent an article to Olof, Jr., that appeared in the Alexandria, Minnesota, newspaper, about the Kensington Rune Stone being a hoax. Olof, Jr., who lived in Viking, Alberta, Canada, wrote back saying essentially, "Dad is gone [Olof died in 1935], Edward is gone [Edward died in 1950], I'm the only one left who was there the day the Stone was found. I should write down what I remember because someday it might be important." His recollection of facts almost sixty years later was amazingly consistent with the other witnesses' statements, right down to his sketch of the tree, the roots and the Stone.

When Olof's letters were included in the Swedish exhibition at the Community Center in Kensington, long-time journalist and skeptic Peg Meier proclaimed to me, "Olof didn't do it."

One important event was the "Ohman Interview" where Darwin and Tom Kolberg recalled their personal memories of the infamous Walter Gran, as Russell Fridley patiently listened. Russ conducted the "Gran Tapes" interview with Walter Gran in 1970 that became known as the "Deathbed Confession." This was the final nail in the Kensington Rune Stone coffin during the tumultuous period of negativity toward the Kensington Rune Stone in the 1960s. As

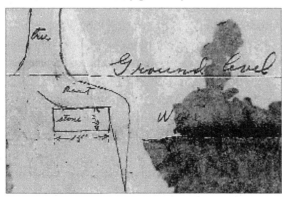

Detail of a letter dated April 2, 1957, from Olof Ohman, Jr., to his brothers, showing a sketch of the tree roots and the Stone. (Letter courtesy of the Ohman Family)

18

the director of the Minnesota Historical Society during this time, Russ presided over the institution that published Theodore Blegen's book that concluded that the Kensington Rune Stone was a hoax. All that was needed was something resembling a confession, and Russ's interview with Walter Gran provided it.

Darwin and Tom's memories of Walter Gran were of a man who was close to the Ohman family for decades, but was by far the least reliable and untrustworthy person in the community. Several recorded interviews with people in the community who knew Walter painted a similar picture. In November of 1983, during a taped interview with Ted Sora, Clarence Larson described Walter Gran with the following words: "He was one the biggest liars that was ever around here."

In spite of Walter's checkered reputation, this may have been the one time in his life that he actually was telling the truth. It was his father who likely made up the story ". . . that the Stone was false and that, you know how we made it . . ." when he thought he was dying in 1927. The factual evidence of the Rune Stone's authenticity proves that his father wasn't telling the truth. John Gran was a wealthy person in the community and reportedly resented the attention Ohman received over the stone. I believe the elder Gran saw an opportunity to take a jab at Ohman and possibly get him to confess by making up the statement to his son. When Walter pressed his father for details, his father said, "Go and talk to Ohman, and he will tell you." Russ asked Walter if he asked Ohman about what his father said. Walter said he had asked Ohman about his father's allegations to which Ohman reportedly replied, "That's a bunch of humbug." I'm still trying to figure out where the confession was that the Minnesota Historical Society found so compelling.

Janet and I brought a gift for the family. In addition to the casts of the Kensington Rune Stone the Runestone Museum had asked us to make for research purposes, Dick and I had an extra cast made and painted for the Ohmans. One of the important discoveries we made was a trail of documents that led to a clear picture of who actually owned the artifact. When and if the Ohman family want to pursue their rightful claim is up to them to decide. Until that day, a replica will have to do.

We also talked with the Ohmans about an idea that had been brewing in the back of my mind: developing the Ohman Farm into a first-class park with a state-of-the-art interpretive center to tell the story of the Rune Stone and the Ohman family. By creating the appropriate facility, eventually the Rune Stone might come back to Kensington where it was originally discovered over a century ago. A few weeks later on January 10, 2005, I got my chance to make a pitch for the park at the community center in Kensington.

I wanted this interpretive center to be a "living" facility. In addition to being a repository for artifacts and documents, it should also be a place to conduct and facilitate related research. Many people and organizations have backed the plan, and it's moving steadily forward. The Kensington Area Heritage Society, the Runestone Museum, and Douglas County have all embraced the idea of making the Ohman Farm into a historical destination.

After this discussion, Darwin pointed to the large, blue plastic tub on the table. He smiled and said, "We'd like you to have a gift." He then reached into the tub and pulled out a very old book with Olof's signature

Darwin handed a book to me. He said, "We want you to have this."

I opened the cover and gazed at Olof's artistic signature on the inside jacket next to the date he had written, October 26, 1886. On the second page was an inscription written in pencil: the names and birth dates of Karin and Olof's nine children, including the death dates of their two sons Oscar and David Ohman.

Most families write the birthdates of their children in the family bible. This book, *Alexander von Humbolt's Life and Travels*, was by a famous nineteenth-century Swedish scientist who wrote about biology, botany, geography, geology, astronomy, and other scientific topics. This book said a lot about the man I had spent so much time trying to understand. It reminded me of a story I was told earlier in the year by the now-late Einar Bakke, a man in his nineties who knew Olof personally. Einar said, "Many years ago, John Gran was walking home from church and came upon Olof Ohman repairing a fence that his cows had knocked down. Gran said to Ohman, 'You know, Ohman, the Lord isn't going to look too kindly on you working on a Sunday.' Olof turned to John Gran and said, 'My neighbor isn't going to look too kindly on my cattle trampling his crops either. So why don't you shove off and mind your own business!'"

I could relate to that part of Olof that I believe symbolizes a big part of the man he was, maybe who John Gran was, too.

3

The Hans Voigt Letter

After my lecture on the Kensington Rune Stone, on September 19, 2006, to the Sons of Norway, an older gentleman came up to me and said, "My grandfather was a friend of Olof Ohman."

The comment instantly caught my attention. Then the gentleman said, "Would you like to see a letter written by Mr. Ohman?" He held up a plastic ziplock bag containing paper yellowed with age. The cursive writing looked familiar. At his invitation, I gently extracted the contents. Sure enough, it was a two-page, dated letter with the name of the city at the top of the page and written in a style I had seen many times before. I turned the page over and looked at the signature at the bottom. I felt the same thrill of discovery and excitement that surged through me with each new Ohman letter I saw back in Hälsinglands, Sweden, during my visits in 2004. The familiar frustration of not being able to read what I held in my hands also came back!

I pulled my gaze from the letter to the man, who introduced himself as Helmer Voigt. He said he had inherited it from his grandfather, who knew Ohman. I asked if any researchers had seen it. He didn't think so. I immediately went into my "document everything while you can" mode, and asked if I could photograph the letter he had brought and any others he might have. Helmer was very easy-going, and said, "Sure." I began to examine what I held in my hands and realized there were actually two letters. One was written by Ohman, and the other by Helmer's grandfather. They were

This letter was written by Olof Ohman to Hans Voigt on May 19, 1910. Ohman thanks Voigt for clarification about a rumor about his carving runes and relays how he "Must laugh at the madness" over the rune stone. (Letter courtesy of Helmer Voigt)

both dated in 1910, and represented an exchange between them. As I scanned the Ohman letter, my eyebrows raised quickly at the few words that I could read: Prof. N.H. Winchell! I quickly took photographs and asked if I could get together with Helmer at another time to get more information, and perhaps be able to scan all the letters he had. He was very agreeable and gave his address and phone number. I drove home that night with my head spinning at the irony of how yet another amazing thing had happened. It was too late to make any calls, but on the way to work the next morning, my first call was to Darwin Ohman. He said what he usually did whenever I had interesting news, "Well I'll be darned."

Darwin was always excited to hear the latest news about the research, but this time it was a little more personal. This was a previously unknown letter written by his grandfather, one that shed light on his feelings about the controversy surrounding his famous discovery. Another interesting point about this letter was that it gave additional context to Hans Voigt's letter to Ohman published in the Minnesota Historical Society's Museum Committee's Report on the Kensington Rune Stone, in 1915. Newton Winchell had been appointed to investigate the stone in 1909-1910. During his three trips to Kensington, Winchell tracked down the source of the rumor about how Ohman reportedly carved runes at Gunnar Johnson's house in 1882. Johnson remembered someone carving runes on a stick and assumed it was Ohman when rumors of forgery surfaced surrounding the Kensington Rune Stone twenty-seven years later. The letter to Ohman clarified that Voigt was actually the one who had carved the runes. Both Voigt, a painter, and Ohman, a carpenter, helped build the home of the obviously confused Gunnar Johnson.

Voigt's original letter was translated by the Minnesota Historical Society as follows:

> Mr. Olof Ohman:
> I clip this from the *Decorah Post*, and send it with the following remarks. Is the Gunder Johnson, in Brandon, who started this rumor that you used to amuse yourself with writing runes, the same as the Gunder Johnson, Hojbergsner, from the town of Mo? If so, then the house referred to was built for him by you in 1882, and I was there and painted it: and if this is so, then I believe you remember me. I had, in fact, a wedding down there, and you were present. At that time I made on a piece of wood some marks which were, after a fashion, to represent runes, as he says. So it seems to me that it is this incident which has popped up in Mr. Johnson's memory. If this is right, then let me hear from you. I had a long time ago forgotten your name. Hans Voigt[1]

I set up a time for Darwin and me to come to Helmer's home, and he seemed genuinely excited. On September 22, 2006, we arrived at his door on St. Paul Avenue, which, ironically, was the same street I took on my way to and from work every day. Helmer and Darwin hit it off right away. Helmer, a kind, soft-spoken man, looked at least a decade younger than his eighty-four years.

> Kensington the 19th May 1910.
> Mr. Hans Voigt
> Mc Intosh.

I have received your letter and I am fairly grateful for your acknowledgement (validation) of the runic inscription, I can not recall drawing any runes at that time. I had more than enough work on his house, without drawing runes. The strangest rumors are circulating about this stone. The most recent is that I have brought forth the runes with Black magic. Sometimes I have become angry and sometimes I have had to laugh at the craziness. I could not make the stone nor could any other emigrant have had enough knowledge to do it. Your letter will be mailed immediately to Prof. N.H. Winchell in St. Paul. I hope that more will listen to you. Högbergsmoen (Gunnar Johnson) thought he was going to sneak a whole week's work from me, but he did not succeed with it, so instead he thought he would succeed here with his intrigues. "Did you know the Gentleman?" What do you work with: are you a painter or farmer? I farm and do a little carpentry sometimes.

Yours faithfully
Olof Ohman
R.R. #1. Box 56 Kensington

[Translation by Ingrid Anderson on April 30, 2007.]

Note

[1]This translation was published in the Minnesota Historical Society Collections 1909 to 1914, The Kensington Rune Stone: Preliminary Report to the Minnesota Historical Society by its Museum Committee, p. 243.

4

Rodney Beecher Harvey

I n keeping with the belief that any new evidence that bolsters the Kensington Rune Stone also supports the Hooked X and everything else related to it, the work of Dr. Rodney Beecher Harvey (May 26, 1890 to November 4, 1945) deserves mention. I was contact-

Dr. Rodney Beecher Harvey (left) prepares to take a photograph of the runes on the Kensington Rune Stone in this 1937 photograph. Dr. Harvey was a plant physiologist at the University of Minnesota and studied the Kensington Rune Stone including photographing each rune in the inscription. Harvey's son (holding bucket) and an unknown assistant apply plaster while making a mold of the Kensington Rune Stone for the Minnesota Historical Society in 1937. (Photographs courtesy of the Duerr/Harvey Family)

ed by Jennifer Duerr-Jenkins, from Colorado. She was referred to me because she had found something that related to the Kensington Rune Stone. Jennifer had a full-size plaster cast of the Rune Stone.

She emailed me pictures of the bone-white cast made in the 1930s by her grandfather, Dr. Rodney Beecher Harvey, who was a professor of Plant Physiology, Agricultural Botany, and Horticulture at the University of Minnesota. Jennifer said her family wanted to donate the cast, and I suggested she wait until we find out when Douglas County planned to build an interpretation center at the Ohman Farm. She was excited by the idea, and then she said, "I know we have some boxes of my grandfathers' full of letters, notes, and photographs from his research on the Rune Stone." I was instantly excited and told her to start looking for them. It would take Jennifer two years to find the boxes, but on October 22, 2007, she emailed me with the good news.

Jennifer emailed a few of the photos, including one of Rodney taking photographs of the Kensington Rune Stone through a magnifying glass.

After learning of the contents of the boxes, two things struck me as especially exciting. The first was a collection of photographs Dr. Harvey had taken of the individual characters. Rodney apparently realized that documenting the inscription was important. One can only wonder if he also noticed the punch marks I had seen. I had been accused of making those punch marks, but Rodney's work in the 1930s completely exonerated me since I was born in 1958!

The second important revelation was a photograph Harvey took that clearly shows the two root leaching lineations on the back of the stone. Being an accomplished botanist, it is reasonable to assume that Dr. Harvey understood the significance of these features and their relationship to the discovery story. It always seemed strange that I never found any reference of anyone before me having documented this obvious feature. I have even wondered why Professor Newton Winchell never mentioned the root leaching marks that he must have seen during his exhaustive investigation in 1909-1910. Perhaps the discovery story was never questioned during his time and the root leaching was obvious. It turns out I wasn't the first and once again my work validates Professor Harvey's work and conclusions that he was immi-

nently more qualified to reach than me.

On February 8, 2008, I flew to Denver, Colorado, to visit Jennifer and her sister Ruth and to look through their grandfather's documents. At Ruth's home, I immediately saw the bone white plaster cast of the rune

Harvey's photograph clearly shows the root leaching on the back of the Kensington Rune Stone. As a botanist, it is reasonable to assume he would have understood the significance of these features. (Photo courtesy of the Duerr/Harvey Family)

Dr. Rodney Harvey and his assistants had the same trouble with air bubbles during the mold-making process as others had had. Pouring the plaster traps air and produces small round beads within the grooves when the cast is produced. Even in the plaster cast made in 1937, the shallow punch in the upper loop of the dotted R (right) is clearly visible. The cast was made within a couple of years of the rune's discovery.

stone sitting on a table. The Duerr daughters and their husbands, Mike Jenkins and Paul Vanees, watched as I reverently ran my hands over the seventy-five-pound replica. The first thing I looked for was the small punch mark in the first "r"-rune on line six. The dotted R was definitely there!

We spent the next four hours talking about their grandfather and scanning documents. We found numerous interesting photographs and newspaper articles. Unfortunately, there were no reports or hand-written notes. A few of the images were labeled, but there was frustratingly little information to add to my research. This experience served as a reminder to me to take lots of notes. I don't want people ever to have to guess at what I was thinking or why.

While going through the photographs of Dr. Rodney Beecher Harvey with his grandchildren Ruth and Jennifer on February 8, 2008, we found an image of the inscription where he had numbered the characters and circled specific runes. Interestingly, he circled nearly all of the Hooked Xs and parts of several runes indicating he studied the Kensington Rune Stone very carefully. Unfortunately, we have not found any notes or reports to give insight into his analysis. (Photograph courtesy of the Duerr/Harvey Family)

Part II

Kensington Rune Stone Codes, Gotland and the Cistercians

5

The Dotted R

Dick Nielsen's focus was primarily on the language and runes. In particular, he wanted to understand the usage of what he called the "palatal R." He explained to me that as the language evolved in Scandinavia during medieval times, new runic symbols were created to represent these new sounds and meanings. In the case of this new R-sound, a dot or punch was added to the upper loop of the rune.

Dick and I scoured the Gotlandic Books of Runic Inscriptions (*Gotlands Runinskrifter*) for examples of this rare medieval rune. What made the dotted R so important was that modern scholars did not know of its existence until 1935 when the Ukna grave slab inscription (Sm 145), circa 1200 A.D., was discovered in Småland, Sweden. There were two examples of the dotted R in the Ukna inscription. This discovery was followed by another find, an inscription carved on a bone excavated from a garbage heap in Lund, Denmark, in 1938. These two important discoveries prompted Scandinavian runologists to publish this previously unknown medieval rune. Dick explained that the examples he found spanned a time period from 1150 to the latest example in 1400. Since most of the examples were found on Gotland, and all the important language, grammar, and dialect features of the Kensington Rune Stone also pointed there, we concluded the author of the stone had to be from Gotland. Therefore, we believed there was a good chance the dotted R could be in the Kensington Rune Stone inscription, though not previously noticed.

In particular, Dick pointed out the word "waR" (were) on line

The dotted R which was unknown to modern scholars until 1935 proves all by itself the medieval origin of the Kensington Rune Stone. (Wolter, 2004)

six of the Kensington Rune Stone. He asked me, "When you did your photo-library of the inscription with the microscope, did you notice a punch mark in the upper loop of the R?"

I responded, "No, I didn't see one."

Dick then said, "We should check it again."

At this point, I became curious and retrieved the full-size cast of the Kensington Rune Stone we had been asked to make from the original artifact by the Runestone Museum, for just this type of research. As it was already dark outside and I wanted a very particular focus, I turned out the lights. With a flashlight, I cast a narrow beam of light across the face of the replica so that the characters jumped out with perfectly clarity. I then moved the flashlight along the face side of the stone to line six, and, with the light shining across at a low angle, highlighted the second word. We looked at the R and both saw the small black hole that instantly appeared before our eyes. The punch was right where Dick predicted it was supposed to be.

It was an exhilarating moment, quickly followed by a sobering, but powerful implication. The fact that the dotted R was unknown to modern scholars until its discovery in 1935 presents a serious dilemma for anyone wanting to claim the Kensington Rune Stone is a modern artifact. How could a forger know about the dotted R when none of the finest scholars in the world knew anything about it? The dotted R proved, all by itself, the medieval origin of the Kensington Rune Stone.

We later came to realize that there were two other examples of the dotted R in the inscription. In the first line of the inscription it appeared in the word "Norrmen" (Northmen). Curiously, most of the small plateau of rock in the upper loop of the second R had spalled away. Upon closer inspection, I noticed a small conical pit where the fracture originated at the point of impact. It looked as if the carver tried to put a punch mark in the upper loop for a dotted R but used too much force on the punch chisel, causing the rock to fracture and spall.

The three dotted R's on the Kensington Rune Stone presented a challenge for the carver likely due to his unfamiliarity with the hard and brittle meta-greywacke rock. The small plateau of rock in the upper loop of the dotted R on line one (left) spalled off from excessive force as the carver tried to make the punch. Apparently being cautious, the carver put the punch between the legs of the second dotted R on line five (middle). A tiny pit in the middle of the plateau in the upper loop is visible where an apparently indecisive carver placed the punch chisel and then changed his mind. Not to be defeated, the carver again made the punch in the upper loop on line six using less force, creating a shallower and less obvious mark (right). (Wolter, 2002)

The second dotted R occurs in essentially the same word on line five, "Norr" (north). This time the carver didn't take any chances and put the punch between the legs of the R, which apparently was acceptable at that time. Dick and I would later find three, previously unknown examples of the punch being used between the legs of the r-rune on Gotland—G 70 Urguda, G 192 Vastergarn, and G 282 Othem. By the time the next dotted R came along in line six, the carver decided to put the punch back in the upper loop. This time he used less force which produced a shallower punch mark that went unnoticed for over a hundred years.

The Urguda inscription on Gotland (G 70, circa 1514), and the Kensington Rune Stone are the only two known runic inscriptions that have both types of dotted R's. Dick Nielsen and I discovered all three known examples of the dotted R with the punch between the legs on Gotland (G 70 Urguda, G 192 Vastergarn, and G 282 Othem).

33

6

The Dating Code

An important discovery within the inscription came on January 19, 2005. Dick Neilsen and I were discussing the mysterious "crossed L" and "crossed U" runes. At first, Dick thought the crossed L could have been an "el" or "le" bind-rune. Bind-runes are when two letters are bound together into a single character. In my mind, that didn't seem right, since there weren't any other obvious bind-runes within the inscription. The carver was very consistent in making well-defined individual runes throughout the inscription. To me, these uniquely crossed runes appeared to have been singled out. It was almost as if they were saying, "Pay attention to me. I'm important." There were other runes with a horizontal line through the middle of the vertical stave, such as the "e" rune (†). However, these two odd ducks had noticeably shorter horizontal bars and didn't seem to belong in these runes.

For years Dick thought there might be a coded date within the inscription. He thought this based on his knowledge of the use of the unique dating method on Gotland. The medieval Easter Table was used extensively by the Cistercian monks on Gotland for calculating important religious dates. There were many examples in the Scandinavian books of runic inscriptions of Easter Table dates on church bells and graves slabs. Dick explained that if the carver had coded a date, the two crossed runes worked perfectly within the nineteen-rune alphabet of that time called the "Futhork." The "U" worked nicely as the Sunday Letter, with the "L" representing the Golden Year. To make a date however, we still needed a column number. Dick then asked me about the photo-library of the inscription I had made sometime earlier, in 2002.

Dick asked, "Of the twelve individual numbers in the inscription, were any of them unusual?"

I said, "Yeah. One, and only one number has a punch mark within the lines." Dick asked me which one it was, and I said, "The very first thing in the inscription, the pentadic number eight."

With slightly raised bushy eyebrows and a wry smile he said, "Let's try it." With a possibility of over 500 years ranging from 1140 to 1671, I was stunned after Dick plotted the three characters. The date he arrived at was 1362 A.D.

At first it seemed incredible, but as it started to sink in, the coded date began to make more and more sense. The discovery of this amazing code quickly led to us to try to figure out why the same date would be inscribed on the stone twice. One possibility we discussed was that the coded date would protect the pentadic date of 1362 from being altered.

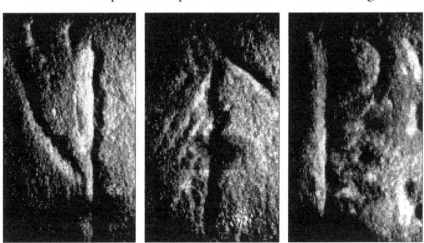

The dating code on the Kensington Rune Stone consists of two curiously crossed runes, the "U" on line 9 (left), the "L" in line 3 (middle), and the 8 on line 1 (right) that has an obvious punch within the second horizontal line. When these runes are plotted on the medieval Easter Table, they equal the year 1362. (Wolter, 2002)

35

It would be easy for someone to take a chisel and carve another horizontal line on the number three for example, changing it to a four. This simple alteration would add a hundred years, making the date 1462. It made a lot of sense to us, but why would anyone have done that? I believe the simple explanation was that the Kensington Rune Stone was carved, and then immediately buried, as a land claim.

As soon as we thought about that, the idea made perfect sense. I then turned my attention to the possibility of physical evidence to support our supposition. During my initial investigation of the Kensington Rune Stone I had spent a great deal of time examining the large, white, triangular-shaped calcite area in the lower left corner of the face side. I looked carefully for evidence of differential weathering in the area below the last line and didn't see any. If the stone had been carved and then set upright in the ground as many investigators assumed, there should have been some evidence of a weathering ground line. The relatively fast-weathering calcite should have exhibited above and below grade differences, even if it had been upright for only a couple of decades. The lack of any observable difference in weathering didn't prove the stone had been immediately buried, but it was consistent with it.

The dating code fit beautifully with the theory of a land claim. It

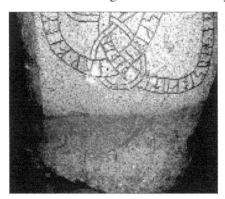

The Viking age Torsätra rune stone from Uppland, Sweden, on display at the Historical Museum in Stockholm exhibits a well-defined weathering ground line since being pulled from the ground (left). The Kensington Rune Stone (right) exhibits no such ground line consistent with it never having been placed upright. (Wolter, 2003 and 2004)

also fit nicely with the message on the stone when viewed from a context that hadn't been considered from before. The inscription says who they were, "eight Götalanders and 22 Norwegians"; where they were at from three different levels; "far to the west from Vinland," "fourteen days journey from this island," and "one day's journey north from this stone." It read a lot like a land deed. The message also says when they were there . . . twice. Once by using pentadic numbers in Arabic placement to make the 1362 date, and the second by use of the Easter Table dating practice prevalent on Gotland at that time. Lastly, it says why they were there; "acquisition business or taking up land."

The land claim theory seemed like the perfect explanation with all the pieces seemingly fitting into place, except for one thing: if the stone was carved and buried as a land claim, how would the claim stakers be able to come back some day and find it? How in the world would they do that? The question gnawed at my brain for only a couple of weeks. This time it was Janet who made the startling breakthrough.

7

Sacred Geometry and the Stone Holes

Relocating the Kensington Rune Stone buried in the ground in the wilderness of North America would have presented a huge challenge for a future returning party. Yet there had to be a way for them to do it. One thing that gave me hope was like everything else related to the stone: if we were right about our theory then there had to be an explanation. It was during this time that Janet and I began reading books about the Knights Templar who were closely affiliated with the Cistercians. One book that we found particularly interesting was written by Erling Haagensen and Henry Lincoln entitled, *The Templar's Secret Island*. Henry Lincoln was the driving force behind the book that first presented the idea that Jesus and Mary Magdalene were married and had a child together entitled, *Holy Blood, Holy Grail*. Dan Brown's wildly successful fictional novel, *The Da Vinci Code*, was largely based on this book.

The premise of *The Templar's Secret Island* was about how medieval Templars constructed several churches at strategic locations on the island of Bornholm, in Denmark. Four of these churches are round in shape, exhibiting architecture similar to the tower above Christ's tomb at the Church of the Holy Sepulcher in Jerusalem. Haagensen and Lincoln discovered that, by sighting off the steeples of the churches and using mathematics, geometry, and astronomy, the Templars had conceived a way to make important symbols, including the seven-pointed star with amazing accuracy. The discovery of this incredible knowledge used by the Cistercians and Templars—something they called "sacred geometry"—was an eye-opening experience for both of us.

The book also talked about how the midline of the geometry on Bornholm extended in a north-easterly direction into the Baltic Sea fifteen miles off the coast to a tiny island called Christainsø. This midline extended through the steeple of a small church there as well. Janet and I were intrigued by the book and were beginning to appreciate the intellect of the medieval military order of the Templars and their Cistercian brothers.

On February 13, 2005, Janet and I were in Duluth for a presentation about our research on the Kensington Rune Stone at the Kitchi Gammi Club. Professor Emeritus Dr. Richard Ojakangas had invited me to give this talk, and I was excited about presenting our recent discovery of the dating code for the first time. About forty-five people in the audience seemed to enjoy the presentation.

Later that night at the Holiday Inn, we both fell asleep with thoughts prompted by recently read books and that evening's talk swirling in our heads. The problem boiling in my brain was the major stumbling block to our recently hatched theory of the Kensington Rune Stone being carved and immediately buried as a land claim. Everything so far had fit together so nicely. The only problem was, wouldn't they have to be able to come back some day and find it? How could they exercise their land claim if they couldn't find the proof they had previously buried? How in the world would they be able to find this tombstone-sized rock in the middle of the continent? We had put the question to the group that night as well, and they were all stumped. The surprising answer came in the wee hours of the morning, as happens so often when the subconscious has time to work things out for the conscious mind.

"The stone holes, the sacred geometry, that's how they did it," Janet said. She had awakened and thumped my chest to get my attention.

Her excitement and formidable swat instantly jerked me from my slumber. I groggily sat up and with a puzzled look said, "What?"

As my brain began to clear and her words fell into place, I was suddenly struck with the same realization. Of course, the triangular stone holes found across much of the upper Midwest and into Canada—we had puzzled over them. The current theory was that they were "mooring stones." Long-time Kensington Rune Stone researcher Hjalmar Holand theorized that the numerous holes found in glacial boulders were used by early explorers to anchor their ships. Primarily due to incompatible water levels, Holand's mooring stone idea never made sense to me. The holes must have been handmade, likely with a straight-edged chisel, for a more practical and logical purpose, and Janet appeared to have come up with one. Our minds went to work over this new supposition. Over the course of the next several hours, we came up with the likely scenario for the mysterious stone holes.

After all, we had read about the Templars and Cistercians, we knew they were intelligent and certainly would have figured out how to relocate something as important as the proof of their land claim. If the stone holes were indeed carved by these people, then they likely served multiple functions. The first usage could have been as a way of marking their routes similar to leaving a breadcrumb trail. With twenty members in their field party (according to the Kensington Rune Stone inscription, there were "10 men by the sea to look after our ships"), the plausibility of such a feat was relatively easy to comprehend. At the start of each day on their trek, one person could start making a stone hole with a hammer and chisel. Depending on the depth and hardness of the rock, the process would have likely taken an hour or two. The "breadcrumb" holes likely had a designated depth. Once the first hole was finished, the carver would start hiking after their party. They probably could have followed the pounding noise of the second hole being made farther up the trail. This method would have allowed the group to keep moving and to make several holes throughout the day.

Upon reaching the desired land they wanted to claim near what is now Kensington, Minnesota, they would have laid out a grid system of intersecting lines by pounding holes, possibly of a different depth or angle than the breadcrumb holes, into glacial boulders that, so conveniently, littered the land. The inscription was then carved into a relatively flat, glacial boulder, after it was first split down to its present shape of almost exactly a two-to-one ratio of length to width. The Kensington Rune Stone was then buried at the spot where the surveyed lines intersected. A returning future party who understood the methodology of the stone holes could then have located the land claim stone in the wilderness even with it buried.

This sacred geometry put Hjalmar Holand's mooring stone holes into an entirely new light. It also meant that all the data supporters of the mooring stone theory had been compiling for decades suddenly become very important. I knew I needed to solicit the help of these people. I had always tried to be respectful of their ideas but could never get excited about the mooring-stone theory. Why would ships be moored on hills at elevations where there was no water 600 years ago? Janet's epiphany had instantly changed all that, giving those holes a completely new meaning.

One of the leading researchers into the mooring-stone holes was a woman, Judi Rudebusch, living in the Whetstone River Valley of South Dakota. Judi, a highly inquisitive and intuitive woman with an insatiable appetite for anything to do with the stone holes, had found many stone holes in glacial boulders near her home and had assembled a data base of the GPS location of most of the known holes in the Midwest. Judi was one of the first people I invited to attend another meeting in Kensington where I wanted to present the latest theory that Haagensen and Lincoln's book had led Janet and me to believe made more sense.

On April 2, 2005, we met with Kensington resident and friend Mel Conrad, at the Ohman farm to check out the interesting cluster of stone holes around "Rune Stone Hill." Half an hour later, Judi Rudebusch and her friend Bruce Kunze, a soil scientist arrived from South Dakota. By 10:00 A.M., Al Lieffort with Douglas County Parks, and his wife, Beth, had joined the party. Bruce and Judi helped locate several of the stone holes they had seen previously. We also used photographs taken in 1941 that Judi found in Hjalmar Holand's personal papers at the Wisconsin Historical Society. A few of the photos helped us locate the original position of a boulder with a stone hole that had been moved up the hill to where the flagpoles were. Ironically, the boulder had originally been in Nils Flaaten's (Ohman's neighbor) rock pile and was moved in 1985 as part of renovations at the park to show visitors what a mooring stone hole was.

Later, at the community center, Marion Dahm, Leland Peterson,

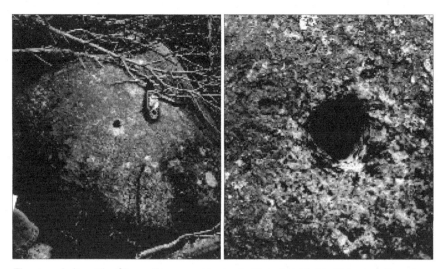

The stone holes at the Ohman Farm were hand-cut with a straight chisel into glacial boulders. They, of course, exhibit some weathering. Typically, the holes were roughly an inch in diameter, had a rounded triangular shape and varied from an inch up to several inches in depth. (Wolter, 2005)

Bob Berg, Cal Corneya, Mel Conrad, Judi Rudebush, Bruce Kunze, and Janet and I shared the information about Gotland, the grave slabs, the Templars, and the "stone hole" theory. I then explained how the information they compiled over several decades suddenly took on a whole new importance and asked for their help. Judi and Bruce Kunze offered to plot all the GPS locations of the stone holes in proximity of the Ohman farm on a satellite map.

A few days later, Judi emailed the satellite map with dots plotted where the stone holes were. Janet and I could easily see where the Flaaten rock pile was and drew a dot on one of the several copies of the map we had printed out, marking the original location of the boulder that had been moved. Janet laid a ruler on the paper and started connecting dots. It took a several tries, but then suddenly everything fell into place. Amazingly, three lines converged in a triangulation pattern with the bulls-eye at a predictable spot. I pulled out the aerial photograph of the Ohman farm that Al Lieffort had given us permission to use with the

On the Nils Flaaten farm in this 1941 photograph, Hjalmar Holand points to a triangular shaped hole in a glacial boulder around which rocks cleared from the adjacent field were piled (left). During our April 2, 2005, visit we found that the same boulder (right) had been moved up near the Kensington Rune Stone discovery site during renovations to the Ohman Farm to show visitors what a "mooring stone" was. (Left: Wisconsin Historical Society; Right: Wolter, 2005)

It was vitally important to document the original location of the Flaaten boulder to test our theory about the stone holes. The 1941 photo on the left shows one of the Flaaten boys standing next to the boulder. On April 2, 2005, we were able to use the same boulder in the lower left of both photos to pin point the original location of the boulder that had been moved. (Left: Wisconsin Historical Society: Right: Wolter, 2005)

discovery site clearly marked and sure enough, the intersecting lines all met at the exact spot where the Kensington Rune Stone had been found.

After drawing the lines, Janet and I stared. I didn't know if I was more amazed by how clever these ancient explorers were to craft such an ingenious plan or that we had actually figured it out. Regardless, we definitely knew we had made a significant discovery. This wasn't just about what was going on at the Ohman farm. We realized that we had stumbled upon what was only the tip of the iceberg with the stone holes and the likely medieval use of what the Templars called "Sacred Geometry."

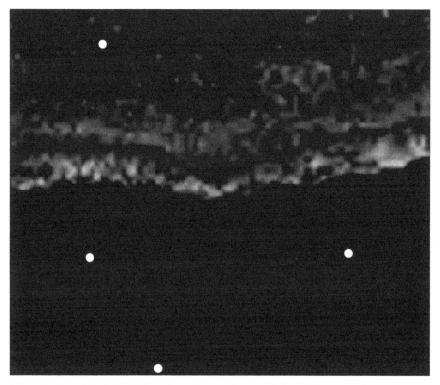

This satellite map includes the south and east ends of the Ohman farm outlined by trees. The locations of the stone holes are marked by dots. The "Flaten 1" stone's original location was found using old photographs and is marked with an arrow. Theoretically, a returning Norse party could survey the stone holes, triangulating to the location where the Kensington Rune Stone land claim stone was buried. Four of the stone holes that are not part of the triangulation are smaller boulders in the ditch next to the crop field and were likely moved by the Ohmans. Very large boulders were not moved. They form a perfect equilateral triangle, which is an ancient symbol of the Goddess, but whether that was intended is unknown.

8

Gotland

After reviewing the published Gotlandic runic inscriptions, Dick Nielsen and I decided that we had to verify that the important features we found did in fact exist. The presence of the dotted R in Gotland was by far the most important. We also thought that if the punch between the legs of the "r"-rune in the word "NorR" was correct, we should be able to find other examples. The other interesting thing that was, if there was sacred geometry involved in the layout of the churches on Bornholm, the same was likely true on Gotland. The only way even to begin to figure that out was to go to Gotland and get GPS readings of every church.

I already had a good friend ready to help out. Since the first time we met him in Minnesota in 2002, Lars Westman, a prominent, semi-retired journalist in Sweden, had been a huge supporter of our research. Lars had helped guide us through the choppy waters of Swedish academic skepticism during our first three trips to Sweden.

On February 27, 2005, I landed in Stockholm. Lars drove me to his office where I was anxious to show him the dating and "Grail" codes. He thought the dating code was great, but I was a little surprised at his somewhat cool reception when I used the word "Templar." Lars would be the first of many who had an instantly negative reaction toward any mention of the possible involvement of the Templars with the Kensington Rune Stone. Part of it was understandable, considering Dan Brown's hugely successful book *The Da Vinci Code*. That novel was based on the premise in the book *Holy Blood, Holy Grail* that Jesus and

Mary Magdalene had been married. Looking back now, it's amazing how our research into the likely involvement of the Templars and the Cistercians coincided with the world-wide hysteria over Brown's novel. At the time of my visit, I had no idea how close the parallel would actually turn out to be. The only difference between Brown's novel and our emerging story was that ours was not fiction!

Lars knew I was serious about this research and offered to take me to the only church in Stockholm dedicated to Mary Magdalene. We arrived at the church just at twilight. Lars introduced me to his friend Göran Kåring, a priest who had just finished presiding over a wedding service. As Göran gave us a tour of his magnificent church, I scanned the walls for symbolism of the ideology I had recently been studying.

The architecture and decorations were beautiful and suggested Mary Magdalene's role in Christianity was more important than her traditional role as a prostitute. I paused in front of the altar to take in the beautiful painting of baby Jesus and his mother Mary (The Virgin?) fawning over him. Directly above the painting was a glowing triangle known as the Delta of Enoch showing the rays of the sun radiating outward. Inside the sacred triangle is allegedly the ineffable name of God in Hebrew.[1] I would eventually learn that this symbol was very sacred to both the medieval Templars and modern Freemasons. There were many more notable symbols, such as Templar crosses and the five-pointed star, sprinkled throughout the church. As much as I wanted to search for more symbols, I knew there would be ample opportunity to look for symbolism in the ninety-nine churches on Gotland. Göran was more than gracious giving us a tour considering his work day had ended with the wedding service. I was very grateful.

The next day Lars and I drove to the Historiska Museum. My agenda at the museum included examining and photographing several rune stones on display, and one inscription I'd made an appointment to review. I felt like I was on a scavenger hunt tracking down the runic evidence Dick and I had hoped to find. Dick had done a tremendous job scouring the books of the runic inscriptions of Sweden to find the runes, words, dialect, and grammar features on the Kensington Rune Stone. My job was to find the actual inscriptions and make sure what we thought was there actually was.

 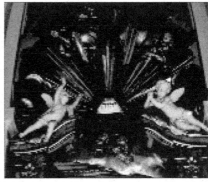

Interesting symbolism was evident as I toured the Church of Maria Magdalena in Stockholm, Sweden, on February 27, 2005. I noticed a five-pointed star centered on a Templar cross incorporated within the design of a gold-encircled crest (left) and the Hebrew Delta of Enoch above the altar (right) which contains the true name of God that appeared within a golden triangle showing the rays of the sun. I would eventually learn these symbols were and still are very sacred to the Templars and Freemasons. (Wolter, 2005)

There were only a few inscriptions at the museum to find and examine, but there was one additional artifact I had to find. In an obscure display case I found the gold-gilded reliquary I was looking for. The exquisite thirteenth-century relic box was adorned with gold M's and W's. It also had small X's filling the trim around the panels on the box that reminded me of the Hooked X on the Kensinton Rune Stone. I didn't know it at the time, but I would eventually discover that all three symbols were intimately related.

At the end of the work day Lars dropped me at the station where I boarded a train to the ferry boat docks in the Stockholm archipelago. It was a three-hour ferry ride from Stockholm to the walled city of Visby where I rented a car for the next part of my journey visiting churches. My list of inscriptions to find and examine was long, and I wanted to stop at all ninety-two churches outside Visby. If there was anything going on with regard to sacred geometry here, the only way to figure it out was to get the GPS location of every church I could.

Each church on the map was designated with a horizontal Christian cross, and they were pretty evenly spread out across the island. I decided to

The religious symbols M and W appeared on this relic case (circa 1200) from Spånga Church in Uppland, Sweden. Notice the repeated X pattern in the trim and the fleur-de-lis along the top ridge of gold. This case is now in the Historiska Museum in Stockholm, Sweden. (Wolter, 2005)

head north along the coast. Within a few miles, I saw the first steeple appear over the treetops. Lummelunda Kyrka (Swedish for church) stood alongside the winding two-lane road between snow-covered farm fields. The purpose of my journey from Minnesota was about to be officially consummated upon entering my first church on the island. As I walked along the neatly snow-shoveled walkway through the stone gate past several old tombstones, I couldn't stop staring at the stone tower. Regardless of how small it was compared to the monstrous cathedrals across Europe and even in the United States, it was in its own way very impressive. The doorway was framed in beautifully carved limestone that curved upward over the door into a pointed peak. The dark-brown, highly weathered wooden door had to have been many centuries old. I grabbed the metal latch but heard a high-pitched "ting" that drained my excitement. The door was locked!

It was the off-season and I already been warned that many of the churches would be locked up. The good news was that I had ninety-one more chances. The fifth door I tried was Rute Kyrka. This time the old wooden door opened. It was beautiful inside with two limestone columns, one round and one square that supported both rounded and vaulted archways. Next to the round column was a baptismal font that was also carved out of limestone. As I walked down the aisle toward the pulpit next to the altar, I scanned the walls and noticed a painted cross that would become very familiar. It was the Cross Pattee or "Templar" cross within a circle that I would eventually see painted on the walls of nearly every church on the island. The crosses certainly inspired my curiosity, but there was an important inscription here I wanted to see that also had this same interesting cross. After exploring the nave and altar, I headed back toward the tower area and noticed four weathered grave slabs leaning against the wall.

The first church on my initial trip to Gotland on February 28, 2005 that was not locked was Rute Kyrka (Church) on the northern end of the island. (Wolter, 2005)

They had been moved inside after centuries of standing in the graveyard. Three of the four grave slabs were extensively weathered, but I was still able to make out the carved areas that remained by shining my flashlight at a low angle. The round Templar crosses were still visible along with a few runes. I didn't remember these inscriptions from the Gotlandic rune books, but I instantly recognized the fourth grave slab. It was in very good condition and had been painted by runologists in the recent past.

The grave slab was stunningly beautiful with the carved lines and runes painted in red and black. Inside the circular inscription was a striking Templar cross that made me wonder where the original grave was that this slab marked, and if a medieval knight was buried there.

Around lunchtime, I pulled into Lärbro Church and parked in front of a snow-covered open shelter covering several old grave slabs. Staring back at me sandwiched between two slabs with Latin inscriptions was another Templar cross.

I circled the shelter and found a couple more Templar crosses on other slabs. As I walked toward the church, I passed the restored defense

The Gothic architecture inside Rute Church on Gotland was evidenced by both square and round limestone columns with curved arches supporting the ceiling (left). Inside the tower was the grave slab with a runic inscription (G 318) that also had a beautiful Templar Cross within the circular inscription (right). (Wolter, 2005)

tower once used as a refuge to protect the local population during raids by pirates. The Baltic Sea was a little over a mile away, and this was one of six defense towers scattered across the island near the coastline. The other five defense towers at Gothem, Öja, Sundre, Fröjel, and Gammelgarn churches, are now in ruins. The Lärbro church tower was unique because it had an octagonal shape with gables, angled at ninety degrees, encircling it about halfway up. They reeked of symbolism that at the time I had only recently become aware of. The gables represented both the alternating "M" for wisdom, and "W" for the Holy Spirit, as well as the "Λ" symbol for the male, and the "V" symbol for the female.

Inside the church, I found the same Gothic architecture with limestone columns and vaulted ceilings. I also found an interesting wall painting of what appeared to be Saint Bernard of Clairvaux holding a coded key in one hand and a Templar cross within a ring in the other.

I knew that Bernard was arguably the most important figure in the history of the Cistercians, and my research revealed many interesting details about this charismatic man and the incredible monastic order he led.

The following passage is a summary of the Cistercian order written by their modern day contemporaries.

> Cistercians are men and women who follow Saint Benedict's Rule for Monks and the Constitution of Cîteaux. Settling in 1098 in a

At Lärbro Church a snow-covered shelter protected several grave slabs including one with a prominent Templar cross. (Wolter, 2005)

51

remote Burgundian marsh (in Latin, a cisterna), the first Cistercians determined to live simply and to balance in their lives common prayer, personal reflection, and manual labor. For guidance they read the Bible, the writings of the Church Fathers, and the docu-

The tower at Lärbro Church is octagonal in shape and exhibits medieval symbolism. The gabled M's and W's represent wisdom and the Holy Spirit as well as the duality of male and female consistent with Cistercian and Templar religious beliefs. The restored defense tower on the right was used by the local population as a refuge from raiding pirates. (Wolter, 2005)

ments of the centuries of Christian monasticism. The literature they created resonates their love of God and their reasoned analysis of the intensely personal experience of growth through self-acceptance to self-knowledge to the perception of God.[2]

Bernard was a very important figure in early medieval history and a person many historians consider the most powerful man in Christendom during his lifetime (1090 to 1153). He was born in Fontaine, France, and sent to be schooled by the canons of Saint Vorles in Chatillon. He chose to live a life of religious service, entering the monastery in Cîteaux in 1113. After only two years as a monk, Bernard was sent by Stephen Harding with a group of monks to found Clairvaux in 1115. Bernard's religious dedication and charismatic nature enabled him to persuade his many friends, family, and followers into the monastic life. So successful was

This wall painting at Lärbro Church appears to show the Cistercian monk Saint Bernard of Clairvaux holding a coded key in his right hand and a Templar Cross in his left. Bernard successfully argued with the pope in 1129 A.D. that a military Order of Christian Knights was necessary. (Wolter, 2005)

Bernard in bringing new recruits into the order that sixty-eight daughter houses were founded during his lifetime. This would eventually lead to the amazing total of around 750 monasteries across Europe, Scandinavia, and into the Middle East. So revered was Bernard that he was offered five bishoprics and refused them all. Many historians agree he could easily have become pope if he so desired. Curiously, he instead enjoyed the authority belonging to those positions of honor. Indeed, no important political decision was made in Europe without seeking his advice.

The Cistercians sought to live a quiet, pious life by building their monasteries in remote wilderness areas away from population centers where they devoted their time to self-sufficiency through prayer and work. Their well-documented meteoric rise to wealth and prominence was simply due to their strict adherence to the motto of the order, "Ora et Labora" (Pray and Work).[3] The "White Monks" began each day by rising at 1:00 A.M. first to pray and then to pursue their given tasks in earnest. Typically, the monks would eat twice a day, and were only allowed meat two to three times per week depending on the particular individual's physical needs to complete their duties. After evening mass, they would retire at 8:00 P.M.

The monks worked at many vocations including farming, gardening, manufacturing, and tending to large herds of cattle and sheep. Sheep were especially important to the Cistercians, who produced high quality wool from their flocks. Merchants preferred doing business with the monks, who produced a consistent quality product, were reliable and easy to deal with year after year.

In addition to selling the wool, they used the skins for vellum, fueling the many scriptoriums where artistic monks spent their days copying manuscripts. Many of these beautiful manuscripts survive to this day. It is within these virtually untapped manuscripts that modern researchers can learn much more about the activities of these amazing monks. Not surprising, the lamb is an important symbol to both the Cistercians and the Knights Templar.

Most people are not aware of the connection between the Cistercians and Knights Templar. Bernard is given credit for establishing the now famous military monastic order designed to fight wars on Christ's behalf. In 1128, Bernard wrote the charter for the order of the Poor Knights of Solomon otherwise known as the Knights Templar, modeled after the Cistercians, and argued successfully for papal recognition at the Council of Troyes in January of 1129. His two main arguments were that military monks were necessary to protect traveling Christians and to remove Muslim infidels from the Holy Land in Jerusalem. Two of the nine founding members of the Knights Templar, André de Montbard and Hugh de Payens, were Bernard's uncles.[4] His support was invaluable to the Templars and paved the way for future military monastic orders, such as the Teutonic Knights, who received their rule, based on that of the Templars, when Pope Celestine issued their charter in 1198.[5]

The Cistercians' strict dedication to their work and their business acumen are what allowed them to accumulate immense wealth. Bernard's personal symbol was the beehive, emblematic of the achievements possible when a community of individuals worked with diligence and cooperation for the greater good. Under Bernard's leadership, the monastic order flourished by efficiently employing the principals symbolic of the beehive.

An unmistakable symbol of the Cistercians and the Knights Templar is the Lamb of God with a flag staff with a red cross on a white mantle. This wall hanging was found at Gothem church on Gotland on May 8, 2005. (Wolter, 2005)

Bernard also preached for the Second Crusade, against heresy and, ". . . justified his involvement in the affairs of the wider Church by what he perceived to be the need to defend it against its foes, both internal and external."[6] He mediated conflicts and spent roughly a third of his time away from his beloved abbey of Clairvaux. Bernard had a hand in the selection of at least two popes. In 1130, he lobbied successfully for the election of Gregorio Papareschi, otherwise known as Pope Innocent II. Bernard would have another ally in the papacy when his former disciple at Clairvaux, Eugene III, was elected as pope in 1145.

Arguably the most important aspect of Bernard was his deep veneration for the Virgin Mary. Innocent II echoed this adoration by his ". . . openly declaring the Virgin Mary to be considered the 'the mother of God' and 'Queen of Heaven.'"[7] Elevation of the Virgin served to satisfy Bernard's zeal for the "feminine" within his faith and likely had its roots in the Egyptian goddess Isis. Legend has it that Bernard gave a sermon where he saw the Virgin Mary come to life. He reportedly said the Virgin put her hand to her breast where drops of her milk with its healing powers dripped into his mouth. Quite likely the breast milk story had its origin in Egyptian mythology. Regardless of the genesis, the veneration of the sacred feminine had a profound impact on Bernard and his followers.

Writers Alan Butler and Stephen Dafoe wrote in their 1999 book, *The Knights Templar Revealed*, that Bernard represented a group of families called the "Troyes Fraternity," whose goal was to alter the patriarchal ideology of the Catholic Church to a matriarchal form of Christianity, by using subversive means to achieve their goals. It appears their goal was to elevate the female component to a more equal level with Jesus. Some have called their religion one that was very ancient and celebrated the duality and balance of male and female, and heaven and earth. When the Cistercians are examined with this theory in mind, their history, from their inception in 1090 A.D. to the beginning of their decline in the middle 1300s, becomes extremely enlightening.

By 1300 A.D., it appears that, along with King "Phillip the Fair" of France, whose primary goal was to seize the Templars' wealth, the Church in Rome had caught on to the plan and realized that if something drastic

THE FLEUR-DE-LIS.

The bee was used as a symbol of royalty by the immortal Charlemagne, and it is probable that the fleur-de-lis, or lily of France, is merely a conventionalized bee and not a flower. There is an ancient Greek legend to the effect that the nine Muses occasionally assumed the form of bees.

The beehive was the personal symbol of Saint Bernard of Clairvaux, the charismatic leader of the Cistercians from 1115 until his death in 1153. (Hall, 1909, p. 87)

wasn't done soon, their version of Christianity would be in serious jeopardy. The Knights Templar had become both a powerful military and economic force threatening to bankrupt the king of France. Historians tell us that Philip the Fair partnered with the pope to condemn the Templars because of the money he owed, which very likely was one of the motives to move against them. However, there was no doubt a more important agenda for the Templars, and their Cistercian brothers, than just money. Both King Phillip and Rome were well aware of the Cistercian umbilical cord-like connection to the Templars that began when Bernard wrote their charter and argued successfully for the creation of the order to the pope in 1128. By eliminating the Templars, by arresting them on "Black Friday," October 13, 1307, torturing and burning as many of them as they could, they severed that cord, leaving both entities permanently crippled.

Although both the Templars and Cistercians had been severely damaged, they were still the ones who were best prepared to endure the next great calamity that was indiscriminate of ideology or religion: the Black Plague. The case could be made that the landscape in Europe had been irreparably changed for the Cistercians after the Templars were put down. In addition to famine and war ravaging during the first decades of the 1300s, the plague, which began in 1348 appears to have delivered the final blow that turned the attention of the Cistercians in a new direc-

This image of Saint Bernard of Clairvaux was painted on wood circa 1600 A.D. The inscription around his head reads, "St. Bernard first abbot of the arch-abbey of Clairvaux." (Könemann, 2006, p. 32)

tion. The continent "far to the west" likely offered the best glimmer of hope for an ideology that was ready to make its next bold move. To venture off into a vast unknown to establish a "paradise" was what the Cistercians had done since their inception. One should almost have expected the Cistercians and the fugitive Templars to be involved in such an ambitious enterprise.

WHEN I ROLLED THE CAR into the walled city of Visby, it was after dark. I'd stopped at thirteen churches. Even though I was only able to get inside a few of them, I took GPS (global positioning system) readings at each one. After reading about the sacred geometry on the island of Bornholm (Denmark), the possibility of similar geometry on Gotland seemed like a good bet.

Perhaps the most important part of my trip was to try to verify the one smoking gun in the Kensington Rune Stone mystery, the dotted R. In the Gotlandic books of runic inscriptions (*Gotlands Runinskrifter*), Dick Nielsen and I had identified several examples that needed to be checked. As it turned out, two of the examples noted in the Swedish rune books, in my judgment, did not appear to be what the experts thought they were. What they thought were dots in R-runes were actually edge chipping (G 57, circa 1150) and pitting in the rock from weathering (G 158, circa 1305). However, I unexpectedly found three examples of the dotted R with the dot between the legs previously unknown to the Swedish scholars. Swedish runologist Henrik Williams, at the University of Uppsala, later complimented Dick and me for the discoveries.

There was no way I could visit all ninety-two churches spread out on the island on my first trip, let alone make note of all the inscriptions I wanted to see. So, on May 4, 2005, I returned to Gotland. The first place I wanted to visit was Lye Church. I'd already made arrangements to meet with pastor Patrik Ahlmark, and as I pulled up to the church, I saw a smiling man walk up with a little girl at his side. Patrik introduced himself and welcomed me to his church. I explained why I had traveled so far just to look at scratches in the plaster and the oldest grave slabs in his church that were mortared into the floor.

Patrik and his daughter, Martina, escorted me into the church where I explained the two things I most wanted to see. There were two important grave slabs here next to the altar. They both contained lengthy runic inscriptions that scholars had designated as G 99 and G 100. I dropped to all fours and started scanning the inscriptions. I started with the G 100 inscription. Moments later I called out, "There it is." Patrik and Martina leaned over as I pointed to the word comprised of four runes. The carved and then painted dot in the second R of the word was obvious and clear. It was a beautiful dotted R!

The other important feature on these two graves slabs was that they were both dated twice to the same year of 1449. The first date was spelled out in runes, and the second by use of the Easter Table Dating method. I smiled as I stared at these amazing inscriptions. It seemed almost too good to be true that the tradition of double dating we found on the Kensington Rune Stone, like everything else in the inscription, was also found on Gotland. I asked Patrik if I could make a rubbing of the inscription, and he graciously gave me the go-ahead. I made rubbings of both grave slabs and photographed the numerous medieval inscriptions carved into the plaster in the tower area of the church. Before heading off to my next stop I took a GPS reading near the tower and then thanked Patrik for his hospitality.

A frustration of my first trip was the numerous locked churches. But this time the tourist season had just begun, and virtually all the churches were open. At Othem Church on the northwest side of the island, I found

The Maltese cross is carved into several grave slabs at Othem Church on Gotland. This particular grave slab in front of the altar has a runic inscription (G 282) that contains a dotted R (between the legs) along with two other extremely rare grammatical features that are also found on the Kensington Rune Stone. (Wolter, 2004)

three grave slabs with striking Templar crosses, and I couldn't help wondering who was buried here. I already knew that the medieval monks at these churches were all Cistercian, but the crosses reminded me that their brothers who carried swords were also here. The Teutonic Knights, the Baltic Region's version of the Knights Templar established in 1185 A.D., also had had a strong presence on Gotland, which was literally the center of commerce in the Baltic Sea in the fourteenth century.

Realizing this made me think back to the first word of the Kensington Rune Stone inscription. Undoubtedly, there were at least one, and perhaps two, Cistercian monks and/or a Templar priest in the Kensington Rune Stone party. The other six "Goths" were likely Teutonic Knights or members of the Order of the Knights of Christ. The twenty-two "Northmen" were probably the Norwegian crew. To many people, the best sailors in the world, back then and today, were Norwegians.

In three days I visited thirty-nine churches to complete the total of ninety-two on the greater part of the island. It was a whirlwind tour for sure, but I made sure to collect the GPS location of every church.

Notes

[1]Knight and Lomas, 2005, p. 348.
[2]Cistercian Publications, Kalamazoo, Michigan, 1992.
[3]Butler and Dafoe, 1999, p. 83.
[4]Butler and Dafoe, 1999, p. 90.
[5]Urban, 2003, pages 12-13.
[6]France, 2007, page xiv.
Butler and Dafoe, 2006, p. 97.

A dotted R appeared in the G 100 inscription, dated 1449, at Lye Church, on Gotland, viewed on May 6, 2005. (Wolter, 2005)

Most of the medieval runic inscriptions on Gotland are carved into grave slabs that have been mortared into stone floor near the altar of the churches. These two important grave slabs (G 99 and G 100) were examined by the author at Lye Church on May 6, 2005. (Wolter, 2005)

9

The Grail Prayer

On October 3, 2005, I received a call from Dick Neilsen, who was in Europe on his way to China for work. He said, "Scott, we have Grail on the Stone."

I said, "Do you mean *that* grail?"

Dick said "Yes," and then explained that, with lots of time on his flight to Europe to think about the punch marks in the inscription, he had puzzled it out. We had both spent time thinking about those marks. What Dick did was simply put the singled-out characters I documented under the microscope in sequence. The first four letters were "g," "r," "a" and "l," which spells "gral." In medieval Old Swedish this means "Grail." The first thing I thought was that no one was ever going to believe us.

Dick's discovery was amazing, yet it was so simple. We then immediately started trying to figure out what the rest of the mysterious message was. The next three letters singled out were the thorn rune "Þ," another "a,"

The first four characters that were singled out with either a punch mark or a short stroke by the carver (red) are "g," "r," "a," and "l." In medieval Old Swedish these letters spell "Grail." (Wolter, 2002)

To have a Cistercian insert the word "Gral" [grail] within the Kensington Rune Stone inscription is perfectly reasonable since it was the Cistercians who wrote the "Grail" legends during medieval times. This fourteenth century painting, circa 1351, from the Cistercian Queste del Saint Graal, depicts the Grail Mass of Josephes. (Gardner, 2001, page 97)

this time with a punch in the bottom of both legs, and a second "r." This "r" also had two punch marks that were at the same elevation as the word separators, and seemed as though the carver was telling the reader to stop spelling. Dick thought the second word could be "these," "those," or the possessive "their." He and I had many discussions about the split at the bot-

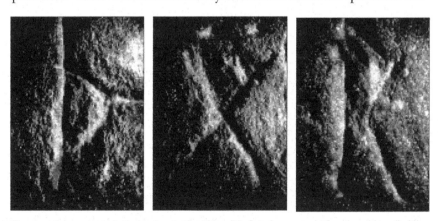

The next three runes singled out were the "thorn," "a," and a second "r" and could spell either "these," "those" or the possessive "their." (Wolter, 2002)

tom of this thorn rune, wondering if it might be a bind rune, or possibly something else. I always believed it was too subtle to be a bind rune, and that it had to be part of a code or secret message. By including it, a logical message began unfolding that started to make sense.

The carver clearly created some kind of message. Dick and I were not in agreement over what the next thing the carver intended to single out. The first Arabic ten on line seven had a very shallow punch mark in the small plateau of rock in the right loop. Apparently, the carver learned from his mistake in the upper loop of the first dotted R in line one, and was very careful not to make this punch too forcefully. This interpretation immediately led us to check the second Arabic ten on the split side. To no surprise, it also had a shallow punch, only this time it was made in the left loop.

Dick thought the dotted tens might denote a mathematical equation hidden within the inscription. However, I believe they were part of a secret message. It is possible that the tens serve a dual purpose: part of the "Grail" message, and an equation that has yet to be solved.

The next character in the sequence obviously singled out was the Latin letter "M" on line eight. It had a punch mark at the bottom of the far right leg. From our research about the Cistercians, Templars, and the Teutonic Knights, we felt confident that the "M" was symbolic for "Wisdom," being derived from the Egyptian belief that the owl carried wisdom with the M symbol derived from the stylized pattern around the bird's eyes. It would have been perfectly consistent for the Cistercians, who embraced much of the religious beliefs and symbolism of the Egyptians, to use the Latin M for wisdom.

The final character in the inscription to be singled out was the "W"-rune on line ten of the split side, in the word "hawet," which means "inland sea" or "lake." We reasoned that, to the Cistercians, the "W" represented the Holy Spirit, symbolic of the sacred feminine and always associated with water. The realization that this was probably correct came to me after Dick made an insightful observation. He asked, "Do you think it's a coincidence that of the ten W's in the inscription, the one that has a punch is in the word that means water?" Could this be considered simply a coincidence? In my mind, the Cistercian or Templar carver definitely meant to single out the Holy Spirit rune in the word it would logically be associated with.

After many hours of sorting through numerous possibilities, it appears the Cistercians had encoded a prayer by spelling out words and symbolism using a series of punch marks and short lines, after carving the inscription. This "Grail" prayer was obviously for the ten dead men and was consistent with Cistercian beliefs. One translation could be, "Grail, these ten [men have] wisdom, the ten [men are with the] Holy Spirit."

The realization of our discovery of this prayer, and how it eerily coincided with *The Da Vinci Code* mania that was sweeping the world, was mind-blowing.

The carver of the Kensington Rune Stone put shallow punch marks in the two Arabic tens that occur on lines seven (left) and ten (right) in the inscription. (Wolter, 2002)

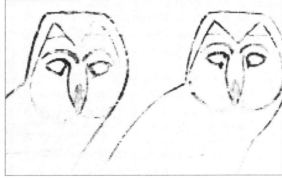

The Latin "M" on line eight of the Kensington Rune Stone inscription has a punch in the lower right leg (left). To the Cistercians and the Egyptians, the "M" was the symbol for wisdom, which was carried by the owl. This Egyptian drawing on limestone, circa 1490 B.C., illustrates how the "M" was derived from the pattern around the bird's eyes. (Left: Wolter, 2002; Right: Peck, 1978, page 27)

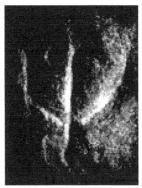 

The "W" rune on line 1 of the split side of the Kensington Rune Stone has a deep punch at the bottom of the main stave apparently singling out the rune in the word "hawet" meaning "inland lake" or "sea." Outside Catholic doctrine, the Holy Spirit was considered to be female and always associated with water. The Birth of Venus is depicted as a Goddess riding across the water in a clam shell. (Left: Wolter, 2002; Right: Sandro Botacelli, c.1485)

Perhaps it was our heightened awareness because of the novel that led to our finding a plausible explanation to the mysterious marks. The prayer seemed to answer the burning question of why the marks I'd found under the microscope existed.

The coded prayer also fit logically within the context of the inscription and our land-claim theory. For an inscribed stone to be used as both an affirmation to the title to land and a memorial is not unprecedented. Scholars point out that Irish Ogham (Ogham is an ancient form of script consisting of vertical and angled lines cut into wood and stone) standing stones dating back to the fifth century, were used to mark burials of both Christians and pagans, and as affirmation to land in addition to delineating terriorial boundaries.[1]

It was also a reminder about was how careful one needed to be when trying to interpret an inscription. Many times I've heard people talk about how the ten dead men were "scalped by Indians." The inscription didn't say that. For that matter, no one can know if it wasn't ten Natives who were ". . . . found dead"? Perhaps the Kensington Rune Stone party came across the aftermath of a battle between two warring tribes. A monk would likely carve a prayer for ten dead souls regardless of race or whether he knew them personally. This also brought to mind the theory of our late friend, Tom Reiersgord, who proposed in his 2001 book, *The Kensington Rune Stone: Its Place in History*, that the "ten men red with blood and death," weren't actually dead. Tom's hypothesis was that they were stricken with the plague, with blood flowing from their eyes, ears, noses, and mouths is certainly valid. We simply don't know exactly what happened.

Many archaeologists, such as Mike Michlovic at University of Minnesota at Moorhead, have argued that nothing has ever been found in the ground at the discovery site. Based on our land claim thesis, I wouldn't expect there to be evidence of an encampment. After lying out the triangulation with the stone holes cut into glacial boulders, the Kensington party buried the stone where they had to. Besides, a lack of evidence proves nothing. We also don't know how long after the referenced tragic event that the inscription was carved. It could have been days, weeks or even months. We just don't know and must be very careful drawing conclusions based on assumptions that might not be correct.

Note

[1]Monk, 1998, p. 27.

Part III

Spirit Pond Rune Stones and the Hooked X

10

The Spirit Pond Rune Stones

The Spirit Pond Rune Stones were found buried together by Walter Elliot who was searching for arrowheads and other artifacts along the shores of Spirit Pond near Popham Beach, Maine, on May 27, 1971. All three runic inscriptions have the Hooked X, which meant they were clearly connected to the Kensington Rune Stone. I flew out to visit the Maine State Museum and the site where the stones were found. Since I knew the stones couldn't be sent to my lab for examination due to museum policy, I decided to bring my lab to Maine. I purchased a specially designed, padded travel case, and packed my stereomicroscope to bring along. The microscope was equipped with a digital camera, and a SPOT software package that allowed me to take photographs using my laptop. To my knowledge, this would be the first time these rune stones would be examined under a microscope.

On March 5, 2006, I arrived in Augusta, Maine, but, much to my chagrin, my new black case with the microscope never came through the luggage chute. With only two days to complete my work, it frustrated me

Walter Elliot holds two of the three rune stones he found shallowly buried together while searching for arrowheads and other artifacts along the near-shore area at Spirit Pond near Popham Beach, Maine, on Saturday, May 27, 1971. (Photo courtesy of the Associated Press)

This picture of the Spirit Pond Rune Stones and the amulet gives an indication of their relative size. (Wolter, 2006)

that I would miss this chance to examine the rune stones with my equipment. I still had the macro lens on my Canon digital camera; it would have to do the job. Having already made arrangements with both the Maine State Museum director J.R. Phillips and archaeologist Bruce Bourque, it didn't take long to get to work. Bruce and his assistant, Bob Lewis, set me up in a quiet, out-of-the-way room with a large table and some good lighting, and then left me alone for the day.

To my pleasant surprise, the half-inch-thick, playing-card-sized digital camera worked out great. Not only was I able to stabilize the camera with the tripod I'd packed in my luggage, but the macro lens allowed me to take excellent close-up images of all three inscriptions, and the mysterious amulet also reportedly found at Spirit Pond sometime after the rune stones. I was also able to persuade Bruce and Bob to collect a tiny piece of the Spirit Pond Inscription Stone for a chemical analysis.

By 4:30 P.M., I had taken over 300 photographs, and made several interesting observations. From a geologic standpoint, the Spirit Pond Inscription Stone was carved into a relatively soft mud-stone that, unfortunately, didn't lend itself to the same kind of relative-age dating work I had done on the Kensington Rune Stone. Subsequent scanning electron microscopy confirmed the mineralogy of, primarily, very fine-grained quartz, and clays, that didn't experience additional measurable weathering. This fact meant that the various aspects of the inscription itself—language, runes, grammar, dialect, and dating—would have to be the primary means of determining its authenticity.

The Spirit Pond Inscription Stone had reportedly been scratched out with a penknife by the discoverer Walter Elliot, similar to what Olof Ohman had done to the Kensington Rune Stone. This inscription appeared altered with many of the carved lines looking as if they had been widened and deepened. The most convincing evidence of Walter's reported handiwork was the smaller and deeper original pits at the bottom of most of the word separators (the vertically aligned double dots between words).

Perhaps the most exciting aspect of the Spirit Pond Inscription Stone was the numerous bars over eight different runes in the inscription. Dick Nielsen wanted me to pay special attention to the bars, with the idea that the carver was using bars instead of dots for the sound variations we'd already seen in the Ukna grave slab. According to Dick, two of the seven barred runes on the Spirit Pond Inscription Stone were extremely rare, the dental "n" (ᚿ̄), and the barred R (R̄). If that barred R was in fact a substitution for the dotted R, that point alone proved the Spirit Pond inscriptions were medieval.

There are eight basic futhork runes, fourteen in total, on the Spirit Pond Inscription Stone that have been marked by a horizontal line over the rune. These appear to represent the classic dotted þ (ᚧ) for the ð-rune, the dotted k (ᚵ) for the g-rune, a dotted unilateral n (ᚿ) for the "dental" n-rune, the dotted i (ᛂ) for the e-rune, the dotted t (ᛑ) denoting a d-rune, the dotted

The Spirit Pond Inscription Stone front and back sides. (Wolter, 2006)

b (ᛔ) for the p-rune and a dotted r (ᚱ) for the R-rune. Seven of these dotted runes appear on the Unka grave slab (Sm 145) from Småland, Sweden. In addition, there are seven (X̄) runes that appear to be synonymous with the (X̆) rune on the Kensington Rune Stone.

The Spirit Pond Map Stone was carved into a relatively flat meta-basalt cobble, and was the artifact that intrigued me the most. The area depicted on the map carved on one side of the stone corresponded with the area where the rune stones were found near Popham Beach where the Kennebec River flows into the Atlantic Ocean. The inscription on the map, according to Dick, said that "Vinland, takes two days" with an arrow pointing to the right, or in the direction of south on this map. As interesting as the map was, the opposite side was even better. The first time I saw the images carved on the back, I was taken aback. Who would carve animals, an Indian face, a canoe, and a bow and arrow onto a rock? It wasn't until I understood that the runes at the top of the stone meant essentially "good land" in the Algonquin language that things started to make sense. This begged another question: why is an Algonquin word being spelled in runes? Whoever carved it appeared to be documenting what things were at this particular location, right down to the amazingly accurate map.

The Spirit Pond Norway Stone. (Wolter, 2006)

What didn't make sense were the carvings at the bottom. On the left side was a strange "X" character that had an arc between the upper two arms. To the right of the arced X was something that some people have called a "ladder." It would be a very strange ladder that had four rungs on the left, and eight rungs on the right! Dick's interpretation was

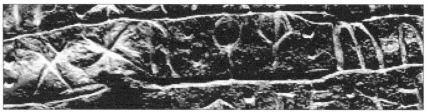

The Spirit Pond Inscription Stone is dated using the medieval Easter Table with the two Arabic tens (ᚠ) indicating the tenth column and tenth row. This yields a date of 1401 A.D. which is immediately confirmed three times with the Sunday Letter for that year of ᚾ. (Wolter, 2006)

The map and symbol sides (Front side, opposite; Back, above) of the Spirit Pond Map Stone. (Wolter, 2006)

that the symbol was simply a different style of pentadic number similar to those used on the Kensington Rune Stone. Based on medieval examples such as in David King's book, the number would be forty-four.

The so-called Norway Stone had only three words carved into a well-rounded, granitic cobble and appeared to have been made by a different person. The tip-off was the use of an "o-r" bind rune. The two runes were bound by a common vertical line, or stave, whereas the carver of the Spirit Pond Inscription Stone separated the two runes in the word—"nor" (North).

I also examined a small basalt amulet with a prominent cross on one side, and three lines of runes and symbols on the other. It was impossible to estimate the age of the weathering at this point, but the drilled hole on one end did appear to exhibit wear, apparently from being worn as a necklace.

I had a much better understanding about medieval history by now, and what the possibilities might be. Dick had previously found four Easter

Table dates on the Spirit Pond Rune Stones, one of 1401 and three of 1402. The only European candidate that I knew who could have been in that part of the North America with a Cistercian monk using runes was a very controversial historical figure, Prince Henry Sinclair, Earl of Orkney and feudal baron of Roslin in Scotland. I didn't know a whole lot about his reported voyage at the time, but I would soon learn a great deal more.

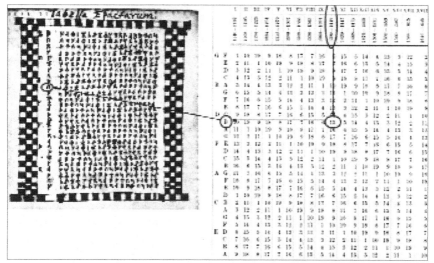

The runic Easter Table on the left has been converted to Latin letters and numbers for clarity on the table to the right. Moving down the tenth column to the tenth row yields a date of 1401 A.D. The Sunday letters are listed on the far left column. When the Sunday Letter for the year 1401 is converted back to runes on the medieval Easter Table on the left it yields u. (Lithberg, 1939 and 1953: Table 65)

The second Easter Table date on the Spirit Pond Inscription Stone occurs on line eight and indicates the tenth column, eleventh row which yields a date of 1402 A.D. (left). This date is not confirmed with a Sunday Letter. The same date appears without a Sunday Letter confirmation on the Spirit Pond Map Stone. (Wolter, 2006/2007)

To learn as much as I could about Walter Elliot, I met with Sue Carlson and Roslyn Strong, members of the organization called the New England Antiquities Research Association (NEARA), and both knew Walter well. Sue, an architect and quite knowledgeable about the Old Icelandic language, had her own translation of the Spirit Pond

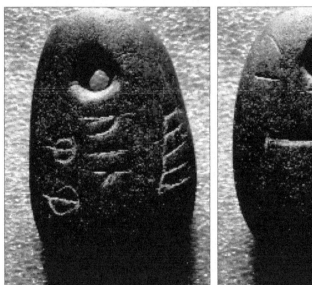

The symbol side and cross side of the Spirit Pond Amulet. (Wolter, 2006)

Inscription Stone. Sue believed the inscription to be a poem intended to be sung in the traditional style. She does not agree with Dick Neilsen's interpretation, which I did happen to agree with.

Both were adamant that Walter could never have carved the inscriptions, as claimed by many opponents, and that state officials had treated him unfairly. They said Walter was a friendly, independent man who had a high school education and served in the Navy. The more I heard, the more amazed I was at the irony of the similarities between Walter and Olof Ohman. In my mind, both men were utterly incapable of being able to do what they were accused of. Sue and Roslyn also told me how Walter had committed suicide in 1994. One of the last things he reportedly said was, "I just want to know what it (Spirit Pond Inscription Stone) says." This certainly didn't sound like the words of a forger to me.

I also asked Sue and Roslyn about the discovery site. Roslyn pulled out photographs from a dig members of NEARA performed at the site where Walter had found the stones. I photographed the photographs. She said that nothing else was found during the dig, but said, "Make sure you look at the sod houses." Bruce Bourque had shared an archaeological report with me about a dig conducted on two sod houses located several hundred yards north of the rune stones' discovery site one year after they were found in 1972. Two depressions within yards of the shore of Spirit Pond were excavated, and samples of wood from within the excavation were collected for Carbon-14 dating. The test results came back and were consistent with colonial habitation (around 1600 A.D.), except for one sample. One of the pieces of wood reportedly came from what was believed to have been the original floorboards of the structure. The date the lab came back with was 1405, plus or minus forty years!

At one point I glanced across the room and saw what looked like a giant book with the Spirit Pond Inscription Stone painted on the cover. Sue explained how she made the book to illustrate her version of the inscription. Sue even sang a rendition of her translation of the inscription, using her best Icelandic tongue.

On March 7, 2006, I drove forty-five miles due south toward Spirit Pond. The road crisscrossed the Kennebec River, which eventually emptied into the Atlantic at Popham Beach. Spirit Pond looked to be about a mile inland from the coast judging from the map. I parked on a trail next to the road and hiked though the woods. I had no problem walking along the marshy edges of the pond because the ground was still frozen. As I gazed over the pond, I thought about what it must have been like thirty-five years ago when Walter was searching for arrow heads.

I made my way south along the western shoreline just as Walter must have done, eventually reaching the dammed southern outlet. The historical pamphlet from the museum said the pond was dammed in the 1830s to harvest ice. Large square blocks of granite had been brought in to raise the water level a couple of feet. I knew I was near the discovery

The accuracy of the map on the Spirit Pond Map Stone is demonstrated by the once water-filled channel to the sea that is now a treeless, swampy channel with a small stream draining the pond. The removal of weight from mile-thick glacial ice has allowed isostatic rebound of the earth's crust and raised the land relative to the sea by several feet in the last 600 years. (Wolter, 2007)

The top arrow is the site where the Spirit Pond Rune Stones were found near a bedrock outcrop by Walter Elliot on May 27, 1971. The lower arrow marks the highly weathered stone hole in bedrock found by the author on March 6, 2006. The age and possible association of the stone hole with the Spirit Pond Rune Stones is unclear but could be centuries old. (Wolter, 2007)

site when I saw the granite blocks. The area looked much like the photos I had, and I easily found the outcrop Sue and Roslyn said Walter sat down on when he found the stones together in a cluster. He had noticed the edge of the Spirit Pond Inscription Stone protruding from the ground.

While trying to understand the geology of the terrain, something caught my eye. Within twenty-five yards from the discovery site, I stared at a highly weathered and several inches deep stone hole! This hole could easily have been made during the ice harvesting days, but it could also be much older based on the advanced weathering of the sides of the hole filled with water. Why did these stone holes always show up around rune stones?

After the excitement with the stone hole, I made my way north along the west shoreline. Roslyn and Sue had pointed out the location of the sod houses on my map. Roughly 300 yards from the discovery site, I found the area marked off like a crime scene with yellow tape. I walked the perimeter and then looked out over the pond, trying to imagine who might have put in the wooden floorboards around 1400 A.D. I also thought about the incredible new connection between the Carbon-14 date of the floorboards, and Dick Nielsen's 1401/1402 Easter Table dates on the artifacts found only a few hundred yards away. The odd early date of about 1400 of the floorboard piece of wood didn't mean much in 1972, when researchers believed the rune stones dated to 1010, but it took on a whole new importance now.

On February 7, 2007, I was back to examine the Spirit Pond Rune Stones one more time, only this time my microscope had arrived safely. My host was David Brody, a practicing attorney and fiction writer who had become interested in the Spirit Pond Rune Stones while conducting research for a novel. As we crossed into Maine, the topic of the Spirit Pond Rune Stones was formost in our minds. David related a story from the night before. At the dinner table with his wife, Kim, and his two daughters, Allie and Renee, David had been telling them about why he was going with me to see the Rune Stones. He explained what they were, and at one point was explaining the orientation of the Map Stone. He asked his girls a question: "If you were making a map like that, where would you put north?"

Renee, his ten-year-old daughter, spoke up first and said, "Well, Daddy, if I was making the map today, I'd put it at the top of the map. But if I was making it in medieval times, I'd put it to the left with east at the top."

David relayed the story matter-of-factly, but I looked at him, stunned, and said, "You're kidding me. She really said that?"

David was taken aback, "You mean you didn't already know that?"

"No!" I said.

Apparently Renee had read an article in a magazine about pirates to learn this very important bit of information. David said that after Renee's comment, he went on the Internet and found

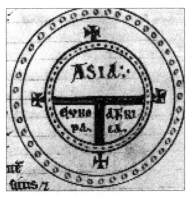

Some medieval maps, such as this "T-O" world map from the twelfth century, were oriented with east at the top, and the Holy Land of Jerusalem depicted as the center of the world. The map carved on the Spirit Pond Map Stone is also oriented with east at the top. (British Library, C5933-06, page f.135v)

a couple examples of medieval maps that indeed did have east at the top. He had printed them out and showed them to me. I would later find numerous examples of these so-called "T-O" maps, which are named for their resemblance of the two letters that has Asia at the top with Europe in the lower left, and Africa in the lower right quadrant of the "T." The vertical bar represented the Mediterranean Sea dividing the two lower continents. The intersection of the horizontal and vertical bars represented Jerusalem, which was considered the center of the world at that time. This Church-inspired map first appeared in the seventh century and persisted into the fifteenth century.

Renee's discovery triggered another thought that serves to help support the map's authenticity. A modern forger would almost certainly carve a map oriented with north at the top. For our time, that was the most logical choice. It seems highly unlikely they would know when the "east at the top" orientation had been the fashion. In this case, we had a brand new example of the old phrase, "Out of the mouths of babes."

D AVID BRODY AND I ARRIVED at the Maine State Museum annex building, in Hallowell, where I had already viewed the stones twice before. The head archaeologist, Bruce Bourque, was out so his assistant, Bob Price, greeted us with good news. "Your microscope arrived safe and sound." This time I shipped it ahead instead of checking it as luggage. The box with the Inscription Stone was already on the table ready to be examined. David opened it.

After studying the artifact for a few moments, David handed it to me to place on the mechanical stage under the microscope. I spent the entire morning examining various physical features, and the runes, on both sides of the Spirit Pond Inscription Stone. I took a couple of hundred photos and noticed several interesting things, including something that came both as a surprise and a disappointment. On the front side of the stone, I noticed four runes that had been scratched with a sharp instrument. Fortunately, I had my photo-library from my visit last March, and when I looked at the same characters, the scratches were not there. Somebody in the past eleven months had accessed the artifact and essentially vandalized four of the runes.

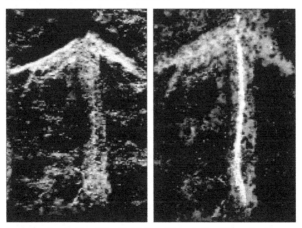

Four characters on the front side of the Spirit Pond Inscription Stone had been scratched with a sharp instrument since my previous examination made in March of 2006. The scratched runes are: L-4, R-67; L-8, N-12; L-10, R-180 and 181. This disturbing vandalism is obvious in these photos of rune 67 on line 4 taken in March of 2006 (left) and February of 2007 (right). (Wolter, 2006/2007)

When I brought the scratches to Bob's attention, he frowned. Under the microscope, I noticed scratches and ink at the bottom of many characters. We took a break for lunch and in the afternoon looked at the Map and Norway stones. By 4:30 P.M. I had taken nearly 400 digital photographs under the microscope, and David had scanned through a good portion of the laboratory's reference books. Thanks to David's daughter Renee bringing it to his attention, he found another medieval map with east at the top!

Another notable observation I made was on the map side of the Map Stone. There were four word separators made with three punches instead of two. A fifth word separator had the normal two-punch marks aligned vertically. What was really strange was that the spacing of the three punches was different in each case, as if they were parts of a code. Having already been down that road with the Kensington Rune Stone, it seemed to me like a natural possibility. If I'd learned anything, it was that whoever carved these stones was capable of just about anything. I also hoped that, eventually, we would figure out what these curious punches meant.

After spending the day with the Spirit Pond Rune Stones, David and I decided to drive down to Popham Beach to see the area around Spirit Pond. On my visit in 2006, I'd spent time hiking around the discovery site and along the shores of Spirit Pond, but I never made it out to Popham Beach. This time, I coaxed David into seeing the Kennebec River area near the beach that is depicted on the Spirit Pond Map Stone. David parked where we could see the ocean so I could take a quick look at the islands and take a few pictures. The wind was howling and felt like cold knives cutting into my exposed ears. The waves were crashing wildly on the shore looking very different from the frozen serenity of Spirit Pond, less than a mile away. That must have been why those medieval visitors wisely chose to make their encampment where they did, instead of here.

My trips to the East Coast helped my understanding of the Spirit Pond Rune Stones immensely. Shortly after my return home, I had a serendipitous encounter that would lead to solving arguably the most important symbol found on five North American Rune Stones. It is the symbol that ties them all together.

11

The Hooked X

O f all the oddities in the Kensington Rune Stone inscription, the one that seemed to haunt me was the Hooked X symbol used for "a." It had also long puzzled runologists and linguists who said it never existed or was invented by a forger. I thought that too simple. It was especially easy to assume this when their mindset was predisposed that it was a fake. My geological work had produced the opposite mindset, which meant there had to be an explanation for everything in the inscription including this mysterious character. The fact that the Hooked X was so radically different from the known runic symbols for "a" (the classic rune for "a" is "ᛆ") meant that there had to be a compelling reason for it. Since the language, runes, grammar, dialect, and dating led us to Gotland, and the Kensington Rune Stone author being a Cistercian monk, the reason for the radical difference in the character had to have been for a religious reason. If so, then the character must have represented important symbolism to the Cistercians.

My obsession with the Hooked X led to a deep plunge into researching medieval religious symbolism. Especially the symbolism associated with Cistercian/Templar beliefs. I found myself purchasing books I'd never even looked at before in bookstores. These books on the occult, symbols, secret societies, codes, medieval and Egyptian history, the Holy Grail, and Freemasonry proved helpful in my understanding what was important to these orders, and why. If I had any chance of figuring out the Kensington Rune Stone, I had to understand how these peoples' minds worked. It quickly became obvious that, although conventional reference material was helpful, it wasn't getting me where I needed to be. If I was going to make headway with the Hooked X, I needed to think about unconventional sources. The most logical unconventional source was the secret society (or as many Freemasons will say, "A society with secrets") that many researchers believe was born after the putdown of the Knights Templar in 1307: modern Freemasonry. Ironically, Masonry met me first!

It all started on December 14, 2005, as I gave one of my regular presentations to an American Concrete Institute (ACI) concrete class in Arden Hills, Minnesota. My lectures are normally about concrete, but since the Kensington Rune Stone book had just come out, the instructors, Dan Frentress and Paul Junkel, asked me to tell the class about our research. I was more than happy to oblige. My head was filled with newly acquired information from my rapidly growing library and at one point I asked if there were any Masons in the audience. No one spoke up, but they seemed to enjoy the new material and Power Point images I'd assembled. After packing up my computer, I noticed one student had stayed behind. He looked to be in his thirties, with a shaved head and a dark mustache. I had an inkling why he had stayed and asked if he was a Mason. He said, "Yes, I'm a Mason."

He introduced himself as John Ross and said he was the Worshipful Master of a Lodge in St. Paul. I asked him, "How'd I do?"

He nodded and said, "Good." John then asked me for my card and wondered if I'd be willing to give a talk at his lodge sometime.

John then spoke with some of his Masonic brothers about my talk. He called and asked if I'd be interested in giving my Kensington Rune Stone talk in front of a larger audience at the Grand Lodge of Minnesota, in St. Paul. My eyes instantly widened and I couldn't say, "Yes," fast enough. He asked me if April 25th would work and if I'd be interested in meeting the current Grand Master of Minnesota at the lodge beforehand. "Yes," came even faster this time.

A couple of weeks later, I met Andy Rice at the Grand Lodge. The hall where the meeting and lecture were to be held was big and had all the now familiar symbols of Freemasonry scattered throughout. I was really looking forward to this presentation and planned to ask for help with deciphering the Hooked X.

Janet and I arrived early at the lodge at the same time that Darwin and Ginny Ohman pulled in. Darwin had heard the Kensington Rune Stone talk several times, but I'm sure he was as excited as we were for this one. A smiling Tom Kolberg greeted us. Russ Fridley arrived with his wife, Metta. Tom introduced me to an older gentleman, Andy Engebretson. "This man has an interesting story to tell you," Tom said. Andy relayed that he was an attorney, and a longtime Freemason, and then he launched into his story. He said his father had been in the banking business, and in 1914 was the banker in the town of Kensington. Andy said, "At that time, the bankers lived at the bank, and during the winter of 1914-1915, in Kensington, there was a bad snowstorm." According to Andy's father, everything was shut down, and nobody left their homes that day. "My dad decided to unlock the bank door since he was going to be stuck there anyway." At one point during the day, a man came in with icicles hanging from his mustache. There was so much snow that the man hadn't wanted to take his horses out of the barn and had walked almost three miles into town to pay off a small loan. When Andy's father asked why he didn't wait until the weather was better, the man said, "The loan's due today, so I'm going to pay it back today." That man was Olof Ohman.

My eyes widened in amazement. "That is a great story," I said. "Would you mind telling it to a couple of friends of mine?"

I then rounded up Darwin and Russ Fridley and asked Andy to repeat the story. As Andy started in, I chuckled to myself as I watched Olof's

The compass and square symbol with the "G" for geometry (and Gnosticism?), is on the outside of the Minnesota Masons Grand Lodge in St. Paul Minnesota. The probable meaning of the Hooked X was realized that night when I asked the Masons for help during my presentation on the Kensington Rune Stone. (Wolter, 2006)

grandson (Darwin), great-grandson (Tom Kolberg) and the most well-known living Kensington Rune Stone skeptic (Russ), listen to this story together. I was also struck by the irony of how eerily similar this story was to another incredible story told by the son of another man about Olof Ohman. In January of 1970, Russ Fridley interviewed Walter Gran who relayed his now infamous "Deathbed Confession" story that his father, John Gran, reportedly told him in 1927. Both were second-hand stories that portrayed Ohman in two completely different lights. The world had certainly heard Walter and Russ's story and it seemed only fair that Andy's and his father's story should also be heard.

After finishing the second time, I asked Andy for his contact information and if he would be willing to let me videotape his story. He said he would be happy to let me record it and gave me his card.

The Grand Lodge hall quickly filled with roughly 130 people, mostly Freemasons from various lodges in Minnesota. Many friendly people introduced themselves, including several men who said they were Knights Templar. Even though I already knew there were modern Knights Templar, this was the first time I ever knowingly met one. Janet and I were seated at the head table along with Darwin, Ginny, Tom, Russ, and his wife, Metta. After the meal, John Ross stepped up to the microphone and introduced me. I started my presentation as the last of the sun's rays faded through the west-facing windows. I took the audience through the factual evidence, and then into our speculation as to who the carver of the Kensington Rune Stone was, where he came from, and why he carved it. I then moved on to the Spirit Pond Rune Stones and the mysterious character that linked them: the Hooked X.

For over five years I'd pondered the meaning of the enigmatic symbol. Dick Nielsen had noticed the Hooked X in Columbus's coded sigla which led to the realization that he was undoubtedly linked to the Templars. Many scholars believe, as I do, that the fugitive Knights Templar simply changed their name to the Knights of Christ after the order was put down in 1307, and continued on. I explained to the Masons how the runic scholars dismissed the Hooked X symbol because it had never been seen before in a runic inscription in Scandinavia. The runic symbol the scholars expected for the "a" sound was "ł." I also explained that since the geology of the Kensington Rune Stone proved the stone was genuine, there had to be a compelling reason why this unique symbol was being used. It seemed that the most logical reason for the deviation from the norm had to be a religious one, since we were confident the Kensington Rune Stone author was a Cistercian monk.

I also explained the basic symbolism associated with the X character. When cut in half horizontally it creates a Λ under a V. The V symbol has been used for thousands of years by many different cultures to symbolically represent the chalice, the vessel, or the womb for the female. The Λ represents the phallic, penis, blade, or the sword symbolic of the male. The Cistercians are thought to have believed that by combining these two symbols into the X it represented the union of male and female.

Near the end of my presentation after telling them about the seven known examples of the Hooked X (the Kensington Rune Stone, the three Spirit Pond Rune Stones, the Narragansett Rune Stone, Columbus's sigla, and the Larsson Papers) and its apparent symbolism, I then asked the Masons, "Does anybody have an idea what the hook means?"

One person, who identified himself as a symbologist, raised his hand and said, "A child?" The words triggered a sudden realization, and I instinctively caught Janet's wide eyes in the front row. She looked at me and silently mouthed the words, "The daughter." I then quickly whirled back to the man and said, "That's great." A few more people spoke up in agreement as the light-bulbs in their heads started clicking on like popcorn.

My mind was racing. I could feel electricity in the room and knew that something important had just happened. The implicit meaning of the Hooked X offered, for the first time, tangible evidence on medieval artifacts consistent with the premise of the book, *Holy Blood, Holy Grail*, that Jesus Christ and Mary Magdalene were married and had at least one child. The symbolism of the Hooked X could very well represent the belief in the union of Jesus Christ, Mary Magdalene, and their daughter in the womb, the little chalice (v) inside the big chalice (V).

This startling revelation was followed a couple of weeks later by another equally startling discovery. On the morning of May 7, 2006, I

Could the scissors arches (1338 A.D.) in the nave of Wells Cathedral in England be symbolic of the "X" representing the union of male and female? (Wolter, 2008)

relayed the story of the Hooked X discovery with the Freemasons, to William Mann, of Ontario, Canada, who agreed with my interpretation. As the author of two books on the Knights Templar, and whose grandfather was the Supreme Grand Master of the Knights Templar in Canada, Bill's opinion on this subject carried credibility. During our conversation, Bill offered a thought about a possible connection of the Hooked X to Egyptian royalty who believed in the matriarchal line. He explained how the Cistercians adopted many of the same beliefs and symbolism as the Egyptians and urged me to look into it.

Bill's words triggered a memory of something I felt compelled to act upon. I looked up Egyptian history. It didn't take long to find what I was looking for, which appeared on the cover of a book entitled,

The Hooked X as it appears on the Kensington Rune Stone used for the letters "a" and "ä." This enigmatic character's radical departure from the medieval runic norm appears to represent a powerful symbol for the ideology of a people who sought refuge on a continent they called "The New Jerusalem." (Wolter, 2002)

Tutankhamen. Emblazoned on the cover was a gold gilded sarcophagus with the crossed crook and flail over the chest. There was no doubt in my mind that this was the inspiration for the symbolism of the Hooked X to the Cistercians and their Templar brethren.

Within the hour, I was back on the phone with Bill, sharing the discovery he had inspired. He explained how the crook and flail represented the Egyptian gods Osiris and his wife, Isis, and that the crossed rods symbolized kingship, royalty, and the belief that the crook held the eggs of fertility. The Hooked X could very well have represented Jesus (kingship), his wife, Mary, (royalty) and their daughter, who many believe was named Sarah, Miriam, or possibly Salome (Fertility).[1]

There is additional evidence consistent with an Egyptian/Cistercian/Templar connection. In at least three Egyptian kings' tombs are wall paintings that could be the inspiration for the white robes of the Cistercians, representing purity, and the white robes with the red pâté cross of the Knights Templar. Tutankhamen, Tuthmosis IV, and Ramesses I all are depicted wearing white clothing with red crosses on their upper bodies.

In the 1974 reproduction of the *Book of Kells* (an illuminated manuscript in Latin, circa 800 A.D.) that contains the four Gospels of the New Testament, author Henry Franciose discussed the recurring pose of religious figures with their arms crossed in front of them in what he describes as "The Osiris pose."[2] Franciose writes that the origin of this pose, ". . . is of course Osiris holding flail and crook-sceptre," and speculates, ". . . these poses were transferred from Christian Egypt to representations of Christ and that from Coptic art they passed into Insular iconography."

Franciose further notes how difficult these links are to make due to missing examples over time. Regardless, the Osiris poses of Christian figures in the *Book of Kells* and an example in the Lichfield Gospels appear to provide strong evidence consistent

This gold gilded sarcophagus found in Tutankhamen's tomb has the crossed crook and flail over the chest. The crook and flail represent the Egyptian gods Osiris and his wife, Isis, and the crossed rods symbolized kingship, royalty and fertility. (Desroches-Noblecourt, 1963)

with an Egyptian origin for the Hooked X symbolism. These books also insert eighth- and ninth-century links into the chain of an ideology that appears to span a period of time of at least 3,300 years (Tutankhamen's reign from 1336-1327 B.C. to the present).

Another parallel is the belief in the spiritual and medicinal powers of breast milk. Egyptians believed that lactating women were considered special, especially if they had given birth to a male child. Their milk could be used to cure a variety of maladies.[3] The Cistercians have a lactation legend associated with their patron saint and founder of the Knights Templar, Saint Bernard of Clairvaux. According to author

These three wall paintings in the tombs of the Egyptian kings Tutankhamen (left), Tuthmosis IV (middle) and Ramesses I (right), all have white dress with red crosses on their upper bodies. The red X identifies the king, signifying royalty. Could this possibly be the inspiration for the Cistercian's white wool tunics and the Knights Templar with a red cross? (Photos from Internet)

James France, "By far the most popular of all medieval images of Bernard was the so-called lactatio or lactation, Mary offering Bernard milk from her breast."[4] How this knowledge could have been acquired from ancient Egyptians can only be guessed. Perhaps the nine knights who spent nine years in the Holy Land, from 1109-1118 A.D., also trav-

These three images are examples of what author Henry Franciose calls the "Osiris pose" that transferred from Christian Egypt to representations of Christ. The first image of St. Luke is from the Lichfield Gospels, circa 730 A.D., and the next two are from the *Book of Kells*, circa 800 A.D. (Franciose, 1974, p. 191-192)

eled to Egypt during this period. If I've learned anything about these medieval monastic orders, it would be a mistake to underestimate them.

Another possible parallel to the Hooked X came to me while listening to a spirited lecture given by William Penhallow, Professor Emeritus of Astronomy and Physics at the University of Rhode Island, at the first symposium on the Newport Tower in Newport, Rhode Island on October 27, 2007. Dr. Penhallow lectured on how the ancients understood that both the heavens and the earth revolved around the axis of our planet. That axis represents a pole historically referred to as the "umbilical cord" of the world.[5] He then explained how the scepter of many kings was symbolic of the umbilical cord joining heaven and earth and representing divine power. Dr. Penhallow's comments made me think about the crosier, or pastoral staff of cardinals, bishops, and abbots that symbolizes the shepherding of the monastic community.

An interesting example of the apparent Egyptian influence on the medieval Cistercians is the belief in the spiritual and medicinal benefits of breast milk as in this model of the Goddess Isis preparing to feed her son Horus (left). In the fifteenth century manuscript drawing (right), Saint Bernard of Clairvaux receives healing milk from Mary's breast for his faithfulness. (Left: Wolter, 2009; Right: France, 2007)

I've seen hundreds of the medieval images of Bernard of Clairvaux carrying an ornately decorated crosier obviously symbolic of his leadership. I couldn't help but wonder if there was another symbolic representation to Bernard and his Cistercian/Templar brothers related to their knowledge of sacred geometry. The allegorical symbolism of the umbilical cord unifying the heavens and earth could very well have been an important symbol to these medieval orders.

Besides being a symbol of his leadership the ornately decorated crosier held by Bernard of Clairvaux in this sixteenth century painting by Allaert Claeyssins could also represent allegorical symbolism of the umbilical cord of the earth unifying the heavens and earth. (France, 2007)

Notes

[1]Montgomery, 2006, p. 48.
[2]Pp. 190-191.
[3]Gahlin, 2001, p. 68.
[4]France, 2007, p. 205.
[5]Michell, 1994, p.13.

12

The Ciphers of the Monks

On June 9, 2006, Kensington Rune Stone researcher Michael Zalar and I met. Michael had said he had something interesting to show me. The excitement in his voice told me he had found something he thought was important. Michael pulled out a folder with several sheets of paper, photocopied pages from a book he had recently read. He relayed how when he read the Kensington Rune Stone book, he decided to do a little surfing on the Internet relating to "Cistercian" and "codes." While browsing, he found a reference to a book entitled, *The Ciphers of the Monks*. The author, David A. King, was a professor of History of Science, at the Johann Wolfgang Goethe University, in Frankfurt, Germany.

The first thing Michael showed me was how Professor King had discovered a system of numerical ciphers Cistercian monks had developed during medieval times. King's research was the result of his examination of numerous Cistercian manuscripts found in cathedrals all across Europe. Many pages were actual photographs of manuscript pages with ciphers in the margins. The numerical system was simple and ingenious and allowed the use of one numeric symbol to represent numbers from 1 up to 9,999.

This Cistercian numbering system was very impressive, but the last page Michael showed me was by far the most interesting. He had copied page 123 from King's book, which showed a photograph of a page from a manuscript with an eye-popping caption, "Alphabetical codes, one based on the Cistercian ciphers, in a fifteenth-century Latin manuscript of German provenance."

Every word in the caption struck a chord as if it were written especially for the Kensington Rune Stone. Michael then pointed to the first symbol in the top left-hand corner of the page. I gazed at the "a" centered directly over a big beautiful "X." I sat stunned for a moment and then the words uttered to me by Professor Henrik Williams when the whole Larsson Papers episode unfolded in 2004 came back to me. "The "X" symbol for "a" has never been seen in a medieval runic inscription, I don't believe it ever existed, and I don't believe you will ever find it." I always knew that it had to exist, but it was a breath-taking moment to actually see it in a medieval document.

I told Michael he had found something really important and then asked, "Will you show me where this book is, like right now?" We made our way to the Wilson Library at the University of Minnesota. Michael led me to the third floor, then down the isle to a yellow hard-bound book published in 2001. I immediately checked it out and thanked Michael profusely for sharing his remarkable discovery. Little did I know, in just a few short hours the best was yet to come!

13

The Arced X

As the evening wound down, I finally had time to dig into King's book. With each page, I found myself amazed at how intelligent those Cistercian monks were. They had variations of variations that created a myriad of symbols and codes. It made more sense than ever how the Templars had learned the use of codes to develop their banking empire during their nearly two-century reign. The book also had numerous examples of pentadic numbers that appeared in the manuscripts, including the same type used on the Spirit Pond Map Stone.

On page 284 I saw a familiar character in bold type. Instinctively, I called to Janet, who had fallen asleep with her head on my shoulder. She jerked awake and said, "What?" It was the mysterious "arced" X from the symbol side of the Spirit Pond Map Stone!

At almost the same instant, my eyes darted to the opposite page where the symbol appeared again. This time it was plain as day in a photograph, etched into the surface of a metal plate from a medieval instrument used to calculate latitude called an astrolabe. I was excited and confused at the same time. I studied the plate and slowly figured out how the symbol was being used. Whoever made the plate had used the symbol to represent the number "40." The word "latitude" was etched on the plate above the symbol with a Latin number "1" next to it. The Spirit Pond Map Stone had the pentadic number of 44 to the right of the arced X symbol. Suddenly, a thought came that immediately turned my atten-

Another variant, found already in Carolingian times, is 𝕏 and the like for ⟨
This form seems to have been particularly popular in Spain: see also the Spani
plate in a composite astrolabe (#191),⁷ where 𝕏 is used (Fig. B.2). In manuscri
its use could lead to confusion with X for 10.⁸

The "arced X" that appears on the symbol side of the Spirit Pond Map Stone appeared on
page 284 of the book, *The Ciphers of the Monks*. The symbol appeared on a medieval astrolabe for the number 40. (King, 2001)

tion to locating an atlas. Janet had joined me. I opened my atlas to a map
of the East Coast of the United States.

My mind was racing with excitement scanning the map for
Popham Beach where the Spirit Pond Rune Stones were found. Just
north of the area was an arcing horizontal line of latitude. Janet and I
followed the line to the far left side of the map. Spirit Pond was located
almost exactly at latitude 44 degrees north!

Janet and I stood in disbelief. We knew we had discovered something important, but I also knew we had a lot more work to do. The next
morning I called Dick Neilsen, and couldn't wait to give him the news.
He was delighted of course, and started peppering me with questions
about what else was in the King book. The next day, I ordered two
copies of the $130 book on the Internet.

The next step with the astrolabe was to figure out where
Professor King found the instrument. King made no reference to what
time period it was from, or what other parts the instrument might also
have had the symbol. The instrument was in the collection of the Oxford
Museum of the History of Science, and King's reference was a book published in 1932 entitled, *Astrolabes of the World*, by Robert Gunther. I
found a copy of the 1976 reprinted version for $300 on the Internet.

The Gunther book arrived on May 19, 2006, a week before the King
book, and it was a beast. Weighing almost five pounds and nearly three inches thick, the 600-page volume contained photographs and information about
the over 300 astrolabes in Oxford's collection. I knew I'd have to look at each
and every instrument to see if the arced X symbol appeared on any of them.

The book was fascinating, and I was constantly amazed at the level of detail, sophistication, and beauty of each amazing instrument. It was interesting to see the cultures that had the older astrolabes, including Persian, Indian, Hindu, Arabian, Moorish, Spanish, Italian, French, Flemish, Dutch, German, English as well as mariner's astrolabes designed to be used at sea.

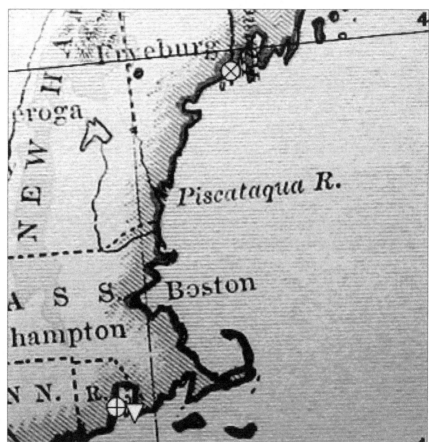

The circled X near the top of the map marks the location where the Spirit Pond Rune Stones were found near Popham Beach, Maine, in 1971. The pentadic number 44 with the "arced X" symbol on the Map Stone appears to indicate the astrolabe derived latitude of 44 degrees north, which is the approximate location where these rune stones were found! The circled cross near the bottom and below the "R.I." (Rhode Island) is where the Narragansett Rune Stone was found and the triangle just to the right marks the location of the Newport Tower in Rhode Island. (Fiske, 1902)

I arrived at the chapter on French astrolabes and spotted the now familiar instrument from King's references. The date of the instrument-was about 1350-1400 A.D., contemporaneous with the dates of the Spirit Pond Inscription and Map stones. The arced X symbol on this instrument was the only one known in connection to the Spirit Pond Rune Stones and these dates provided another piece of critical evidence.

The instrument was described as 5¾ inches in diameter and ³/₈ of an inch thick. The "rete," which is the ornately designed piece that fits onto the

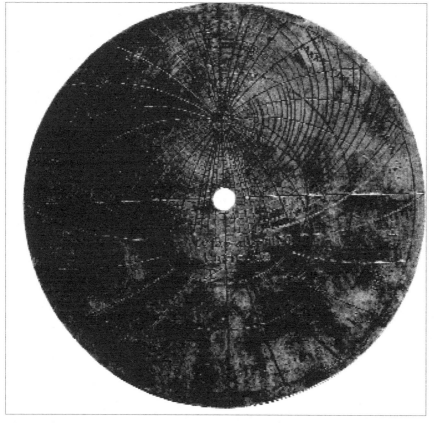

This plate from a medieval astrolabe was made for the latitude 41 degrees north, appears on page 285 of *The Ciphers of the Monks* by David King. The mysterious "arced X" symbol on the Spirit Pond Map Stone appears three times on this plate representing the number 40. (Wolter, 2006)

face of the instrument and points out stars on the zodiac on each plate, is of a Gothic design (see page 156 for a photo of the assembled instrument). The text described the instrument as having individual plates made for the latitudes of 38, 41, 45, 46, 47, 48, 49, 50, 55, 57 and 58. What struck me was how the arced X symbol (X̄) was ingeniously being used for the number forty by combining the Roman number X for 10, and the medieval Hindu-Arabic number ᛉ for 4. The proof this was the correct interpretation was on the plates. Where the symbol was used along with Roman letters, they added up to the proper latitude illustrated on the plate.

The photograph in the book only showed four of the eleven latitude plates listed. This meant there was more to the instrument than was pictured. At this point, this astrolabe was the only thing in the world directly connected to the Spirit Pond Stones and provided definitive proof of their medieval origin. I knew that I had to examine the instrument myself and there was only one way to do that.

On October 25, 2007, researcher David Brody and I spent the day at the NEARA Library housed at the New Hampshire Technical College in Concord, New Hampshire. In a NEARA file labeled "Runes," I found a paper that included a translation of the Spirit Pond Map Stone written by Wilhelm Schröder from Hamburg, Germany. Schröder translated the arced X as indicating latitude and the pentadic number as 44 degrees. He apparently did not realize the origin of the arced X being a combination of the Roman 10 (X) and the medieval Hindu-Arabic number 4 (ᛉ) for the number 40 (X̄). My discovery in 2006 of the apparent meaning of these two symbols for 44 degrees latitude serves as independent validation of Mr. Schröder's work in 1983.

14

Columbus's Mysterious Sigla

One of the biggest ironies of the Kensington Rune Stone saga (as well as the Spirit Pond and Narragansett Rune Stones) is the argument over who discovered America. Most Americans are taught that explorer Christopher Columbus was the first European to discover North America when he ". . . in 1492 Columbus sailed the ocean blue." That paradigm long held sacred by many scholars is now shattered, but I'm sure Columbus, or whatever his real name was, has been laughing in his grave at this notion for over 500 years. Researcher Dr. Manuel Da Silva believes he has deciphered the mysterious sigla and that his name was actually Cristobal Colon. Dr. Da Silva also asserts that Columbus was in all likelihood of Portuguese descent and a member of the medieval order in Portugal that followed the Knights Templar after they were put down in 1307: the Knights of Christ.

Columbus, who reportedly sailed to Iceland in 1477 and may have even reached the shores of North America then, likely knew all about the New World from his "brothers" in the Knights of Christ military order established in Portugal in 1318. Contrary to what many believe, the Templars really did simply changed their name and continued on. It is certainly no accident that both orders shared the same original seat in Portugal at the monastery in Tomar, founded in 1159.[1] In depictions of his three ships, the *Niña*, *Pinta* and the *Santa Maria*, all have the red Templar/Knights of Christ cross emblazoned on their sails.

Columbus's likely connection to the Knights of Christ no doubt aided in his ability to make his successful voyages. His first wife, Dona

The original seat of the Knights Templar in Portugal was founded in 1159 at the monastery castle of Tomar (left). After the Knights Templar was dissolved in 1307 a new order called the Knights of Christ was founded that was essentially the same thing. Speculation that Columbus was a Knight of Christ is well-founded given the cross of the order was emblazoned on the sails of ships, as seen in this model at the Dighton Rock Museum in Berkley, Massachusetts (right), that sailed to the Caribbean in 1492. (Photo by Cristian Chirita, posted on Wikipedia, Wolter, 2008)

Felipa Perestrello e Moniz, was of noble blood. Columbus and his wife lived with her mother. Dona's father was also a sea captain and upon his death his mother gave Columbus her husband's navigational instruments, writings and maps.[2] Some modern researchers assert that Columbus used a map to find his way to the west and kept two ship's logs of his initial journey. The correct log was kept secret in case he was captured by enemy ships. His father-in-law's maps likely included information from earlier Templar and Norse expeditions.

One of the likely Templar sources can be traced to Columbus's connection by marriage to Prince Henry Sinclair, who reportedly sailed to North America in 1398. Prince Henry's grandson, John Escorio (the Scot) Drummond (born circa 1402), was himself an explorer who likely passed on stories of his grandfather's exploits to his son John Affonso Escorcio Drummond (born 1430). John Escorio's second wife, Dono Gulmar De Lordello (born 1400), was previously married to Triston Vas Teireira, Jr. (born 1400), whose aunt was Guimar Teixeira (born 1420). Guimar married Bartholomew Perestrello (born 1410), and it was their daughter, Felipa Perestrello (born 1450), who married Columbus.[3]

As confusing as this connection is, it must be remembered that after

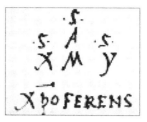

Three examples of Christopher Columbus' sigla clearly show the Hooked X, which appears to be code of his allegiance to the medieval order of the Knights of Christ. The sigla on the left is from a 1501 document requesting money [Civica Raccolta stampe A. Bertarelli, Castello Sforzesco, Milan]. The middle sigla appears on a manuscript in the Rábida monastery. The example on the right is from the Bettmann Archive. (Left: Novaresio, 2002, p. 67 Middle: Bellic, 2000, p. 87 Right: Morison, 1991, page 94)

the discovery of the Madeira Islands by Bartholomew Perestrello and Tristan Vaz Teireira, and accompanied by John Goncalves Zarco, in 1419, each man settled and raised families there.[4] Intermarriage was common in the close-knit community that included many explorers and early exploration of family descendants like Prince Henry would certainly have been discussed. In light of this genealogical background, to speculate that Columbus had a map of the New World (perhaps one of Prince Henry's) on his famous voyage is not only possible, but a virtual certainty.

What appears to be a tell-tale sign that Columbus was indeed a member of the Knights of Christ is the previously unnoticed Hooked X in his mysterious sigla. This discovery brings out an interesting irony. The now 110-year-old debate about whether the Kensington Rune Stone party beat Columbus to North America by 130 years, is no longer in doubt (to say nothing about the Viking Age Norse explorers at L'Anse aux Meadows in circa 1000 A.D.). It turns out Columbus was likely a member of the same highly secretive and successful medieval orders.

Notes

[1]Schütz, p. 70.
[2]Chapman, 1991, p. 186.
[3]Brown, 1993.
[4]Brown, 1993

15

The Larsson Papers

During our first trip to Sweden in October of 2003, when Dick Nielsen, LuAnn Patton, then director of the Runestone Museum, and I brought the Kensington Rune Stone, there had been extensive media coverage in Scandinavia. A retired professor, Tryggve Sköld, listened to a radio interview about the Kensington Rune Stone with then curator Helmer Gustavson at the runic department of the National Heritage Board in Stockholm. The discussion of the unusual runes and strange numbers sparked the memory of a lecture Sköld had heard on the Kensington Rune Stone more than a decade earlier.

Professor Sköld recalled seeing two sheets of paper from a recently donated collection to DAUM (Institute for Dialectology, Onomastics and Folklore Research in Umeå) that contained Swedish writing interspersed between two rune rows, a strange box code alphabet, and the same pentadic numbers used in Arabic placement as on the Kensington Rune Stone. The first sheet was dated December 1883, the second April 16, 1885, and originated from Edward Larsson (1867 to 1950), reportedly a tailor by profession. His grandchildren donated the papers along with pictures, letters, music scores, and books to DAUM in the mid 1990s.[1]

Amazingly, the characters in the second rune row of each sheet were strikingly similar to the Kensington Rune Stone runes and were described in the paper as the "secret style." Sköld concluded that the secret runes were Masonic codes used by traveling tradesmen to communicate. He wrote two papers outlining his conclusions. The papers were brought to the attention of Gustavson and other runic scholars, who immediately concluded that Olof Ohman, or some other immigrant, brought the secret

The Larsson Rune Rows from 1883. (Courtesy of the Institute for Dialectology, Onomastics, and Folklore Research in Umeå [DAUM])

runes to America in the latter part of the nineteenth century and carved the Kensington Rune Stone. The Larsson Papers became the smoking gun the Swedish scholars were looking for to make the Kensington Rune Stone, along with Dick Nielsen and me, go away.

What was most annoying about this episode, was that Dick and I didn't find out about the Larsson Papers until a day before the Swedish expert's negative opinion hit the Swedish media. To make matters worse, a few weeks later a negative story about the papers hit our local newspaper, the *Minneapolis Tribune*, which cast a dark shadow over the Kensington

The Larsson Rune Rows, April 16, 1885. (Courtesy of the Institute for Dialectology, Onomastics, and Folklore Research in Umeå [DAUM])

Rune Stone. We were told the negative Swedish report had been quietly forwarded to the newspaper by a professor of archaeology and well-known Kensington Rune Stone opponent from Moorhead, Minnesota, Mike Michlovic. Why he didn't inform us about the report reeked of ill intent. Regardless, for the next several weeks, Dick and I were on the defensive. Nobody wanted to hear what we thought about the Larsson Papers and what the implications might be for the Kensington Rune Stone.

The first thing we pointed out was that the original Kensington Rune Stone opponents' claim that Ohman had invented seven of the previously unknown runes was incorrect. In fact, the Larsson Papers proved that the runes had existed all along. Dick also noticed that Edward Larsson, who was eighteen at the time, didn't understand the meaning of some of the characters due to mistakes he made copying them. He apparently copied the rune rows from another document that he could have found in clothing he repaired. That clothing may have been the costume belonging to someone, possibly even a relative, who was a Freemason or member of a secret society. We also suggested that the papers Larsson copied could themselves have been copied from earlier documents that originated in medieval times. When we eventually shared these alternate possibilities, the scholars in Sweden scoffed. We didn't know it at the time, but the silver bullet that would kill their hoax claims would soon be discovered.

The discovery of the dotted R on the Kensington Rune Stone was the smoking gun that finger-printed the inscription to medieval

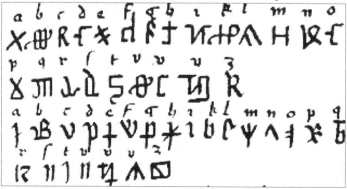

Kensington Rune Stone researcher Michael Zalar found the "X" symbol for "a" in a coded alphabet in a fifteenth-century Cistercian manuscript of German provenance. (King, 2001, page 123)

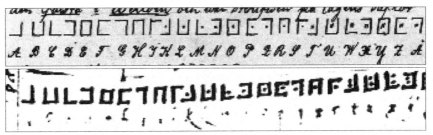

The same Masonic box code in the Larsson Papers from 1883 and 1885 (top) was also found in a fifteenth-century Cistercian manuscript of German provenance (bottom). (Bottom: King, 2001, page 349)

times. The fact that the dotted R was not found in the Larsson Rune Rows cuts the heart out of the theory that a late nineteenth century Swedish immigrant carved the Kensington Rune Stone.

The "o" (ᚭ) rune with the open horizontal bars facing to the right had previously never been seen except on the Kensington Rune Stone. Yet it was found in the coded alphabet in a medieval Cistercian manuscript of German provenance, and is also present in the Larsson Papers. This demonstrates that our claim that the Larsson Papers could trace back to medieval times was correct.

Another powerful piece of evidence was the Masonic box code alphabet we had speculated was medieval, which turned out to be true. On page 349 of King's book, I found the exact same box code in another fifteenth century Cistercian manuscript of German provenance.

The King book offered still another important connection between the medieval Cistercians, the Kensington Rune Stone and the Larsson Papers. The pentadic numbers used in the Kensington Rune Stone are a direct link to the Cistercians who chose a numbering system where they didn't have to use zero. Robert Lawler wrote the following in his 1982 book, *Sacred Geometry*, "Some of the monastic orders resisted the adoption of this system of decimal notation with zero, claiming particularly that zero was a device of the Devil. Among those who refused it was the Cistercian Order whose mystic and Gnostic philosophy was the inspiration and foundation of the Gothic cathedrals, the cosmic temples of the Piscean Age."

Both the Cistercian author of the Kensington Rune Stone and Edward Larsson used pentadic numbers in Arabic placement. However,

Type	1	2	3	4	5	6	7	8	9	10	11	12	Example
A													Calender dated 13 in Nuremberg
B													Calender in Den Hague (late 14th century)

King lists fourteenth-century examples of pentadic numbers similar to the Kensington Rune Stone and Larsson Papers. That Larsson put zero under the Arabic 10 suggests that he likely copied the papers from an earlier document.

Larsson tips his hand about his lack of knowledge of the numbering system by placing a zero under the Arabic number ten. This is one point that suggests that Larsson likely copied the papers from an earlier document.

These were perfect examples of what we feared might happen once the documents were studied. The knee-jerk reaction of scholars in Sweden turned out to be very premature. What they initially thought (and hoped) would be the demise of the Kensington Rune Stone inscription turned out to be important evidence to support its authenticity. Our speculation of the "secret" Larsson alphabet that actually contains six hooked characters might be connected to a Masonic organization also appears to be true. The fact that these characters (including the Hooked X) had never been seen before by scholars, yet obviously did exist, can only be explained that they were indeed secret symbols likely originally used by the medieval Cistercians and their associates.

Note

[1]Henrik Williams, 2004.

112

Part IV

Sacred Geometry, Rosslyn, and Freemasonry

16

The Horn and Knife Rocks

Judi Rudebusch, fascinated with stone holes for almost a decade had started off as a follower of long-time Kensington Rune Stone researcher Hjalmar Holand. Holand believed the stones holes were made by "Viking" explorers who sailed into the Midwest and anchored their boats by cutting holes into rocks, inserting a metal ring and tying them up. He claimed the water levels were much higher 600-plus years ago and, therefore, it made sense to him that the holes had to have been used for mooring their ships. He also claimed the mooring stones were evidence that supported the authenticity of the Kensington Rune Stone. Unfortunately, his mooring stone claims did more to hurt the Kensington Rune Stone than help it. He simply didn't have the factual evidence, and his opponents used it against him. To this day, some opponents argue that the Kensington Rune Stone is a fake because the stone holes could never have been used for mooring boats.

I had moved beyond believing that the holes were used for mooring ships, mainly because modern water levels in Minnesota pretty well match what they were 600 years ago. Most of the stone holes are found at elevations where water could only have existed during the period of the melting of the glaciers, at least 12,000 to 15,000 years ago. Regardless, whatever the use of the stone holes, they are a separate issue from the Kensington Rune Stone, which must either stand, or fall, on its own merit. That's not to say that they are not linked.

One of Hjalmar Holand's most ardent supporters was Marion Dahm, who lived in the community near Kensington until his death on July 30, 2006. Some time after his death, when his family was ready to deal with the vast quantity of data he had compiled, they invited Judi Rudebusch and me to take a look through several boxes of maps, photographs, letters, and reports of the dozens of holes he'd studied. When I presented the theory that the holes could have been made by medieval monks as breadcrumb trails, land boundaries, and locator stones using sacred geometry, Marion at least understood that, no matter what their use, they were important.

Judi Rudebusch, from near Milbank, South Dakota, started as a "mooring stone" person but was one of the few to embrace our new ideas and hasn't looked back. Her interest was stimulated by the fact that there are several stone holes, in both bedrock and glacial boulders, in her area. Ever the curious researcher, Judi worked tirelessly trying to find answers. On May 12, 2006, I took Judi up on her invitation to show me around.

Joining us on the trip were journalists David Porter and Bent Are Iversen, originally from Norway and who was writing an article for a Scandinavian magazine about our research. I had previously met Bent, and it was obvious from our discussions that he was skeptical of the Kensington Rune Stone and medieval Scandinavians in North America.

We met in Milbank, not far from the north/south continental divide in North America. Judi was excited that we see what turned out to be two of the most interesting carvings I'd ever seen. Judi led our small caravan of cars along a fence to a metal gate, behind which dozens of cattle milled around a hay feeder. We slowly drove into an open field with dozens of glacial boulders ranging in size from a couple hundred, to a couple thousand pounds. The land sloped downward toward a small, spring-fed creek.

Judi stopped near a group of boulders and pointed to one of them and said, "Take a look at that."

I immediately saw the carving. At first I was puzzled by how perfect the horn shape was and quickly noticed that it even appeared to have a handle. Bent was taken aback by the carving and immediately started taking pictures while David Porter stood back, filming the overall scene.

"What do you think of it?" Bent said, as I kneeled down for a closer look.

I was instantly struck by the advanced state of weathering. The rock was a type of granite or granite gneiss, and for such a relatively hard and resistant rock the weathering of the carved surfaces let me know it was very old. I said, "Well, it definitely isn't modern. It's at least a hundred years old and probably much older. This thing has been here for along time."

Bent was also impressed by the weathering and pointed out a feature I hadn't noticed. Being Norwegian, he was familiar with drinking horns and said they typically had a round metal ball at the pointed end. Sure enough, the tip of the carving was wider and rounded. During the Viking Age through medieval times in Scandinavia, it was customary to exchange drinking horns when an important land transaction took place. Could this be what this carving represented? It was impossible to know. The carved stone was located near a spring, and I thought about how the Cistercians always built their abbeys on rivers, streams, or near springs. Could the land have been marked with the carving as a future site for an abbey or settlement?

Judi then showed us another boulder about 100 feet away. This rock was a little smaller and had an obvious man-made carving in it, only this one looked exactly like a narrow-handled knife. Once again, the rock was granitic in composition, and the weathering of the carving was very advanced. In fact, the weathering looked identical to the horn rock.

In January of 2009, Judi forwarded an academic paper that included new information about medieval land claim practices that might be relevant to the horn and knife rocks. Scholar M.T. Clanchy wrote the following about medieval land transactions in a 1980-1981 paper:

> To win over the public, writings had to seem as impressive as the knives, horns, silver cups, finger rings, and other objects which were customarily used in conveyance of property. The fact that writing did the recording job with greater precision and ease may not have seemed as overwhelming a point in its favor as it does to us because against that had to be set the fact that a document might not look as durable as a knife or a horn and furthermore it might be distrusted by those who could not read.

Upon reading this article, it seemed reasonable that, if a transaction occurred with Native Americans, a written document would have been worthless. The permanence of symbols like these carved into rock would likely have more impact. The following quote by Mohawk elder,

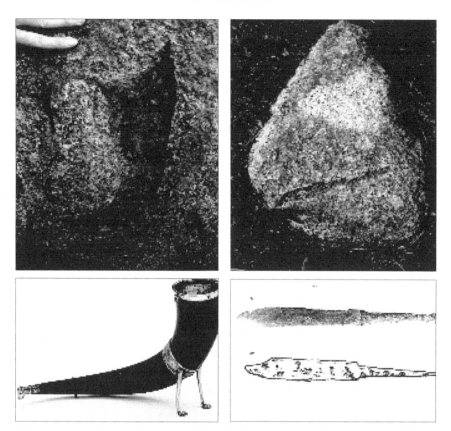

We saw two amazing carvings on glacial granite boulders in a cattle pasture near Milbank, South Dakota, on May 12, 2006. Both were reminiscent of a medieval drinking horn and table knife, and exhibited advanced weathering that could easily be many hundreds of years old. (Top right & left: Wolter, 2006, Bottom left, Internet; Bottom right, Seaver, 1996, page 174)

Ernest Benedict, of Akwesasne, Ontario, was uttered in June of 1992, and could explain the origin of these incredible carvings: "I have heard the Elders say that when the terms of the treaties were deliberated the smoke from the pipe carried that agreement to the Creator, binding it forever. An agreement can be written in stone and stone can be chipped away, but the smoke from the sacred pipe signified to the First Nation peoples that the treaties could not be undone."[1]

The next day Judi had more stone holes to show us. We stopped at seven different sites, and saw about twenty stone holes of different types. Several exhibited a radiating fracture pattern emanating from the hole, suggesting a dynamite blasting pattern, or possibly a lightning strike. We also saw several round holes suggesting a recent origin, as well as triangular shaped holes. A couple of sites had clusters of glacial boulders with stone holes at the edge of farm fields, suggesting they had been moved, but the stone holes appeared highly weathered, suggesting significant age. Many of the other boulders appeared to be in their original locations with the hole cut into them exhibiting advanced weathering.

At a location just west of the town of Wilmot, South Dakota, Judi led us into a secluded, boulder-strewn valley surrounded by fifty to sixty-foot hills with a small spring-fed stream meandering through the grassy lowland. Halfway down a draw on the south side, Judi pointed out three boulders with triangular-shaped stone holes arranged in a near-perfect equilateral triangle roughly 100 feet apart. This triangular pattern of stone holes was eerily reminiscent of the equilateral triangular pattern of stone holes found just north of Rune Stone Hill at the Ohman Farm.

Within the triangle of stone holes was a large couch-sized boulder that had what appeared to be a man-made basin designed to hold water. On either side laying several feet away were two large pieces from the boulder that defied a natural explanation. On one end of the basin was a milk-carton-sized block of the boulder that could have served as an altar. I carefully scanned the edges of both the basin and protruding block for evidence of purposeful impact marks. In spite of the advanced weathering, there did appear to be impact marks along the perimeter of the protruding block of rock. This mysterious intentionally fashioned boulder fueled my speculation that the stone block could have been crafted to serve as an altar over the cistern-like basin. My speculation was apparently supported by the fact that the stone block was aligned to the east.

During a second trip in May of 2009 to film these stone holes for the documentary film, the glacial boulders took on a whole different perspective. Armed with new knowledge about the practices of the Cistercians, I saw the stone holes and the basin boulder as the possible

119

scene of a sacred religious ceremony that included some type of ritual bathing. What exactly might have occurred here is unclear. However, if a fourteenth-century Cistercian monk had been here considering a future abbey site, this valley would serve as a prototypical location.

That night at Judi's farm, we talked about whether stone holes were found in other countries. We had no direct knowledge then. However, some interesting examples did materialize. After Marion Dahm passed in 2006, his family made his personal papers available to researchers. In them, Judi found correspondence from Scotland that included photographs sent to Marion by Robert Wilson that included a three-inch deep stone hole at the top of a 200-foot tall cliff at Cape Wrath in northernmost Scotland.

The origin and purpose of this stone hole is unknown. However, Scotland has a well-known medieval Knights Templar history and one cannot help but wonder if there is a connection.

Another place where the medieval Knights Templar were known to frequent was the Baltic Sea island of Bornhom in Denmark. During a

This couch-sized glacial boulder appears to have been intentionally quarried out to create a basin to hold water. The milk-carton sized piece of stone appears to have been made into an altar located on the east end of the boulder. This interesting structure is located within an equilateral triangle of stone holes roughly 100 feet apart and is similar in size to the equilateral triangle of stone holes at Rune Stone Hill at the Ohman Farm. The southern most stone hole is seen at the top of this image. (Wolter, 2009)

Looking north down the draw past the triangle of stone holes (marked with white arrows) with the basin boulder, one sees a beautiful valley with a meandering spring-fed stream. This beautiful spot would likely have enticed a medieval Cistercian monk to consider building a future abbey. (Wolter, 2009)

trip to the island in August of 2008, while filming for a documentary, we visited the largest castle in Northern Europe. Hammershus Castle is believed to have been constructed in part by Templar stone masons for King Valdimar II in the thirteenth century.

While walking around the courtyard inside the castle walls, I scanned the intermittent areas of glacially smoothed granite bedrock protruding through the grass. Danish author Erling Haagensen, whose book, *The Templars Secret Island*, had inspired Janet's sacred geometry with the stone holes at the Ohman farm was our guide along with his friends Ole and Susanna Sveigaard. After spotting the first stone hole, the others quickly helped find the other five. The discovery of these stone holes prompted a short lecture about their possible purpose and connection to the stone holes in the United States. Our Danish friends were quite intrigued and we all agreed the stone hole pattern was reminiscent of the constellation Orion.

These European examples of stone holes and their possible association with the Knights Templar are identical in size and depth to those found in America and represent yet more mysterious smoke billowing near what appears to quickly becoming a very hot fire.

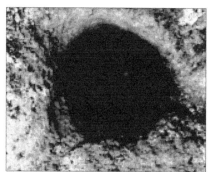

On the top of a 200-foot cliff at Cape Wrath, the northern-most point of mainland Scotland, there is at least one highly weathered stone hole. Could the stone holes found in the Midwest region of North America be related? (Photographs courtesy of the Marion Dahm Family)

Hammershus Castle overlooking the Baltic Sea on the island of Bornholm in Denmark. Several stone holes were found carved into bedrock within the courtyard of the largest castle in northern Europe. (Wolter, 2008)

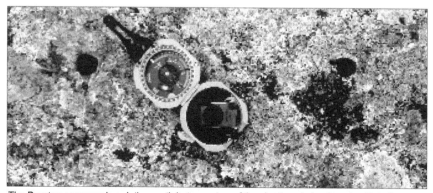

The Brunton compass is pointing north between two of the six stone holes found cut into the granite bedrock exposed in the courtyard of Hammershus Castle on the Baltic Sea island of Bornholm in Denmark. The six holes formed a pattern reminiscent of the constellation Orion. (Wolter, 2008)

My mind kept going back to the Kensington Rune Stone. Whatever happened to the other probably larger piece of the slab that was skillfully broken off by the carver? Could there be another land claim stone still buried somewhere and marked by a triangulation of stone holes, with this triangle of stone holes? Maybe the Kensington Rune Stone party intended to claim a larger tract of land by eventually fitting the two stones together? I couldn't help but wonder if some of these stone holes were hiding an important secret. One thing was certain: our theory of another land claim stone associated with the Kensington Rune Stone still out there somewhere would be conclusively proven if another buried rune stone was found using the stone holes.

Note

[1]http://www.indianclaims.ca/client/site/includes/print.asp?lang=en&print=1& url=%2Fabout%2Faboutlogo%2Den%2Easp

17

Jim Mueller's Discovery

The realization of how extensive and complex the use of sacred geometry was throughout Europe and Scandinavia amazed all of us involved in this research. That we had discovered it was also present in North America was even more exciting. As thrilling as the discovery of the triangulation of the stone holes at the Ohman Farm that pinpointed the burial site of the Kensington Rune Stone, it was only a precursor of what was to come.

I met Jim Mueller at a book signing in Alexandria. He'd read the Kensington Rune Stone book and had discovered something. He said, "After reading your book and how you found the sacred geometry at the Ohman Farm, I thought I could trust you with the sacred geometry I think I've found."

I said, "Well, show us what you found."

Jim, a graphic designer and an artist with a calm and quiet demeanor, laid out a map of the Lake Minnetonka Area with the City of Excelsior situated on the lake at roughly the center of his map. He said his quest had begun in 1999 while doing research on Captain John Johnson, a steamboat pilot on Lake Minnetonka from 1881 to 1910.

I asked Jim, "Isn't that the same man whose name is on that monument in Excelsior near the old amusement park site?"

Jim nodded and pointed out how Johnson had three residences in Excelsior. Jim had noticed on the map that these made a straight line running roughly east and west. Jim explained how he then noticed the old railroad tracks in town, running parallel to the "Johnson" line, had a unique looking curve. "The interesting thing about the railroad is that it has a configuration that reminded me of the one-half design in sacred geometry of a cup [grail design]. The cup shape appears to conform to the golden ratio," he said.

In the book *Sacred Geometry* by Robert Lawler, I'd read how the ratio of the growth pattern of many things in nature, such as the spiral of a shell or the growth of trees, as well as many other natural phenomena, were known by ancient cultures and held sacred. This mathematical equation was also important in Freemasonry. I asked Jim if he knew if Captain Johnson was a Freemason.

Jim looked at me with a surprised look and said, "Yes he was."

Jim said that after plotting the mid-line of his "golden ratio cup" it became his north-south line. However, this line did not run exactly north-south geographically. The north end tilted slightly to the west, roughly six degrees. From there, Jim saw that his north-south line ran through a very prominent island on Lake Minnetonka called Big Island. He figured it must have something to do with the apparent geometry he was finding and then extended the lines east-west, perpendicular through the island to see what would happen. Jim said, "I used mostly intuition and months and months of playing around."

Eventually, he realized that equidistant, east and west from his midline, through Big Island he found two streets named Cardinal Road and Cardinal Cove. Working on and off over the course of six years Jim discovered geometric patterns with lines intersecting at streets with names associated with Freemasonry and apparently the legend of Prince Henry Sinclair like Mason Road, Red Oak Drive, and Rose Street as well as other streets and roads with a very familiar name: Sinclair!

Eventually, an incredible geometric pattern emerged. However, it didn't quite line up with the level of accuracy Jim felt it should. He then relayed the discovery that helped him find the missing piece. He recalled reading a book about a mysterious inscription in a church in France that was found to contain an important historical clue. The clue applied to a painting where geometry was discovered when the hidden pattern was rotated three degrees. Jim then said, "After experimenting for a while with my lines drawn on a piece of clear plastic over the map, I pivoted the plastic six degrees on the eastern most street [Cardinal Point]." Jim then demonstrated his discovery on the map. When he rotated the plastic, the familiar pattern burst off the map to reveal a symbol aligned perfectly north-south. That symbol was the six-pointed Star of David also known as the Seal of Solomon.[1]

Janet and I were stunned; then our minds began racing with ideas and possibilities. By this time we were no longer skeptical of the concept of sacred geometry, although having it right here, literally in our own back yard, was a big surprise. Looking a little closer I noticed that Highway 101, which runs due north-south right next to our property, was directly on the eastern vertical line of Jim's symbol.

I've brought Jim's work up to Freemasons I know who have said nothing to suggest that his work was not valid. In fact, they reinforced the geometry and essentially confirmed that there is much more to it. Washington, D.C., is the most well-known example of sacred geometry incorporated into an American city. Jim had discovered that same type of incredible geometry within the street system of the Twin Cities.

During the time of settlement in America and the subsequent growth of the major metropolitan areas, it appeared that smaller scale, city-sized geometric patterns were constructed within a larger matrix previously mapped out centuries before. Some people believe the medieval Templars were responsible for the original mapping of North America. If the medieval Templars and modern Freemasonry were indeed connected, as authors like John J. Robinson in his book, *Born in Blood,* have effectively argued, then it is likely the early Freemasons had knowledge of the older, large-scale matrix and simply added onto it. The large-scale grid system in North America, which predates the founding of the United States, is likely part of a world-wide grid system author Ashley Cowie calls, "The Rosslyn Matrix."

This worldwide mapping system theory seemed more plausible the more I learned about it. One fact that lent support is the locations of Rosslyn Chapel, in Scotland, and Minneapolis/St. Paul, in Minnesota. Rosslyn is located three degrees west of the prime meridian of

Jim Mueller's Lake Minnetonka Templar grid includes interesting street names where lines inter-sect: A – Quamoclit ("Cardinal Climber" Vine), B – Hazeltine National Golf Course, C – Firethorn Pointe, D – Black Friar's Road, E- Lafayette Club, F – Sinclair Place. Street names that appeared in Jim's original mapping pattern of the Lake Minnetonka grid include Cardinal Cove Drive, Cardinal Road, Cardinal Avenue and Drive, Cardinal Lane, Circle and Court, Sinclair Road and Court, Cardinal Lane and Mason's Pointe. (Courtesy of Jim Mueller)

Researcher Jim Mueller made a stun-ning discovery of sacred geometry in the Lake Minnetonka area of Minnesota. Where two lines intersect at the north-west point of the sacred symbol he found, are two small roads that bear a familiar name. (Wolter, 2007)

Greenwich, England. The Twin Cities are located ninety-three degrees west of Greenwich, exactly ninety degrees, or one quarter turn of the earth west of Rosslyn. These locations could mean Rosslyn and the confluence of the Minnesota and Mississippi rivers [Twin Cities] are worldwide Cardinal points and allow for interesting global geom-etry that appears to have been under-stood by the Templars. There is no way to know for sure, but the stone holes could certainly be related to all of this.

Centuries-old knowledge of the Rosslyn Matrix would certainly be consistent with the long speculated passing on of knowledge through time within secret organizations. This could also explain the prior knowledge of the New World explorers like Columbus likely had and acquired through these secret organizations that can be traced back to the early Norse explorers prior to 1000 A.D.

Note

[1]King Solomon was ruler of the Kingdom of Israel around 1000 B.C. and is credited with building the first Temple in Jerusalem. This magical seal reportedly gave him power to control demons.

The imprint of Freemasonry is very prominent in Minneapolis, Minnesota. The ornately carved sandstone entrance to the Lumber Exchange Building in downtown Minneapolis includes numerous symbols of Masonry including the six-pointed Seal of Solomon, the same symbol Jim Mueller discovered in the western suburbs. This building is located across the street from the original Masonic Temple on Hennepin Avenue. (Wolter, 2007)

The Green Man, an ancient pagan and Masonic symbol, are carved into the Lumber Exchange building entrance on Hennepin Avenue in Minneapolis (left) and the interior of Rosslyn Chapel in Scotland (right). (Wolter 2007 & 2006)

18

Iceland's (and Kensington's) Ring World

In June of 2007, a researcher from Iceland, Valdimar Samuelsson, joined Judi Rudebusch, Peter Tomlinson, Michael Zalar, Jim Mueller, Janet, and me on a field trip to various sites within Jim's "Templar Matrix" around Lake Minnetonka. Afterward, we convened at our Chanhassen home for lunch and discussion. Valdimar found Jim's work extremely interesting and shared his own incredible research involving ancient sacred geometry that he called a "Ring World."

Valdimar explained how stone cairns and triangular-shaped holes, similar in size and shape as those found at the Ohman Farm, and near Judi's home in South Dakota, were used as boundary markers in Iceland beginning in the tenth century. The method typically started with the construction of three stone cairns in the south-western edge of the tract of land. From this point, a line was drawn to the northeast following the angle made by the rising sun on the summer solstice. Valdimar explained that the distance the line could be were 108,000, 216,000, 432,000, 864,000, and up to 1,728,000 feet, or approximately twenty, forty, eighty, 160, and 340 miles. These figures come from old mythology that some say dates back to the Sumarians dating back as far as 5000 B.C. The circular land layout formula was believed to have been passed down from the Romans and eventually to Denmark, and was believed to have been used for the last time on Iceland according to Samuelsson.[1]

To complete the circular ring of land being claimed, a second line

129

is drawn the same distance in length following the winter solstice that mirrors the summer solstice line. The end points of the solstice lines are marked with either hand-chiseled triangular shaped stone holes or stone cairns.

Valdimar then discussed how, at the west settlement in

Valdimar Samuelsson stands next to one of many ancient stone cairns used as land boundary markers found on Iceland. Similar stone cairns were found in South Dakota and Red Wing, Minnesota. (Left: Courtesy of Valdimar Samuelsson; Right: Courtesy of the Goodhue County Historical Society)

Greenland, in 1342 between 5,000 to 10,000 people suddenly disappeared and were never found. All they left behind were livestock and heavy furniture, everything else was taken. He wondered if some of those people made it to the interior of North America. He and Judi were investigating the similarities of stone markers in South Dakota, and the possibility of their use as land boundaries in a similar way.

Judi pointed out that in the Whetstone Valley near her home was a farm that had three stone cairns on its land. When they investigated, three generations of landowners led them to the remains of the stone cairns and shared stories of playing on and around them in their child-

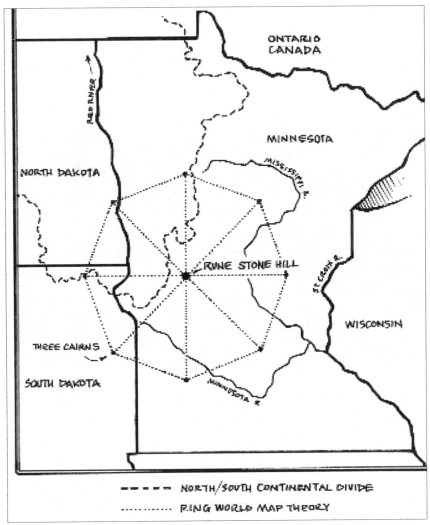

Icelandic researcher Valdimar Samuelsson is currently investigating evidence of a possible medieval land claim remarkably similar to those made in Iceland. Three stone cairns recorded by settlers in South Dakota appear to mark the southwest part of a circular land claim 160 miles in diameter with the Kensington Rune Stone discovery site at its center. Within this area over 125 stone holes cut into glacial boulders and bedrock could be connected to the Ring World as either boundary or survey markers, or "bread crumb" trail markers. The north-south continental divide snakes through a large portion of the possible Ring World, consistent with some medieval land claim practices involving the headwaters to major river systems. (Drawing by Dan Wiemer)

hood. Valdimar then drew a line on a map from the farm following the summer solstice angle at that latitude. To his amazement, after a distance of 432,000 feet, the line hit right on Rune Stone Hill. He then continued the line another 432,000 feet and then drew a circle with Rune Stone Hill as the center point. Judi pointed out that within that circle over seventy stone holes have been documented. This seems to be more than just a coincidence.

Other parallels to the ancient theory that are found both here and in Iceland are fertile land to the southwest quadrant of the ring world and forest land to the southeast quadrant. Both Judi and Valdimar expressed a desire to look further into this possibility that an ancient ring world could be centered over the Kensington Rune Stone discovery site.

As their theory unfolded, my mind went back to my land claim theory and how a returning party might re-locate the Kensington Rune Stone buried in the ground. Perhaps the stone holes within the ring world were made as a bread-crumb trail that ultimately led to Rune Stone Hill where the triangulation of stone holes there would pinpoint the land claim stone. Here again, logic dictates that if the Kensington Rune Stone is indeed a land claim, then the party that carved and buried it must have had a way for the stone to be relocated. The ring world theory works beautifully both practically and historically.

Note

[1]Samuelsson, 2007.

19

David and Gloria
Sinclair-Bouschor

Throughout the 2006 summer, I increased my library of Freemasonry and the history of the Cistercians and the Knights Templar. Authors William Mann and Steven Sora, among others, have written books on the medieval presence of Templars in North America. Gradually, my understanding of Freemasonry began to grow. As someone more a "concrete sequential" type, the allegorical and esoteric aspects of Masonry were difficult for me to grasp. My curiosity was piqued to the point that when I was asked to join the Masons, I seriously considered it. However, I resisted the urge for fear that my research would be dismissed by opponents eager to paint me as an advocate and not an unbiased and objective researcher.

Jim Mueller shared his discoveries, and he also provided feedback on our research. He suggested we learn about Prince Henry Sinclair Clan and his legendary voyage to North America in 1398[1] to point us to the most likely candidate associated with the Spirit Pond Rune Stones. To my surprise, I found out that the former president of the Sinclair Clan in America was in Duluth, Minnesota. I decided to give Mr. David Sinclair-Bouschor a call.

Mr. Bouschor listened patiently as I explained my reason for calling. I was hoping that he'd find the Spirit Pond Rune Stones and their possible connection to Prince Henry interesting. He did.

On July 31, 2006, we met with David and his wife, Gloria. David, a retired judge, told us stories of his days behind the bench including his presiding over the Condon murder trial in the 1970s.

David had read the Kensington Rune Stone book I sent him, and he expressed empathy for Olof Ohman for what he and his family had gone through. He also wanted to hear about our research on the Spirit Pond

Rune Stones. He showed us a framed life-size paper rubbing of a knight that looked familiar. I asked him about it, and he said it was from a grave slab at Rosslyn Chapel. I'd seen this grave slab in the book *The Sword and the Grail*, by his relative Andrew Sinclair. David then pointed out a life-size full suit of armor with a real sword that he had in his living room.

David explained how the family knew there were hidden chambers, tombs, and tunnels underground at Rosslyn, but factions within the family couldn't agree on whether or not to do any digging. Many authors over the years had speculated on what might be hidden beneath Rosslyn Chapel. The most popular theories suggested items such as the Templar's treasure of silver and gold, Templar knights buried in full armor, religious relicts like pieces of the True Cross, ancient scrolls, the Ark of the Covenant, even the heads of Jesus and John the Baptist.

David also told us about the 600-year anniversary of Prince Henry Sinclair's voyage to North America held in the Orkney Islands of Scotland in 1998. He said the highlight was when the leader of the First Nation Mi'kMaq Indian delegation from Nova Scotia presented their flag to the Sinclairs, which according to David was a virtual mirror image of the medieval Knights Templar battle flag.

After hearing David's tales about the family's quest to have Prince Henry recognized for his accomplishments, I explained how the most compelling evidence yet might just be the arced X symbol we found on the medieval astrolabe that was also found on the Spirit Pond Map Stone. To find it on only one astrolabe in the world was incredible, and I told him I wanted to go to England to see it with my own eyes. David quickly said, "I know someone who can help you get around over there. Niven Sinclair. He'd be tickled to take you to Oxford." Niven's name had cropped up numerous times in my readings.

In David's office, he showed us numerous swords he'd collected. I noticed several familiar red crosses on the certificates on his walls. It was obvious that he was a Freemason and a prominent one at that. Janet told me later that Gloria said that David was the Grand Master of the Freemasons in Minnesota.

On November 14, 2006, David and Gloria Sinclair-Bouschor met with us again and shared some historical information about the

At a 1998 ceremony in the Orkney Islands in Scotland the leader of the First Nation Mi'kMaq Indian delegation from Nova Scotia presented their flag (left) to the Sinclair Clan. According to Judge David Sinclair-Bouschor it was a virtual mirror image of the medieval Knights Templar battle flag (right). (Sinclair, 1998)

Sinclair family in Scotland along with more info about Rosslyn Chapel and Rosslyn Castle. I filled them in on all the new Kensington Rune Stone/Spirit Pond/Narragansett/Newport Tower research. We also talked about what the Sinclair Clan could do to help us establish if there was a connection with the Sinclair voyage of 1398 and the Spirit Pond Rune Stones. David knew the rune stones might be the best opportunity to convince the world that Prince Henry's trip really happened.

Darwin Ohman had also joined us. There was an interesting parallel between the two families, both of which had been chastised and dismissed for defending their family's honor. Most scholars didn't believe the Sinclair voyage ever happened, just as they dismissed Olof Ohman's claim that he hadn't carved the Kensington Rune Stone. I believed there was now enough evidence to vindicate both families.

David answered some of my questions about Freemasonry. At one point, he said, "You'd be a good Mason. Why don't you join the order?"

It was highest honor for an invitation to come from David, but I was torn. I said, "David, I'd be honored to join, but I can't. I'm afraid that if I become a Mason, opponents will say I'm an advocate and that my research is tainted."

David looked puzzled for a moment and then slowly smiled. He said, "Of course. This is probably not the right time." He added, "How about we revisit this question when you get a little older?"

Instantly relieved, I said, "You're on, David!"

Note

[1]Pohl, 1974.

20

The Minneapolis Scottish Rite Temple

My curiosity about Freemasonry had been seriously aroused, yet I knew that if the research presented in this book was to remain completely independent, I could not join the order at this time. This didn't mean I couldn't learn from Freemasons, or members of the modern-day Knights Templar. Peter Tomlinson, a Scottish Rite KCCH, Templar and Masonic Rosicrucian, was a "Brother" I met in Duluth the night I gave my Kensington Rune Stone talk at the North Star College. Peter said he had recently purchased an eighteenth-century page from a manuscript that had an extensive table of runes. He said I was welcome to examine it. A couple weeks later, we met to have a look.

The document included dozens of examples of each letter in the runic alphabet (futhork). Most of the runes on the Kensington Rune Stone and the Spirit Pond Rune Stones were listed on the page including the enigmatic "o" rune (ᚬ). The page was a reminder of how much information is available.

Peter Tomlinson, a quiet, reserved, but very friendly person, was also very dedicated and proud to his order. I feel fortunate that he has taken time to work with me. He was extremely helpful in my understanding of the more esoteric and symbolic aspects of Masonry. Peter, definitely a "right brain" type, was very in tune with the artistic, emotional, and symbolic aspects of life, which certainly lends itself to an understanding of the allegorical nature of Freemasonry.

Tomlinson has helped me without ever telling me things directly. Certain things learned within Freemasonry are only revealed to brothers through ceremonies and their associations as members within the "craft." He acted as a guide, suggesting references where I could find the answers to my questions. Our conversations are less question/answer than question/discussion. Somewhere in those discussions would be a reference or a clue that pointed me in the direction to answers.

Peter also allowed me access to both libraries at the Scottish Rite Masonic Temple in Minneapolis, Minnesota. As head librarian of the temple, on May 6, 2007, he gave Janet and me a tour of the Temple. Originally a Methodist Church constructed in 1890, it was acquired by the Scottish Rite Freemasons on January 1, 1915.

The Scottish Rite Temple in Minneapolis, Minnesota. The United States flag waves crisply on a windy day beneath the Rose window on the north side of the Temple. (Wolter, 2007)

Our tour of the multi-storied temple included two impressive, theatre-style rooms where ceremonies were held for the various Masonic degrees. Having read previously about some of the ceremonies, I could imagine an initiate being overwhelmed inside this beautiful temple. We also saw the libraries filled with books, magazines, photographs, and artifacts, most of which one would not find at a local public library. As Peter led us down the aisles of the larger library in the basement, I scanned the titles in amazement, imagining the weeks I could spend in there. I would eventually get my time for research, but I would only scratch the surface of the vast quantity of material.

Peter suggested titles that have yielded valuable information. Each book led to a new understanding of the importance of symbolism and reinforcement of William Mann's advice. In Freemasonry, virtually nothing has only one specific purpose or meaning. I constantly reminded myself to think on multiple levels, such as the celestial, terrestrial and spiritual. Knowing how adept the ancients were at astronomy, geometry, and mathematics, I've learned to consider these aspects and how they are usually all incorporated into just about everything.

One evening at the temple, I presented to a few of the brothers some of what I saw shortly after returning from my trip in May 2007 to a mysterious old stone structure in Rhode Island called the Newport Tower. My explanation of the two symbolic keystones and a granite orb I observed in the west-northwest facing archway generated comments. At one point, I showed a picture of an egg-shaped keystone and asked for input on why the builders put it on the inside of the Tower. Someone suggested, "Some things aren't meant to be seen."

Only a few months ago, the comment would have sounded cryptic, but that night it made a lot of sense. It reminded me of how the detail of the stone carvings on the exterior of the great cathedrals, and other important religious structures, increases with height. This at first appears odd, until considering the splendor and beauty of the carvings wasn't necessarily intended for people on the ground to see.

This difference in perspective could also explain why many symbols and patterns laid out across the globe lay unseen to the average person. Even for those who know what's there, such as Jim Mueller's geometry in Minneapolis and the symbolism throughout Washington, D.C., it's something generally unseen. The original architects of this sacred geometry on the planet appear to have intentionally made it visible only when viewed from above.

The Scottish Rite Creed:
The cause of human progress is our cause, the enfranchisement of human thought our supreme wish, the freedom of human conscience our mission, and the guarantee of equal rights to all peoples everywhere, the end of our contention.

One of the most captivating images I found in the Scottish Rite library appeared in the 1909 book *The Secret Teachings of All Ages* by Manley Hall. If this depiction of an initiate's symbolic crucifixion in fact dates back to the time of the Pharaoh's in Egypt, then the Christian story of the crucifixion by the Romans may have been borrowed from the Egyptians. The man on the cross in the form of an "X" appears to represent important symbolism to the Egyptians and later the Cistercians.

21

The Trip to Oxford and Scotland

I felt it imperative to examine the incredible astrolabe with the same arced X character that appears on the Spirit Pond Map Stone. This meant going to the Oxford Museum of the History of Science. On that trip I also planned to visit Scotland and see Rosslyn Chapel. I would be meeting Niven Sinclair, who would accompany me to the museum. Niven was the patriarch of the Sinclair Clan across the Atlantic. He would provide invaluable information about the chapel and castle at Roslin.

It almost seemed like destiny that my research would take me to Scotland where it seemed there was the best chance to confirm a connection to the Kensington Rune Stone and the Spirit Pond Rune Stones. Everything seemed to point that way. If the 1401-1402 dates on the Spirit Pond Stones were correct, then the only logical known candidate in history likely connected to them was Prince Henry Sinclair. Prince Henry was the first Sinclair Earl of Orkney, which, along with the Shetland Islands at that time, was still part of the Kingdom of Norway. Judge Bouschor told me that Prince Henry was also a Templar and very likely a grand master with plenty of knowledge about the New World.

His grandson, William Sinclair built Rosslyn Chapel in 1446 for reasons that have engendered speculation by researchers for centuries. In my opinion, the most reliable information about Rosslyn Chapel and its meaning would come from the Sinclairs. The family says one of William's primary reasons for building the chapel was to honor Prince Henry's voyage. Some of the evidence consistent with this voyage was reportedly carved in stone within the chapel. If there was any credibility to the Prince Henry story, which most historians dismiss, I wanted to investigate it myself.

After reading John J. Robinson's book, *Born in Blood*, I felt a plausible scenario had emerged that might explain the historical context for the Kensington party, which included a Cistercian monk, to come to North America. Robinson's theory is that the put-down of the Templars in 1307 A.D. created a need for the surviving members to escape and develop a system of secret communication. Over time, he asserts that the fugitive Templar ideology, under persecution from the Church, eventually evolved into what is now known as modern Freemasonry. He presented a convincing case.

Most historians believe the Templars who escaped France fled to one of three destinations. Those in the Baltic region aligned with their brothers the Teutonic Knights, some fled to Portugal where their original seat in Portugal is located at Tomar, but most are believed to have ended up in Scotland along with the Templar fleet. This scenario made logical sense since it is estimated that only about ten to twenty percent of the Templars in France were arrested. The remaining members of the order were in areas of Europe and Scandinavia that were unaffected, or they escaped. It only makes sense to me to try to learn first-hand what likely happened.

My plane landed at Heathrow Airport around 10:00 A.M., on October 2, 2006. After debarking, I spotted my name on a sign being held by a smiling young man in his twenties of East Indian descent. I shook his hand and said, "I'm Scott Wolter. You must be with Niven Sinclair?"

As the young man introduced himself as Niven's driver, I noticed a distinguished looking older man standing behind him. The man was impeccably dressed in a dark suit and tie. Niven smiled and introduced himself, "Welcome to England." He was pretty much as I pictured him. We got into his car, and Niven said, "Junior, please take the quickest route to Oxford."

I asked about Rosslyn Chapel, and he gave me a synopsis about its history with the Sinclair Family. He also lamented about all the craziness associated with Dan Brown's book.

It took Junior about an hour to get us to the Oxford Museum of the History of Science. Niven led me to a very old sandstone-block building. We had an appointment with Lucy Blaxland.

Lucy led us to a small library room. Bookshelves lined the walls surrounding a large table that had a laptop-sized flat box on it. Lucy said, "The astrolabe is ready for you to look at." She handed us each a pair of purple sanitary gloves. I hovered over the box, certain it contained evidence essential to prove the Spirit Pond Rune Stones were medieval artifacts. Niven was just as excited, knowing the instrument inside the box could provide support of his family's claim that his ancestor had indeed made the historic voyage. I opened the box and gently picked up the relatively small brass instrument.

I held the fully assembled instrument, marveling at its intricacy and detailed engravings. I scanned the plate beneath the points on the rete and caught a glimpse of the all-important arced X symbol etched on its surface. I wanted to take the plates out to look more closely at them but I realized that I didn't know how. I gently tugged at the pin in the middle that appeared to be holding everything together. It didn't move. I pulled the pin again with a little more force, gently angling the pin upward. It finally slid free allowing me to disassemble it.

I placed the seven plates on the protective bubble-wrap already laid out and began to examine and photograph each plate as Niven intently watched and asked questions. Both sides of each plate were engraved with arced lines designed to represent the horizon and the sky. The open hole in the middle of each plate was designed to represent a specific latitude. After a few moments, I realized something interesting. The twelve finished sides were specifically designed for the latitudes of 38, 41, 42, 45, 46, 47, 48, 49, 50, 55, 57 and 58 degrees north. One could effectively argue these plates could have been used to help navigate a voyage from the

The astrolabe (#191) at the Oxford Museum of Science was fully assembled when Niven Sinclair and I examined it on October 2, 2006. Fortunately, I was able to disassemble it and examine each of the seven brass plates. (Wolter, 2006)

Orkney Islands of Scotland, to Iceland, Greenland, Nova Scotia, and then south toward Maine and eventually to the Cape Cod/Narragansett Bay area. This was important information that I hadn't expected and wasn't included in Gunther's *Astrolabes of the World*. This new fact alone made my only hours-old trip worth it.

Lucy searched her computer for information about the instrument, but found little beyond what we already knew. I noticed Niven quietly taking in the possible implications of the instrument. I said, "You know, Mr. Sinclair, there's no reason not to believe that your ancestor could have held this very instrument in his hands on that historic voyage."

A smile formed on Niven's face as he stared at the instrument.

This astrolabe was the only known thing in the world that had the arced X symbol that appears on the Spirit Pond Map Stone. This fact alone refuted any argument that the Spirit Pond Rune Stones were a modern hoax. Niven had told me that early Templars in America planted red and white oak trees at strategic locations in the New World. He said these oaks were not indigenous to North America and brushed aside opponents' theories of their presence without human intervention with a simple response, "Acorns can't swim."

My favorite story from Niven was his describing the experience in 1995, after arriving in Chedabucto Bay, in Nova Scotia, in Canada, where Prince Henry Sinclair was believed to have anchored his ships. Niven said that when he looked across the bay he heard a voice inside him ask: "What took you so long?"

Niven Sinclair took a moment to reflect after examining the astrolabe. It is quite possible that his ancestor, Prince Henry Sinclair, could have held that very instrument during his voyage to the New World in 1398 A.D. (Wolter, 2006)

22

Rosslyn

My next stop was Edinburgh, Scotland. Small, older churches were on nearly every block, but it was the tall steeples of the cathedrals and the majestic fortress in the distance I wanted to see: Edinburgh Castle.

The geologist in me was immediately impressed with a massive outcrop of volcanic rock with the castle perched on top. Later in the week, I took a tour of the impressive castle and walked the famous Royal Mile littered with majestic cathedrals and churches. The building that impressed me the most was the Church of St. John in the heart of the city. The exterior didn't particularly stand out amongst the grandeur of the city. It also looked small sitting in the shadow of the towering castle in the distance. But the massive stone columns and vaulted ceilings did impress me. I suddenly had a great appreciation for the skill and motivation of the people who built these amazing structures so many centuries ago.

The numerous buildings in Edinburgh, constructed mostly of sandstone, were impressive. However, they were just an architectural warm-up for the main event, and my primary motivation for coming here. On October 10, 2006, I visited the small, out-of-the-way town that had recently been thrust onto the world stage by Dan Brown's *The Da Vinci Code*. The movie had made my destination one the most famous religious structures in the world. My first impression of Rosslyn Chapel was that it was dwarfed by the steel canopy draped over it. Construction began on the building in 1446, and the reddish-brown sandstone showed the ill effects of five hundred sixty years of weathering in the harsh Scottish climate. They were letting the structure dry out slowly before beginning repairs designed to preserve the highly porous sandstone.

Niven had briefed me about what to look for that might help my under-standing of who built the chapel, and why. I had read that there was evidence carved in the interior that could only exist if Prince Henry Sinclair had been in North America. Upon entering the north doorway and taking my first look around, I was overwhelmed by the thick jungle of

Edinburgh Castle looms majestically in the distance as St. John's Church sits solemnly during rush hour in Edinburgh, Scotland, on October 6, 2006. (Wolter, 2006)

detailed stone carvings covering the walls, columns and ceilings. While methodically making my way around the chapel I occasionally glanced at the grave slabs and large stone tiles that made up the floor. Both Judge Bouschor, and Niven, told me about the caves and tunnels beneath the chapel and what artifacts and treasure might lie below. One thing for cer-tain was that the local geologic terrain, predominantly soft sandstone, was very conducive to man-made caves and tunnels.

A carving that caught my eye was a ceiling beam with aloe leaves carved into the limestone, on the south side. This indigenous American plant was unknown in Europe and Scandinavia at the time William Sinclair, grandson of Prince Henry, began building Rosslyn Chapel in 1446. The notion of Columbus being the first to North America sud-denly seemed farfetched. This carving dispelled that all by itself. One window bay to the east of the aloe beam was another carving that con-firmed Columbus as a "Johnny come-lately." The limestone arches fram-ing the window had six carvings of maize. This is another American plant that, while pre-Columbian carvings existed in India and Egypt, it

145

was likely unknown at that time in the British Isles and Scandinavia. These carvings provided compelling support of Prince Henry's voyage.

As obvious as the implications were for these well-known carvings, there was much more to be seen and learned. One of the people pointing out some of the more subtle features of the chapel was a retired gentleman who was also a Freemason. In the west end of the chapel above the altar, he pointed to a curious carving quietly tucked into a recess. It was a face that the Freemason said was the death mask of King Robert the Bruce.

This name featured prominently in the time period that was of greatest interest to me. John J. Robinson convincingly wrote that Robert the Bruce had been aided by an infusion of fugitive Templar Knights who helped him defeat the English in the famous Battle of Bannockburn in 1314. This location was an hour's drive north from the chapel. Prince Henry's grandfather, Sir William St. Clair, his great-grandfather, Sir Henry St. Clair, and his great-granduncle, William St. Clair were Templars who all fought valiantly alongside Robert the Bruce at Bannockburn.[1] The face carved in stone that initially seemed out of place now made perfect sense. While its presence was appropriate, I couldn't understand how anyone

Inside Rosslyn Chapel aloe plants, indigenous to the Americas, are carved into one of the stone beams. This plant was not native to Europe or Scandinavia and was unknown in 1446 when William Sinclair started construction of the chapel. (Photograph by Scott F. Wolter with kind permission of the Rosslyn Chapel Trust, 2006)

Although pre-Columbian examples of maize are found in India and Egypt, the plant indigenous to the Americas was unknown in Europe and Scandinavia when the Chapel was built, yet six ears of corn are found carved above a window on the south side. Knowledge of these plants could have been brought back by members of Prince Henry Sinclair's party that reportedly traveled to the North America, in 1398 A.D. (Photograph by Scott F. Wolter with kind permission of the Rosslyn Chapel Trust, 2006)

today could determine if it was actually King Robert's face. My question was answered the next day inside Dunfermline Abbey, roughly twenty miles northwest of Edinburgh. Inside a glass case near King Robert's tomb was a plaster cast of his skull. His actual skull had been on display as an important relic for centuries, until 1818. Modern facial reconstruction methods could easily verify the face in Rosslyn Chapel from the cast alone.

The Bruce's death mask appears to confirm Robinson's speculation of a strong Templar connection to the Sinclairs and the historic battle. The carvings in the chapel confirmed that the Templars, in the form of Prince Henry, very likely did reach North America at the end of the fourteenth century. Of course the Kensington Rune Stone being a Cistercian document means that the likelihood is that the Templars were along on that trip too. Whether the cross emblazed on their white woolen mantles was red (Knights Templar) or black (Teutonic Knights) makes no difference. What matters is that the ideology they all embraced had arrived to the New World.

147

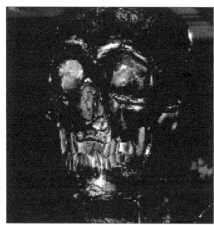

King Robert the Bruce's death mask (left) is carved into the stonework at Rosslyn Chapel. Verification of the mask's authenticity could be done using Bruce's skull. A plaster cast of the skull (right) is on display near his tomb in Dumfermline Abbey in Scotland (Photograph by Scott F. Wolter with kind permission of the Rosslyn Chapel Trust, 2006; Wolter, 2006)

The other thing that struck me at Rosslyn was a carving visible from the inside, but had more impact when viewed from the outside of the chapel. At the top of four windows in the east end of the chapel an "X" was carved with cupped engrailing, a telltale symbol of the Sinclair Family. The beautiful carving hit me as a likely symbol of their core beliefs, the duality of male and female, and heaven and earth. The only thing missing was a little hook in the upper right arm. Perhaps its absence was due to William Sinclair's caution about tipping off a visiting bishop from the Church. The curious hook would have raised eyebrows in his time and likely served as an unnecessary risk.

Later I contacted Niven Sinclair for clarification on a couple points relative to my trip to Oxford. I also shared my interpretation of the Hooked X. Niven responded with what appears to be validation of my speculation about the engrailed "X" that had been carved at the top of four windows outside of Rosslyn Chapel.

From: Niven Sinclair
Sent: Wednesday, November 21, 2007 11:47 A.M.

To: Wolter, Scott
Subject: RE: Name of Bay in Nova Scotia

"The hooked "X" is not dissimilar to the engrailed cross of the Sinclairs."

The Engrailed Cross

The name Saint Clair is derived from the Latin Sancto Claro which means Holy Light . . . In the engrailed cross of the Sinclairs, the esoteric female symbol "V" represents the chalice of life (the womb) whereas its male counterpart which is a "V" in reverse represents the spear of virility. When conjoined one above the other ("X") they indicate unity and the engrailed sequence denotes Generation. An engrailed cross is, therefore, indicative of Holy Generation.

It may also indicate the union of two Royal Houses in so far as Jesus belonged to the Royal House of David whilst Mary Magdalene belonged to the Royal House of Benjamin. She is also "seen" in Rosslyn Chapel where she is represented by the five-petal rose—the sacred feminine.

At the top of the window on the south side of the east end of Rosslyn Chapel is one of four carvings of an engrailed X. The symbol could represent the duality of male and female, and heaven and earth. (Photo by Wolter with permission of the Rosslyn Chapel Trust, 2006)

More commonly, the engrailed cross has been described as being indicative of the protection of the True Cross. The True Cross is seen as being encased with a grail or grille, i.e. engrailed. The Sinclairs were said to be the protectors of the Grail which gave rise to the (erroneous) belief that the Grail was concealed within the Apprentice pillar.

Sufficient be it to say, the engrailed cross has appeared on the coats-of-arms of most branches of the Sinclair family for many centuries. It has appeared on the shields of our warrior forebears, on the sails of our ships, on the ceilings of our castles and, above all, in the intricate architectural splendour of Rosslyn Chapel.

It is a striking symbol which should be displayed with pride wherever and whenever Sinclairs are gathered together.

Niven Sinclair

As if Niven's revelation about the engrailed X at Rosslyn Chapel wasn't enough, the Hooked X would appear again only a few weeks later. English author Simon Brighton wrote *In Search of the Knights Templar*— Janet had made this important discovery in a bookstore. She pointed to a picture the author wrote was a mason's mark. My eyes instantly fixed on the familiar character. It was a Hooked X with a slight modification in the form of a diamond shape hanging below the intersection of the crossed lines. The Hooked X was found at Rosslyn Chapel!

After digitally scanning the Hooked X character at Rosslyn, I emailed the image to David Brody, Judi Rudebush, and a few other NEARA members for their input. Judi quickly made contact via the Internet with a European expert on mason's marks named Robert Cooper, who offered the following possibility for the mason's mark at Rosslyn Chapel on January 8, 2008.

"What I think is shown here is a mason's mark which has been modified by his son by adding a 'V' shape below the centre of the cross to form a diamond shape. A mason chose his mark which was then his alone and no other stonemason could ever use it. If a son also became a stonemason he could not use his father's mark and so would have made a slight change or addition to make it 'the same but different' if you follow me. If a grandson became a stonemason, he too would use his father's mark but make another slight change. Where many generations of stonemasons worked on the same building (say a cathedral) some masons' marks are quite complicated as each new member of the stonemasons' family added to the mark of his father. In other words, I think that these two marks are that of father and son."

Cooper's opinion was very interesting. Given the relative dates of origin for the marks, 1362 for the Kensington Rune Stone and 1446 for the beginning of construction at Rosslyn Chapel, his theory could explain the differences.

A few days later on January 16, 2008, Judi helped us contact Simon Brighton in England. Simon was very interested in our research including our focus on the Hooked X character he photographed at Rosslyn. He forwarded his original un-cropped photograph that helped us determine that the mark was on a column inside the chapel. The weathered appearance that led us think it might have been carved on the outside of the chapel was actually deposits within the grooves of the "lime wash" that was applied to the inside in an effort to help conserve the building in the 1950s.

The left Hooked X character is found on the Kensington Rune Stone. The right one was found used as an apparent mason's mark inside Rosslyn Chapel in Scotland. The meaning of the diamond in the lower part of the X is unclear. Mason marks expert, Robert Cooper, suggested the character found at Rosslyn could be an addition to a stonemason family's mark by a son or grandson. (Wolter, 2002; Photo by Scott F. Wolter with permission of the Rosslyn Chapel Trust, 2008)

The Rosslyn Hooked X held my attention for weeks. I wanted badly to personally examine it, and, as fate would have it, that opportunity materialized during the latter part of March 2008. Andy Awes with Committee Films and I reached an agreement to make a documentary film based on the research in this book. He was excited to start the project, and on March 25th our four-man crew landed in Edinburgh. After picking up the van and filming equipment, Andy; Bo Hakala, the cinematographer; Ben Krueger, the sound and lighting guy; and I drove the half hour south of the city to the village of Roslin.

Niven was anxious to get things moving. He told me how excited he was and that he had already found the Hooked X symbol carved into one of the pillars. He breezed past the ticket counter as the cashier flashed a "Niven can do as he pleases smile," and I followed behind. We entered the north door. Niven led me to a stone column in the south-east end and pointed to a roughly three-inch tall carving at about waist height.

Even though I knew exactly what I was seeing, it was still hard to believe. Of all the places in Europe or Scandinavia where the Hooked X could be, to find it at Rosslyn was unbelievable. On the other hand, in light of everything we'd studied, it was almost expected.

As amazing as this discovery was, this example was different from the symbol we'd come to know. My first thought was it could be a symbol indicative of latitude. Scottish author Ashley Cowie in his 2006 book, *The Rosslyn Matrix*, explains the historic origin of lozenges in a simple and coherent way. Ancient Egyptian priests, who were essentially astronomers, performed a simple exercise to graphically illustrate latitude by simply using a staff. The priest started by drawing a circle in the sand and then held the staff or rod, on the east side of the circle at sunrise. If the sun was rising on the summer solstice in the northern most point in the eastern sky, the staff would project a shadow across the southern half of the circle. At the end of the day when the priest held the staff on the west side of the circle, another shadow would mirror the morning shadow projecting in the opposite direction. If the priest performed the same exercise on the winter solstice two lines of shadow would mirror the summer solstice in the northern half of the circle. Where the lines intersect in the middle of the circle they complete a lozenge with a shape unique to that latitude.

At the latitude of Jerusalem (31 degrees, 47 minutes North) the angle of the lines projecting from the east and west is sixty degrees. If two vertical lines are drawn connecting the shadow endpoints on the circle, two equilateral triangles create the Star of David symbol. The shape of the lozenge gets taller when this exercise is performed at higher latitudes moving north. Curiously, at the latitude of Rosslyn Chapel (55 degree 85 minutes North) the shape of the lozenge created by this exercise is a perfect square!

Cowie explained his theory for the meaning of a mysterious carving on the south wall inside the crypt below the chapel on the east end. This carving looks something like a metal power-line tower with four progressively taller lozenges aligned vertically at the top. Cowie makes a persuasive argument that these lozenges correspond to latitude. A short time after viewing the Rosslyn Hooked X, I examined the lozenges in the crypt and wondered what latitudes and possibly significant places they

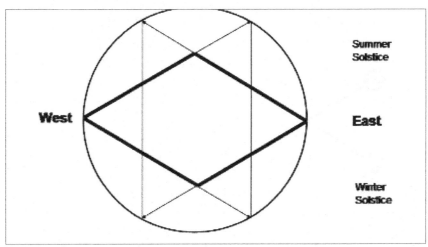

If a rod is placed on the east side of the circle at sunrise, the rising sun on the summer solstice will project a shadow across the southern half of the circle. At the end of that same day the setting sun will cast a shadow of the rod in the opposite direction that will mirror the morning shadow. If the same exercise is performed on the winter solstice, two lines of shadow will mirror the summer solstice in the northern half of the circle. Where the lines intersect in the middle of the circle they complete a lozenge with a shape unique to that latitude.

This mysterious carving is the top part of a tower-shaped design found on a wall in the crypt at Rosslyn Chapel. It is thought to represent a map of navigational gridlines marking specific lines of latitude and longitude. The bowl shape curved lines likely represent the pattern Venus makes as it moves through the sky as a morning and evening star. Venus is depicted as a five-pointed star, which is the pattern it makes during its eight-year cycle. The vertically aligned lozenges in the middle depict latitude. As the lozenge gets taller it depicts more northerly latitude. (Photo by Scott F. Wolter with permission of the Rosslyn Chapel Trust, 2008)

might represent. The Hooked X "lozenges" at Rosslyn might also be a clue to an important specific location. On the other hand, it might simply be a fifteenth century mason's mark.

A couple of months later when I was thinking about the lozenges at Rosslyn, something occurred to me. As my research had progressed on the Knights Templar and Freemasonry, two geographic locations keep reappearing as vitally important to these two groups: Rosslyn Chapel and Jerusalem. The east-west lozenge angles at these two latitudes are sixty and ninety degrees. My attention turned to the most common symbol of Freemasonry—the compass and the square—and I wondered if there was a connection. Is it a coincidence that the angle of the compass is usually sixty degrees and the square is ninety?

Note
[1]Niven, Sinclair, personal communication, 2009.

23

The Mystery Stone

S imon Brighton's wonderfully illustrated book, *In Search of the Knights Templar*, contained a few other photographs at known Templar sites in England that triggered ideas about possible new connections in North America.

During a research trip to the East Coast, David Brody and I drove to the New Hampshire Historical Society on April 6, 2007. We saw a mysterious, roughly four-inch long, egg-shaped stone with several interesting symbols and shapes carved into the very dense and hard rock that looked like quartzite. The stone was reportedly found in 1872, "by construction workers who dug up a suspicious lump of clay near the shore of Lake Winnipesaukee, and Seneca A. Ladd of Meredith discovered this intriguing carved stone within the clay casing."[1]

At the time, neither of us had any clue as to what the symbols might mean or who had made the artifact. However, two photos in Brighton's book prompted me to go back and look at my photos. At the Templar sites of Royston Cave in Hertfordshire, Denny Abbey in Cambridgeshire, and Temple Bruer in Lincolnshire, Brighton wrote how M's had been scratched into

The "Mystery Stone" was found in 1872 by construction workers near the shore of Lake Winnipesaukee. (Wolter, 2007)

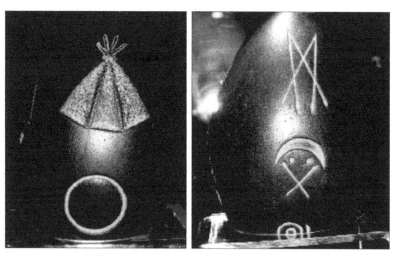

The "Mystery Stone" tepee (with tepee ring?), and symbol sides. (Wolter, 2007)

walls as pleas of protection symbols likely evoking Mary Magdalene or the Virgin Mary. The M symbol on the Mystery Stone looks hauntingly similar with one noticeable difference. The four legs of the M are angled to make the "double axe" symbol commonly made to rid spiritual evil.

The striking M's conjured up thoughts that the symbol could be related to the mirrored pattern of the horns of Venus. Perhaps the M represents the path Venus traces in the night sky as a morning and evening star. If so, then the Mystery Stone could have been made by people who venerated the Virgin Mary or Mary Magdalene.

Note

[1] New Hampshire Historical Society website, Mystery Stone, p. 2.

Wall scratches at Templar sites in Britain represent pleas of protection from Mary Magdalene or the Virgin Mary. Could the "M" symbol on the Mystery Stone in New Hampshire, be a stylized combination of these two symbols as a reference to the Goddess and the horns of Venus? (Brighton, 2006, page 163)

Part V
Archaeopetrography

24

Andy Engebretson Interview

Not long after returning from Scotland, I received a call from
Andy Engebretson. He said he had finally tracked down the
information he was looking for relating to his father's story
about Olof Ohman paying back the loan. Andy said his father only lived in
Kensington for a couple of years and then transferred to another bank in
South Dakota. Andy became concerned when he read in our book that
Ohman had gone to Sweden to visit his family in 1912 and returned on the
infamous ship the *Lusitania* in August of 1914. Andy wanted to verify that
his father was indeed in Kensington at the same time as Ohman and had
found the documentation he was looking for. As a still-practicing attorney,
Andy didn't want to leave any stone unturned that might someday come
back to haunt him, his father's story, or Olof Ohman.

We agreed to record the interview at my office in St. Paul, on
October 19, 2006. Andy and his wife drove down from Superior,
Wisconsin. I noticed he walked with a cane very slowly and gingerly. He
informed me that since we first met at the Masonic Lodge his condition
had deteriorated. His doctor said he likely wouldn't improve, and I felt
a twinge of guilt for pressuring him to travel down here. He politely
brushed off my apology and said, "This was important and a little pain
in my legs isn't going to stop me." Andy did a professional job telling
his story. He definitely came across as credible, and I'm sure his father
would have been proud.

Darwin Ohman and I met Russ Fridley for one of our regular

lunches on October 24, 2006. Russ was aware of the Engebretson interview and understood how this story essentially negated his 1970 interview with Walter Gran. I didn't even bother to argue Andy's superior credibility over Walter's because it really didn't matter. By this time I'd accepted that Russ wasn't going to change his mind about Ohman.

On May 16, 2007, at another of our lunches, Chris Owens, an aspiring journalist, met with us to ask questions before his three-part article was published. (*Chanhassen Villager*, June 28, July 5, and July 12, 2007) Near the end of our meeting, Russ interjected with a surprising unsolicited comment. "Scott [and Dick Nielsen] deserves credit for taking the Rune Stone research in a completely different direction because of one rune. It changes 'Journey of discovery' to 'Journey of acquisition or taking up land,' and I think that's important."

I always felt that either the Hooked X or the dotted R were the key runic symbols that most impacted the new research. I hadn't thought about how much impact the Þ-rune changing from "d" to "t" would have in other people's minds. As it turned out, this memorable moment was only a prelude of things to come.

Three months later on August 15th we met for another lunch that included Chris Owens, Bill Bowell, Russ, Darwin and me. At one point, Darwin spoke up to tell us about a meeting he recently attended at the History Center regarding the latest plans for developing the park at the Ohman Farm and said, ". . . and we all know Olof didn't carve the Rune Stone."

As the words came out of Darwin's mouth, I instinctively looked over at Russ. Gently nodding his head he said, "Yes, I would agree."

25

American Institute of Professional Geologists

People often talk about "watershed moments," when something happens that is epiphany-like or triggers a significant change. An important watershed moment for Dick Nielsen and me came at the American Institute of Professional Geologists (A.I.P.G.) national convention social dinner at the Science Museum in St. Paul, on September 27, 2006. Our local chapter hosted the week-long event. Field trips, short courses, and other social events had all been well attended. This dinner was the culmination of the week, and I was asked to give a presentation about the Kensington Rune Stone. I was very excited about giving this talk in front of not only my Minnesota peers, but geologists from around the country.

It was an exciting opportunity, and I invited Darwin Ohman and Dick Nielsen to attend. I also invited Steinar Opstad from Norway. During the dinner, Steinar told me he was a twenty-five-year member of the Knights Templar in Norway. I couldn't help but think about another of Henrik Williams's comments a couple of years before about how he didn't believe there were secret societies in Sweden. I thought to myself, if they exist in Norway, they exist in Sweden. It turns out the current World Headquarters for the Knight Templar is in Stockholm, Sweden. The dinner also provided an opportunity to meet Bill Siok, past president of A.I.P.G. National, who had written a favorable review of our Kensington Rune Stone book in the May/June issue of *The Professional Geologist*.

At the end of my talk, Steinar raised his hand and asked if he could address the audience. To my and everyone else's surprise, he eloquently said, "I want to say that I fully endorse this work and will ensure that scholars and others in Norway will hear about this research." He then added, "I would also like to publicly apologize to Darwin and his family for the way some Scandinavian scholars have treated them."

This night also marked the end of my joint research with Dick Nielsen. We both knew that for him to continue to pursue working with the world's top runologists, he had to distance himself from "Templar" research. Dick had worked long and hard to get to this point with these scholars. Even though I supported his position, I had to follow the path the Hooked X was taking me.

26

A Disturbed Young Man

One of the neat things resulting from the rune stone research is the numerous calls and emails I receive regarding other artifacts and inscriptions. The weathering studies that worked so well on the Kensington Rune Stone prompted many inquiries as to whether we could generate similar relative-age dating information on other mysterious man-made surfaces. In many cases the potential is good; in others there is very little we can do. The effectiveness of our forensic methods is dependant on several factors. One of the most important is provenance of the artifact. Knowing the history behind an artifact is critical. If there are gaps in the history or very little is known, it can cast a shadow over the data or potentially even make it useless. That is why documenting the history behind an artifact, especially details about its discovery is so important. Relative-age dating can also work the other way by documenting evidence consistent with man-made surfaces not being very old. In spite of the challenges, I am very excited about the future possibilities of this emerging science that I call "Archaeopetrography."

On May 28, 2007, I received an intriguing email from researcher Michael Zalar that put my relative-age dating methods to the test. Mike forwarded six photographs that had been sent to his Kensington Rune Stone website by the owners of an inscribed stone found in Northern Vermont. The photos showed what looked like a rather large, flat stone upright in the ground with carved symbols that included runes and Hebrew script. There was also a spiral symbol reminiscent of those seen at megalithic sites like Newgrange in Ireland. It was impossible to tell the rock type from the photos, but it looked like it might be some kind of sedimentary rock.

I sent the photos off to several people, including David Brody, and they all came back saying the artifact looked very intriguing. After several conversations, David and I agreed it was worth following up. We made contact with the owners of the stone, Dawn and Steve Lawrence. They were very cooperative and seemed just as curious as we were to learn more. We headed to Boston. On June 24, 2007, David picked me up at the Boston airport. It was a three-hour drive to the quiet little town of Lyndonville.

We were excited to be the first researchers to see this inscribed stone and prepared ourselves to do the best job we could of proper documentation. If genuine, this would be the first inscription of its kind ever found in North America.

Dawn and Steve lived about fifteen miles outside of Lyndonville, but the windy roads into the woods made it seem a lot farther. We found the roughly four-foot long by nine-inch-wide stone lying on a picnic table in their yard. We could easily see the inscription, including the darkened area at the bottom where it had been in the ground. The light was fading quickly so I grabbed two flashlights. I always assume it might be the only time I'd get to examine an artifact, so I took dozens of photographs of the inscriptions on both sides of the stone. I also studied the rock, which appeared to be graywacke type of sandstone. I had brought along a new piece of equipment, a portable microscope. It was essentially a microscopic lens adapted to fit onto a digital camera.

Once I had enough photos, we asked Dawn and Steve for an interview. David and I asked as many questions as we could think of about the history of the stone. We also asked if we could visit the site where the stone had been found. They said a friend of theirs found it, and he was willing to talk to us.

Back at the hotel I downloaded the photographs and spent time looking at the magnified images I'd taken with the portable microscope. The stone was a greywacke and looked like it was relatively soft and poorly cemented. This bothered me a little, but I didn't spend a lot of time worrying about it, knowing I might be able to get a sample into the lab at some point and learn more. David had experience with Hebrew and thought the script looked good, but he couldn't translate it. Several of the characters looked like legitimate runes, but others looked a little strange. Not being a

The mysterious inscribed stone in Northern Vermont turned out to have been carved into a relatively soft, and rapidly weathering, greywacke sandstone by "a very disturbed young man." (Wolter, 2007)

runic expert, I knew better than to draw any conclusions. We'd have to wait for detailed analysis. Still something made me uneasy.

We met Dawn and Steve the next day, and they led us even farther into the Northern Vermont Mountains. After driving past a small early twentieth-century cemetery, we pulled into the driveway of their friend who had found the stone. He was busy until the early afternoon, but gave us permission to walk the field next to his house. Steve led us into a cleared field with waist-high grass and pointed out where he was told the stone had been found. David asked if Steve knew anything about the history of who owned the land. To our surprise, he knew the woman who owned the property going back almost forty years. He said she lived on the other side of the field. David and I suggested we speak to her since we had some time.

As we pulled in to the neighbor's yard, two women met us. One, Claire, using a cane, turned out to be the property owner. David began explaining the reason for our visit. When David mentioned the inscribed stone, Claire flashed a knowing smile. She said in the late 1980s she sold a parcel of land to a woman who had a daughter and a son. She said the son was into the occult and Cabalism and "very disturbed." Claire also mentioned he was into Zoroastrianism that apparently was a 1980s New Age fad. When the family moved out in the late 1990s she remodeled the house that she herself had lived in previously. The boy, who was in his late teens/early twenties, had carved symbols into the wooden doorways inside the house and a human eye into the floor. I asked if he had carved symbols into rocks and she said, "Yes." Apparently, he had assembled a circle of rocks in the field with standing stones placed into the ground for strange rituals. She pointed to the field we had just been in.

I could feel David's heart sink as Claire's story unfolded and I certainly felt disappointment as well. On a scale from one to ten, this woman's credibility was an eleven. However, much like I felt the day I was told the AVM Stone was modern (the fake rune stone carved near the Kensington Rune Stone site by University of Minnesota graduate students in 1985), this story also made sense based on what I'd seen on my computer screen the night before. Even though the stone had a weathered appearance, the poorly cemented greywacke sandstone could easily have taken on a weathered appearance in the roughly twenty years it was exposed since it was carved.

After thanking Claire, Dawn, and Stephen for all their help, David and I drove back to his home in Westford. We tried every angle to find a hole in the conclusion staring us in the face, but there was none. Eventually, we agreed the inscription was a folly rather than a hoax. A hoax is something that is intended to deceive. This was the act of an eccentric young man who never realized the future confusion his handy-work would cause. He also didn't realize his inscription now served as a great control sample for future research. The good news about this experience is that it demonstrates exactly how archaeopetrography should work. These methods should be able to help identify hoaxes, as well as history.

Part VI

New England Artifacts and Sites

27

The Newport Tower

Another important connection to this story that I knew I had to see was the Newport Tower. The mysterious stone structure in Newport, Rhode Island, kept coming up in the books I was reading. As the summer of 2006 was starting to wind down I decided to go see it. Sue Carlson and Ros Strong suggested I contact NEARA member Rick Lynch who lived in Rhode Island. Rick said he would be glad to show me some other interesting things as long as I was out there.

Rick was familiar with my geologic work on the Kensington Rune Stone and asked if we could employ our laboratory methods on some of the East Coast artifacts. One of my goals was to try to develop new petrographic methods that could be used for understanding the age of weathered man-made surfaces in rocks: inscriptions, carvings, petroglyphs, dressed stone, and other intentionally broken surfaces.

Rick took me to Touro Park, and I saw the rather crude-looking, two-story Tower built from field stone and mortar. From a distance it looked rather small, but as we walked closer it began to be more impressive.

Being a geologist, the first thing I focused on were the rocks used to build the Newport Tower. Most were glacial cobbles comprised of granite, gneiss, various sedimentary rocks, and an intermittent piece of white quartz. The rest consisted of flat, elongate slabs of slate, phyllite, and schist. All the rock types used in construction appeared to be indigenous to the area. I also spent time studying the mortar. The inside of the Newport Tower had obviously been tuck-pointed at least twice, and there were several areas where the

This photo of the Newport Tower shows its eight-columned, two-storied, stone-and-mortar construction and was taken in Touro Park in Newport, Rhode Island, on September 12, 2006. (Photograph courtesy of Richard Lynch)

mortar looked relatively new. Even if the structure was built in Colonial times, which I doubted, finding the original mortar would be a challenge.

One of the things that surprised me was the numerous rectangular recesses, or niches, scattered throughout the inner walls. There didn't seem to be any order for the placement of the recesses or for the three largest windows on the east, south and west sides of the Newport Tower. The most impressive aspect of the interior was the fireplace. Rick explained that there were two flues in it that vented smoke to the outside through two exterior holes constructed near the top of the structure. Whoever built it knew exactly what they were doing.

After examining the tower for roughly an hour, Rick then hurried me along to our next stop on the west side of Narragansett Bay. We had an appointment to meet with three other researchers to view an inscription I was very anxious to see.

28

The Narragansett Rune Stone

The second site we visited was to see the Narragansett Rune Stone, located near Pojac Point on Narragansett Bay. There we met NEARA member Jim Egan, researcher Duncan Laurie, and Rhode Island State Archaeologist Paul Robinson.

The five of us walked along the gravelly shore about 150 yards when Rick pointed to a spot where the water swirled awkwardly over something roughly sixty feet offshore. "Unfortunately there's a large storm in the Atlantic, and it's making the tide higher than we expected. Do you still want to try to see it?" Rick said.

There was still about twenty minutes before the tide would begin to rise, so I said, "I don't know when the next time is that I'll be here, so let's do it."

With rubber boots on, I followed Rick out to the submerged boulder. The very top of the rock was beginning to protrude out of the water, and I could see it was a large, relatively flat, glacial boulder that probably weighed at least two tons. I climbed on top of it to see if I could locate the nine-character long inscription. With small waves breaking over the stone, I felt the the carved lines. The characters were about two inches tall and maybe half an inch deep. The first rune I saw was the "h" (*), which allowed me to orientate myself to find what I wanted most to see. As the water receded between waves, I suddenly saw it clearly and then felt it with my hands just to make sure. The Hooked X I'd heard and read about in this inscription was definitely there!

Paul asked, "How old do you think it is?"

I said, "I think it's medieval."

Paul said, "Really? That's the first time I've heard that. Most people tell me that it's Viking age."

I then explained. "The Hooked X has only been seen on four other rune stones, and they are all dated to that period." I didn't tell him the other reason why. I figured he would find out about the Cistercians and the Templars in due time.

We talked about the uniqueness of this inscription in spite of its short length. I explained to the group how opponents could not claim this inscription had been copied from either the Kensington Rune Stone or the Spirit Pond Rune Stones. Only three of the nine characters, the "s" (ᛋ), "h" (✳) and the Hooked X (X) were found on the other four inscriptions. Even though it may be difficult to pinpoint the origin of this inscription, the presence of the Hooked X is a tell-tale sign that it was carved in medieval times.

On the hike back to the cars Paul and I talked about the importance of preserving the inscription. He agreed that until the inscription was properly studied, it should be treated as an unknown and protected. I suggested that the boulder be removed from the bay to stop the weathering

The Narragansett Rune Stone inscription contains only three of the same runes found on the either the Kensington Rune Stone or the Spirit Pond Rune Stones (ᛋ for "s," ✳ for "h" and the hooked X for "a") and is a unique inscription that was clearly not copied. (Wolter, 2008)

process, adding that it wouldn't be all that difficult to do. Paul explained that there would be some bureaucracy that had to be dealt with before such an effort could take place. I could certainly understand that there is a certain amount of red tape to be dealt with. However, I also knew that if enough people really wanted something worthwhile to be done, it could happen. Paul could be an important ally for just such an effort.

The next day, I met up with two other locals who graciously agreed show me three more interesting artifacts.

I felt good about the prospects of getting that stone out of the bay and to a secure location for study. Rick was right about Paul. Unlike many archaeologists I had met he appeared to have an open mind to the possibility of pre-Columbian European exploration in North America.

29

The Westford Knight (Sword)

O n the morning of September 13, 2006, I drove to the Westford, Massachusetts, Library to meet Elizabeth Lane, a local expert on the Westford Knight, and David Brody. Elizabeth said the outcrop with the knight carving was only a few blocks away, so the three of us set off on foot through the quaint New England town. After walking about four blocks we came upon the bedrock outcrop surrounded by a fence made of five stone columns with chains. It was situated only a few feet from a well-traveled road. Even with the area in shade, it didn't take long to find the image. I carefully examined the man-made carving on the glacially striated, mica-schist bedrock. We each took a turn crawling over the surface looking closely at the numerous, well defined, closely spaced, eighth-inch-deep circular pits that made a pattern of the hilt end of a sword. The pits were clearly man-made and exhibited extensive weathering that appeared similar in color and texture to all the other glacial aged (roughly 12,000 to 15,000 years old) surfaces on the outcrop. The hilt, handle, and guard of the sword were pecked out to incorporate a long, straight ridge of glacially striated bedrock obviously intended to comprise the blade.

Elizabeth pointed out areas on the bedrock that were supposed to be where the face and shield of a medieval knight had been carved. I looked carefully at these highly weathered and deeply pitted areas. Nowhere did I see evidence of the man-made peck marks so obvious in the handle of the sword. When I voiced my opinion, a concerned look came to her face. She had related many details about a Scottish family crest on the shield and how some people could even see the outline of a body along with a helmet above the face. As hard as I tried, I couldn't see any evidence of anything man-made other than the sword. Elizabeth and David commented that perhaps weathering made the other features hard to see or even had completely removed them. This was certainly a possibility, but my skepticism was rising rapidly. David would later tell me that he couldn't see anything but the sword either but had saved his comments until we had time to speak privately. He didn't want to upset Elizabeth, who was clearly troubled by my comments.

On a subsequent trip to the site on November 12, 2006, for the Fall NEARA conference, Janet and I arrived with a group of five people, including David Brody. The late-afternoon sunlight was shining across the bedrock surface at a low angle that brought out the pecked lines perfectly. The sword looked the same as it did during my last visit, and seeing it in this different light reinforced the opinion I had reached the last time. I was asked, "So Scott, what do you think? Is there a knight there or not?"

I've never sugar-coated my opinion, and I wasn't going to start now. I explained that there were no obvious man-made peck marks in the areas reported to comprise an image of a knight. I also said I didn't buy the idea that these areas had experienced severe weathering, and were easier to see in the past. I said, "If that was true, then why is the sword so clearly visible and everything else gone? If there had been something else there before, there should still be something left, and I just don't see it."

I wasn't worried about this group getting upset with my opinion that the carving long thought to be medieval knight was in reality only a sword. However, I also explained that for people who wanted to argue that the effigy was carved to honor a fallen

The Westford Knight (Sword) under ideal daylight conditions on November 12, 2006. (Wolter, 2006)

Templar knight, they still could. Many Templar graves in Europe had nothing but a sword carved on their grave slabs. It also seemed prudent to make the suggestion that maybe it should be called the "Westford Sword." By insisting there is a knight that nobody can see, supporters open themselves up to criticism from opponents. Everyone in the group understood the point.

30

The Westford Boat Stone

After crawling over the roadside outcrop of the Westford Knight, Elizabeth reminded us that the library would now be open and we could go see another artifact called the Boat Stone. We walked the few short blocks back to the J.V. Fletcher Library. In the lower level they had a 200 to 300 pound glacial granite boulder resting on a metal stand. Staring at the curious artifact, I was instantly struck by the lack of any discernable difference between the color, texture, and weathering of both the glacial and man-made surfaces of the stone. I had already seen a photograph of the Boat Stone in a book where the man-made lines looked fresh. Seeing the artifact in person instantly changed that. These carvings were old.

The images of a boat, an arrow, and three carved characters looked like the numbers 1, 8, and 4. All had been made using a pecking technique similar to the Westford Sword. The stone had been found only a couple of miles from the library in 1932 by a landowner named William Wyman. He moved the Boat Stone into a shed and kept it in his possession until one of his descendents gave it to the library in the early 1960s. The fact that the pecking technique was similar to the Westford Sword didn't mean the carver was the same person, but could be an indication of the particular period when they were made. I was certain the weathering of both the Westford Boat Stone and the Westford Sword were not made in the past several decades and could very well be many hundreds of years old.

I asked Elizabeth if the lights in the room could be turned off, and she found a custodian to help us. Once the room was dark, I pulled a flashlight out of my backpack to highlight the physical relief of the carved characters. At first glance, they looked like the numbers 184. Closer inspection revealed that the upper loop in the "eight" did not appear to be closed. This character was a little confusing due to the presence of a prominent crack several inches long that ran right through it. After studying it carefully, I was convinced it was not the number eight and the upper loop was definitely open.

The three of us discussed the possibilities of what the character could be and what the carver intended by using it. If the carving was old, perhaps it was made to aid a returning exploration party. The open eight symbol could be the astrological symbol for the constellation Taurus. The third character, which looked like the number four, could also be the Arabic number five or possibly the astrological symbol for the planet Jupiter.

Elizabeth and David said that some thought the arrow pointed out the direction to a boat, and the characters represented the number of paces to it. Without knowing the exact location where the boulder had been found made any interpretation difficult. However, the reported location was the base of the hill within 184 paces of a body of water capable of floating a boat like the one depicted on the Westford Boat Stone. The possibility of using constellations as directional indicators seems more plausible to me.

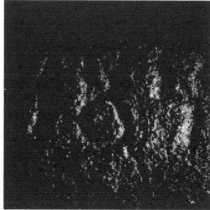

The Boat Stone resides in the J.V. Fletcher Library in Westford, Massachusetts, and was found by a landowner clearing brush to widen a road in the early 1930s. (Wolter, 2006)

178

31

The Tyngsboro Map Stone

Our final stop that day was at a private residence where another artifact, the Tyngsboro Map Stone, was located near the Merrimac River. I had never heard of it before, and my curiosity was piqued. An attractive woman in her thirties answered the door, and was more than happy to lead us to the site. After a short hike into the woods, she stopped in front of a very large granite boulder. She then began pointing out the very prominent and relatively deep, man-made lines. The boulder was heavy with lichen, making the lines hard to see at first. After a few moments, though, the map became obvious. The relatively deep, approximately three-quarter-inch-wide-by-half-inch-deep grooves, appeared to represent rivers with polygonal-shaped depressions representing local lakes.

Here again, I was struck by the advanced stage of weathering of the man-made lines. I peeled back some of the lichen, and there was virtually no difference between the cut lines and the glacial surfaces. The weathering actually surprised me. Whoever carved this did it long ago.

"Hey Scott, take a look at this," said David, as he pulled out a map of the area and started tracing the rivers and lakes that appeared to match the carvings in the rock with amazing accuracy.

David had been born and raised in the area and immediately recognized the curved shape of a river as the Merrimac River and the large trough on the top of the boulder as Lake Winnipesaukee. I said, "I'm more impressed by this than anything else I've seen all day. We need to return here after dark so we could take pictures using low-angle light." Later that evening, we spent a couple of hours examining both the Tyngsboro Map Stone and the Westford Knight after dark which really helped confirm what we saw during the day.

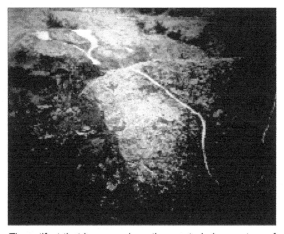

The artifact that impressed me the most, during my tour of sites in Massachusetts, was the Tyngsboro Map Stone. The deeply carved and highly weathered lines were an amazing match to the Merrimac River/Lake Winnipesaukee watershed. (Pendergast, 1992, p. 63)

32

The NEARA Annual Conference

T he NEARA annual conference in November of 2006 was the first-ever joint conference with the New England States Archaeologists. I found a copy of a NEARA publication of technical papers on the Newport Tower. The first article was written by Sue Carlson, who compared the architecture of the Newport Tower with several different European structures with octagonal footprints, including several Cistercian lavatoriums.

Lavatoriums were unique and important structures to the Cistercians that contain freshwater fountains where monks washed their heads, hands, and feet, before and after meals.

The Knights Templar, brethren of the Cistercians, not surprisingly also incorporated the same architecture into over a dozen round medieval churches they built in England after their return from Jerusalem in 1119. These churches were modeled after the tower over Christ's tomb in the Church of the Holy Sepulcher. Only four remain, two of which exhibit the same octagonal footprint in the circular nave as seen in the Newport Tower (St. Sepulcher Church in Northampton, and the Holy Sepulcher Church in Cambridge).

The Knights Templar built over a dozen round medieval churches in the United Kingdom modeled after the tower over Christ's tomb in the Church of the Holy Sepulcher in Jerusalem. Of the four that remain, the St. Sepulcher Church in Northampton, and the Holy Sepulcher Church in Cambridge, England, have the same octagonal footprint of the columns with rounded arches enclosing the nave as the Newport Tower.

At each Cistercian abbey, the lower level of the lavatorium within the cloister had freshwater fountains where the "White monks" washed their hands, head and feet, before and after meals. This two-story octagonal structure at Maulbronn Abbey, in Germany, was built incorporating similar architecture as the Newport Tower. (Photo by Francisco Ruiz Valdés)

Though in ruins today, the lavatorium at Mellifont Abbey, in Ireland (left) exhibits similar architecture as the Newport Tower. (Wikimedia Commons) This two-story architecture was likely inspired by the two-story tower above the Christ's tomb, in the Church of the Holy Sepulcher, in Jerusalem (right). (Photograph courtesy of Richard Lynch)

182

The same two-story octagonal architecture is found in the Baptistry of the Templum Domini, now know as the Quabbat al Mi'ray, in the yard of the Church of the Holy Sepulchre in Jerusalem. In 2008, NEARA member and Freemason Rick Lynch traveled to Jerusalem and shared his photographs at the NEARA conference in November. Rick photographed a number of twelfth-century crusader-built octagonal baptistries reminiscent of the Newport Tower architecture.

Two eight-sided baptistries at Templum Domini in Jerusalem were constructed in the 1140s when Jerusalem was under the control of Templar crusaders. The structures were built by the Templars in the Holy City and display Romanesque archways reminiscent of the Newport Tower. (Photo courtesy of Richard Lynch)

Curiously, there is a twelfth-century Cistercian abbey (daughter abbey to Melrose Abbey in southern Scotland) on the uninhabited island of Eynhallow (Holy Island), in the Orkney Islands of northern Scotland. The Romanesque-style archway within the nave of the church was built using flat-stone construction virtually identical to the Newport Tower. The Cistercian connection is likely not a coincidence. According to documents provided by Niven Sinclair, Henry Sinclair of Rye (1127 to 1178) changed his name to Laurence upon entering the Cistercian order at the age of nineteen in 1146.

The circa 1150 A.D. flat-stone Romanesque-style archway leading into the nave at Eynhallow Church in Orkney, Scotland (left), is strikingly similar to the rounded archways constructed in the Newport, Tower (right). At the far end of the nave at Eynhallow, a triangle-shaped keystone, structurally and spiritually, ties the second archway together. (Mooney, 1924; Wolter, 2007)

If the first-floor ambulatory around Cambridge Round Church in Cambridge, England, were removed, the two-story tower with eight heavy pillars exhibits virtually the identical architecture of the Newport Tower in Rhode Island. (Wolter, 2008)

184

The Knights Templar built over a dozen round medieval churches in the United Kingdom modeled after the tower over Christ's tomb in the Church of the Holy Sepulcher in Jerusalem. Of the four that remain, the St. Sepulcher Church in Northampton, and the Holy Sepulcher Church in Cambridge, England have the same octagonal footprint of the columns with rounded arches enclosing the nave as the Newport Tower. (Wolter, 2008)

At the age of twenty-seven in 1156, ". . . he became abbot in charge of the remote Cistercian monastery of Eynhallow in Orkney with instructions to enforce the rigid Cistercian rules, but also to ensure the security of some physical artifact, a relic or document of immense religious significance."[1]

The remote 185-acre island of Eynhallow is guarded by dangerous shoals and reefs with treacherous tides and currents. It would have served as an excellent twelfth-century hiding place. This brought to mind the possible connection to another religious building in Scotland with underground tunnels and tombs thought to contain important religious relics or documents—Rosslyn Chapel. Both are connected to the Sinclair name, which means "Holy Shining Light" (Venus). Rosslyn was built by William Sinclair in 1446. The other notable fact is that both Eynhallow and Rosslyn Chapel are located on a similar longitude (3 degrees, 7 minutes west and 3 degrees, 9 minutes west respectively), suggesting a sacred geometrical connection to a large-scale grid system spanning, in this case, 290 years between the constructions of the two structures. The connections between these two religious sites that include the Sinclair family, remote hiding places, longitude, and mysterious legends seem to be much more than coincidence.

One glaring difference between the four surviving round Templar churches and the Newport Tower was the lack of a ground-floor ambulatory. With the exception of the exterior cap-stone ledges at the top of all eight columns in the Newport Tower, no other evidence has been found suggesting it ever had an ambulatory. That is, until November 7, 2008.

A capstone ledge, such as the one pictures here on the north column, is found at the top of all eight columns in the Newport Tower and likely served as structural support for a wooden ambulatory. The discovery of the remains of two wooden posts equidistant from the columns during an archaeological dig in the summer of 2008 provides convincing evidence consistent with medieval Templar construction. (Wolter, 2006)

At the fall NEARA conference held in Newport, Rhode Island, researcher Jan Barstad, president of Chronognostic Research Foundation, presented findings of a brief archaeological dig conducted the previous summer. The decades-old asphalt walkway around Newport Tower was replaced with concrete. Before the concrete was placed, "salvage archaeology" was conducted in two small areas that yielded surprising results.

To an audience of about one-hundred people, Jan summarized the key findings of the dig conducted by Steve Volukas and other volunteers. "What we have been able to find that William Godfrey (who conducted an archaeological dig inside the tower in 1948) never could have found, is two possible wooden posts at the right distance from the columns to form an arcade (ambulatory). We have no idea what the dates are except for one thing. Remember when I told you about that little foraminifera shell we found? It had a little bit of mortar on it. It dates to about 1450 A.D., plus or minus thirty years."

The shell with the mortar attached was an incredible find, and it raises the level of importance for a complete archaeological dig under the walkway. How ironic that for decades, critical evidence was directly underfoot of countless onlookers pondering the origin of the structure.

As compelling as the Cistercian and Templar architecture was, the example the author listed that struck me the most was the church altar inside the sixteen-sided fortification at the monastery at Tomar,

Arguably the finest example of architecture resembling the Newport Tower in Rhode Island is the church altar in the monastery at Tomar, Portugal. (Photo by Joaquim Alves Gaspar, posted on Wikipedia)

Portugal. The monastery castle at Tomar was the original seat of the Knights Templar in Portugal in 1159. The two-story altar, with an octagonal footprint of columns inside the church, is strikingly similar to the Newport Tower. According to Bernard Schütz, in his 2004 book, *Great Monasteries of Europe*, "The whole structure (altar) is an original reformation of the church of the Holy Sepulcher in Jerusalem." Schütz adds, "After the successful completion of the Reconquista, the Portuguese King Dinis I was eager to protect and expand the young Portuguese nation, and in 1318 he founded the Order of the Knights of Christ 'to defend the faith, to fight the Moors, and to expand the Portuguese monarchy.'"

I would later reflect on the incredible resemblance of the altar at Tomar to the Newport Tower. Its purpose as an important religious structure opened yet another avenue to explore with regard to the Newport Tower. William Mann had recently told me when considering the Templars, always think in multiple levels. I took those words to heart and they have served me well and would soon find they were certainly true when considering the multiple purposes of the Newport Tower.

The bulletin also included an interesting article by Professor Emeritus William Penhallow about astronomical alignments in the Newport Tower. This aspect was one of the "levels" I would soon learn more about from the open-minded scholar who had written the article.

David Brody and Elizabeth Lane joined us for the first of two lectures at the NEARA conference by the state archaeologists for Rhode Island and Massachusetts, Paul Robinson and Brona Simon. At the start of Paul's lecture he flashed a picture of the Newport Tower onto the screen. This structure has been the source of heated debate between archaeologists, who generally consider it a colonial structure, and other researchers, including many NEARA people, who think it's older. Paul stood silent for a good ten seconds, which gave me a chance to gauge the crowd's reaction that was predictably divided. Paul said, "I don't know what this is. It's in my state, but nobody can tell me when it was built."

Brona Simon gave her presentation after Paul about an archaeological dig in a heavily developed urban area. After her talk, I thought I'd introduce myself as a way to network. When I said my name she said, "I want you to know that I'm not into rune stones." That wasn't the first time my rune stone research led to a cool reception by an archaeologist.

Later, I met archaeologist Edward Lenik. I had placed a phone call to him a few months earlier after reading his report about the 1972 dig of the Spirit Pond sod houses. He said that both sod houses had been excavated. He relayed a story about Einar Haugen, a linguist who stud-

The missing piece of the map stone had fallen off and laid just a few feet away. After running my finger along a highly weathered man-made groove to the center of the surface that was part of the original map, I found a three-inch deep, triangular stone hole November 11, 2006. (Wolter, 2006)

ied the Spirit Pond inscriptions shortly after their discovery. Ed had met Haugen at a conference. The Spirit Pond Rune Stones came up, and Haugen offered an interesting comment. "You know, I'm not going to figure these things out (from the linguistics at that time), you guys are going to have to pull something out of the ground."

The following day Janet and I headed off to Westford with a researcher from Nova Scotia, Terry Deveau. We met at the J.V. Fletcher Library with Elizabeth Lane, David, and his wife, Kim, along two other NEARA members, Peter Anick and Dan Kelly and went to see the Tyngsboro Map Stone. Having already made arrangements with the property owner, we all marched up into the woods to the large granite boulder.

Aside from David, Elizabeth, and me, everyone else was seeing the Tyngsboro Map Stone for the first time. While David was explaining the layout of the map to our friends, I turned my attention to something that had bothered me the first time I saw the stone in September. A large, roughly triangular piece on the top side of the boulder appeared to be missing. It looked like the missing piece might contain more of the map, so I looked around to see if I could find it. Lying just a few feet away was what turned out to be the missing piece. The shape looked right, and, when I looked more closely, I saw what looked like lines of the map. The others began to notice what I was looking at. We all saw that the highly weathered surface had a long, straight groove that looked to be man-made. As I ran my finger along the groove that ended at the center of the surface, the area felt soft. I then began to scrape away dirt and organic material and realized there was a small depression. I asked if anyone had a pocketknife, and David tossed one to me. As I began removing the soft material, I suddenly realized I was digging out a three-inch deep stone hole!

I was stunned that it had happened again. First at Spirit Pond and now here in Tyngsboro was another stone hole associated with a man-made artifact. After cleaning the hole out, I felt the walls with my finger. It was roughly an inch in diameter and triangular in shape. Everyone was stunned and excited at the uncanny occurrence that seemed to be happening with ever more frequency.

Note

[1]Sinclair, Niven, *Beyond Any Shadow of Doubt*, 1998.

34

Jim Whittall

On April 26, 2007, Rick Lynch sent me a DVD with three video programs including one on the Newport Tower recorded in 1998. Rick said there was a video from his good friend, renowned NEARA researcher the late Jim Whittall. I had heard many stories about this man. Even though I never met him, I still felt as if I knew him. His final words on the video, spoken barely a month before he succumbed to cancer, eloquently summed up one of the important points of this book.

"Now I don't say we have the final answer, but we certainly have gotten a lot closer, and it's up to other scholars, other researchers, to dig in and pursue it further, to try to find out more data. And I mean research, go out and really do the work. But research today is kind of a real lazy word. It takes a lot of work, and a lot of time and dedication."

The Newport Tower in Touro Park in Newport, Rhode Island, was constructed in the style of Norman-Romanesque architecture, inspired by architecture of the Holy Sepulcher in Jerusalem brought back to Europe by returning Crusaders. In its own unique style, the tower was further influenced by a combination of the architecture of the temples of the Templars, the round churches of Scandinavia, and local architectural traditions from whence the builders came. Architectural features found within the construction of the tower would date it in the broad range of 1150 to 1400 A.D. However, some specific features limit it to a period in the late 1300s. In the course of six years of research I have found the best parallels in the tower architectural features to exist in the Northern Isles of Scotland which were under Norse control during the time frame mentioned. Other features relating the tower to Scandinavian round churches and Templar buildings have been published by Hjalmar R. Holand, Phillip A. Means, and F.J. Allen.

The following are Jim Whittall's twenty conclusions reached after his many years of research:

1. The architecture of the tower was preplanned. The concept was not conceived on site and built in haste.
2. The architecture is completely involved in sacred geometry.
3. The masons were completely familiar with the material on hand with which to construct the tower.
4. The tower was aligned to east and each pillar (8) was placed on a cardinal point in the manner of the Templars. It was not constructed using a magnetic compass. Today designed pillar designated as 1 is 3 degrees west of the North Pole star.
5. The tool marks created in the dressing out of the stone work can directly be related to tools before 1400. These marks are unique and unknown when compared to tool marks noted in colonial stonework.
6. After extensive comparison with ancient units of measurement, we have found that the unit of measurement for the construction of the tower is best suited to the Scottish Ell or the Norwegian short Alen. A photogrammetric survey made in 1991 showed that the unit of measurement for the tower was 23.35 cm, which supports the idea that the Scottish Ell or the Alen was used in constructing the tower. The English foot wasn't used. This doesn't necessarily mean the tower was built using this unit, but it could have been used.
7. The single and double splay windows have prototypes in Medieval Europe and the Northern Isles of Scotland in the 1300s in churches and the Bishop's Palace in Orkney.
8. The arch and lintel design noted in the tower is to be found in Orkney, Shetland, and Scandinavian round church architecture before 1400.
9. I have found in extensive research, that the triangle keystone feature of the arches in the tower only seemed to have been found in buildings in Orkney, Shetland, and Greenland (1 example), and to a very limited degree in other buildings in the Scottish Isles (3), and in Ireland (2).
10. Built-in niches in the tower have parallel examples in Medieval construction in Orkney and Shetland. Features basically unknown in New England architecture except in some post 1700 stone chambers.
11. The plinth, pillar, capital, arch architecture of the tower has no prototype in New England Colonial architecture, yet is found in Kirkwall Cathedral in Orkney.

12. The design of the fireplace with its double flues dates to the 1300s and was out of fashion after the 1400s. There are prototypes of this design in Scotland. Research has indicated the probability that the fireplace and its relationship to the west facing window was used as a lighthouse and probable signal station. The same can be said for the windows on the third level.

13. The walls were covered with a plaster stucco finish both interior and exterior. Stucco finishing started in the 1200s and is a feature known in Orkney and Shetland.

14. The probable layout and design of the floor joists with corbels has parallels in Medieval Scotland.

15. Probable first floor entry by ladder through the window/entry 3. A trait found in the Round Churches of Scotland.

16. Some architectural features in the tower have been organized to utilize astronomical alignments as a calendar event. Some of the alignments fall on Holy days of the Norse and Knights Templar. There are prototypes in Northern Europe.

17. Probability of an ambulatory around the tower (planned for but not necessarily built). Examples in Templar construction and round churches.

18. The tower is located at approximately the same latitude of Rome. This would make it an ideal reference point for exploration and mapping.

19. There is no archaeological parallel in Colonial England for the Newport Tower and its specific architectural features.

20. I suggest that the tower was built as a church, observatory, lighthouse, a datum zero point for future exploration in the New World.

There are other traits, features, concepts, which are still under serious study, but for the moment it seems that the prime candidate for the building of the Newport Tower is Jarl Henry Sinclair. It is more than feasible that it was constructed under his guidance in 1398.

Part VII

Venus Alignments and the Sacred Feminine

34

Astronomical Alignments

On February 12, 2007, my field tripping moved from Maine down the coast to a now familiar Touro Park where David Brody and I were to meet with Leo Titus, a structural engineer with Engineering Consulting Services, Ltd., Jim Egan, professor emeritus of Astronomy and Physics at the University of Rhode Island William "Bill" Penhallow, and then NEARA President Dan Lorraine.

We were all very interested to hear what Bill had to say about the astronomical alignments in the Newport Tower. Bill had written an article about his study that was published in the 2006 NEARA bulletin. I was looking forward to asking him questions. At one point, Bill said one of the alignments could best be viewed at a distance from the Newport Tower about fifteen feet above the ground. Sure enough, when I climbed a tree near the spot he pointed out, I could see the opening through the two windows. Bill offered a comment that came as a complete surprise. "You know, the alignments aren't as tight as they were in the past because the stars and other bodies move around," he said.

I looked at him, a little puzzled, and said, "When were the alignments best for the openings in the tower?"

He said, "Between 1200 and 1600 A.D."

At first I was surprised, but the more I thought about it, the less surprised I was. Bill's statement was very important and served as powerful new evidence of a pre-Colonial origin, and 1400 A.D. fit very nicely for a destination recorded on the Spirit Pond Map Stone of two days sail south from Popham Beach and with the reported voyage of Prince Henry Sinclair. Even if the alignments ultimately date to 1400, it doesn't prove that Prince Henry built the Tower, or that he was even there. However, somebody built it and the circumstantial evidence of Prince Henry's involvement keeps getting stronger.

There were a couple of additional aspects related to the Newport Tower that came to light in September of 2007. Dr. Mark Holley, an underwater archaeologist from Traverse City, Michigan, had worked on standing stone sites on the Island of Mull, in Western Scotland. Dr. Holley lamented how, after spending years performing excavations at these sites, there was nothing to find. The only thing his crew did find were, "White quartz chips scattered everywhere throughout the site." He then said, "The reason these sites are devoid of artifacts is because the people who built them considered these sites sacred, and kept them in pristine condition."

When our conversation turned to the Newport Tower and the likelihood that it served among other things as a religious altar to the builders, Mark smiled and said, "Well, if this is a religious site, in all like-lihood it'll be sterile archaeologically."

Dr. Holley also commented on the fireplace in the Tower after viewing several photographs I showed him. He said, "That's the same fireplace architecture I've seen in medieval castles in Scotland."

The archaeological dig performed on the grounds surrounding the Newport Tower by researchers Jan and Ron Barstad, in October of 2006, yielded nothing older than Colonial-aged artifacts. The Barstads performed another dig in October of 2007 and, once again, found nothing pre-Colonial. In light of Dr. Holley's comments and experience, failing to find artifacts or evidence of a pre-Colonial date may be consistent with a medieval origin after all!

Dr. Holley also said something else I found very prophetic regarding the puzzling attitude of most archaeologists in North America. He said, "Archaeologists in North America look at the Atlantic Ocean as this vast, impenetrable barrier. Archaeologists in Scotland look at the Atlantic as a superhighway."

Yet another interesting piece of information caught my attention during a lecture by researcher Jim Egan at the first symposium on the Newport Tower in Newport, Rhode Island, on October 27, 2007. Jim presented slides that demonstrated how each year on the morning on the winter solstice the rising sun cast its light through the east facing window (identified by researchers as W2) of the tower and projects a rectangular box of sunlight onto the inner west wall. As the sun continues to rise, moving slowly westward, the box of light moves downward in a northeasterly direction. Eventually, the box of sunlight hits a cream colored, egg-shaped keystone in the west-northwest archway. The keystone glows brilliantly as the box of morning sunlight illuminates this apparently important symbolic feature to the original builders.

My mind raced with possible explanations. It was well established that many ancient stone chambers in Europe and North America were carefully constructed to intentionally allow the light of the sun, moon, and Venus to pass through an opening into the chamber and project onto a wall or altar, often constructed of high-white quartz. When light hit the white quartz, typically during annual solstice or equinox events, the chamber was illuminated as part of a sacred religious rite. If the builders of the Newport Tower were the Cistercians and Templars, astronomical alignments would be very important and indeed expected.

After the symposium, one of the issues discussed was if the wooden floor in the tower would have prevented the light from hitting the keystone. The conversation then evolved to how the builders would have accessed the first floor that was probably about ten to twelve feet above the ground. Most of us agreed that access was likely by ladder through an opening in the floor. The obvious problem with the floor was it would have prevented sunlight from hitting the keystone. We then discussed if the illuminating keystone was as sacred as we thought, the access opening in the floor was likely constructed to allow a clear path for the sunlight to hit the keystone at the time of the winter solstice. We all agreed that, if the builders wanted the winter solstice sunlight to hit the keystone, they would have found a way to do it.

35

Venus Alignments

During Janet's and my education through reading as many books as we could about subjects related to the Cistercians and their ideology, we came upon a title that proved invaluable. *The Book of Hiram*, a 2005 publication by Freemasons Christopher Knight and Robert Lomas, traces the origin of Masonic rituals to prehistoric astronomy that wound its way through the development of Christianity. The authors present a convincing case with supporting evidence taken from religious sites across the globe going back to the Grooved Ware People who lived around the Irish Sea (5500 B.C.). Perhaps the most enlightening information from the book was the importance these people placed on the planet Venus and its movements through the sky when viewed from Earth.

There are several cycles associated with Venus that ancient cultures were well aware of and incorporated into their belief systems and architecture. The first is the eight-year cycle where Venus appears in the western sky for four years as an evening star, and four years as a morning star in the eastern sky. The pattern Venus traces in the sky in both cases is in the shape of a horn. The horns mirror each other over that eight-year cycle and are called, "The Horns of Venus" and are found in many cultures including the symbolism within the artwork and hieroglyphs of the Egyptians. There are some who claim that this pagan symbolism triggered a response by the Catholic Church, which tried to demonize the symbol by putting horns on the devil.

When viewed from earth, Venus completes the pattern of a five-pointed star every eight years. The Venus "pentagram" is the likely origin of the symbol so important in mystic religions and Freemasonry. After completing five eight-year cycles, or a period of forty years, Venus then returns to its original position in the sky. Ancient astronomers knew that the planet Venus was the most accurate indicator of the time of year in the

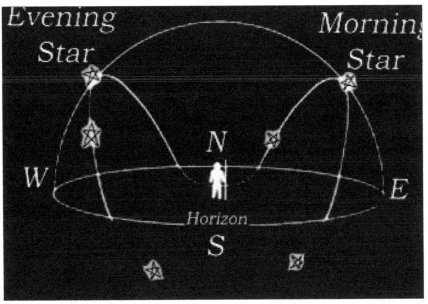

The planet Venus spends six months every year rising in the eastern sky as a morning star and six months rising in the west as an evening star. The pattern traced in the sky by Venus makes a symmetric pair of horns that many ancient cultures documented and revered. The Egyptians venerated the horns of Venus which are commonly depicted with the sun disk cradled within the horns (in this image on the head of Isis) in the allegorical union of heaven and earth. (Cowie, 2006, page 88; Internet)

199

solar system. Every eight years it marked a point when the solar calendar, the lunar calendar, and the sidereal calendar coincided to within a few minutes. Knight and Lomas wrote, "After exactly forty years, when Venus completes five of its eight-year cycles, it synchronizes to within fractions of a second, providing a calendar and clock that was used to set the time of day until the 1950s when even more accurate atomic clocks were invented." The precision of these cycles was profound on ancient cultures and in part explains why the planet Venus was such a sacred heavenly body.

The early observers of the rising of Venus are believed to have associated the planet with love, sex, reproduction, and restored life at the time of the spring equinox. The annual restoration of life in the spring, after being dormant in winter, is believed by many researchers to be the genesis of the Christian belief in the resurrection. The capturing of Venus alignments at important points within its cycles are evidenced in sacred human structures across time. These include the early stone chambers and standing stone sites, alignments incorporated into Solomon's Temple, and the great Gothic cathedrals across Europe and Scandinavia.

I am unaware of any researchers who have investigated Venus alignments in the Newport Tower. In May of 2007, I specifically asked Professor Penhallow if all the niches and openings in the Tower were accounted for with the lunar and solar alignments he had documented in his research. Bill said, "No."

I asked if he had considered Venus alignments. He said he wasn't even aware of them. Most people are unaware of the importance of the brightest star in the sky to many cultures tracing back thousands of years.

The pentagram has long been a symbol of the devil to the Catholic Church, yet the five-pointed star has also been a symbol worshiped for thousands of years. The five-pointed star can easily be seen at the top of the window in the north transept of Amiens Cathedral in France, and makes one wonder why the builders put this symbol in such a prominent place. (Photo courtesy of James E. Mitchell)

Eventually my curiosity about possible Venus alignments in the Tower had piqued to the point where I felt something needed to happen. The Newport Tower symposium had been largely responsible. Bill Penhallow had given an inspired presentation about his alignment work and told me privately that he was still very interested in Venus alignments, but had not spent any time researching them yet. Upon returning home from the symposium, I immediately pulled up the couple hundred photographs of the tower I'd taken over the last year and a half.

Clearly visible in several photos was a small rectangular window near the top of the tower located directly over column P-4 facing southeast. At its highest point at sunrise during the horn-shaped path it traces across the sky, Venus reaches an altitude above the horizon of about twenty-two degrees. By following this angle through the small window identified as W-6, in a northwesterly direction, the line hits a niche labeled N-4 on the west inside wall.

On the west side of the tower is another small window about the same size as W-6 and labeled W-7. If the builders constructed the opening

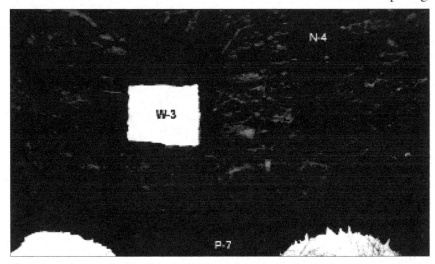

On the west inner wall of the Newport Tower, niche N-4 sits directly above the egg-shaped keystone (Orphic Egg of Freemasonry?) in the archway between columns P-7 and P-8. If a line is drawn from N-4 to the southeast, angling up at twenty-two degrees, it passes through window W-6 and into space in the general direction of the planet Venus. (Wolter, 2006)

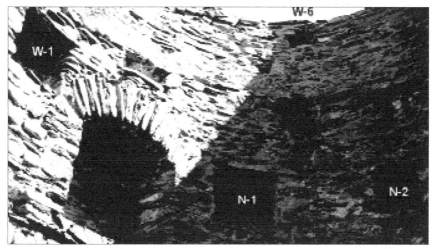

On the southeast inner wall of the Tower, niches N-1 and N-2 sit above the archways between columns P-3 and P-4, and P-4 and P-5. (Wolter, 2006)

The left arrow marks the line from the inner wall niche N-4 to window W-6, which points toward the planet Venus when it is a morning star in the southeastern sky. The right arrow marks the line from the inner wall niche N-1 to window W-7, which points toward Venus in the west-northwestern sky. The angle of both lines from horizontal is about twenty-two degrees. (Wolter, 2007)

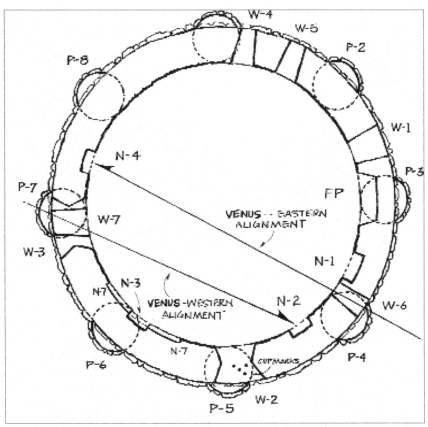

This diagram shows a birds-eye view of the path the light of Venus travels through the window (W-6) in the upper southeast wall to the niche (N-4) on the inside of the west wall. As an evening star, the light of Venus travels through the window (W-7) in the upper west wall to the niche (N-2) on the inside of the southwest wall. (Re-drawn by Dan Wiemer from Penhallow, 2006)

to capture the light of Venus as an evening star during the summer months, then there should also be a corresponding niche on the inside wall on the east side. Sure enough, there are two niches (N-1 and N-2) that could catch a line angling down at roughly twenty-two degrees through W-7.

Upon realizing there did indeed appeared to be Venus alignments in the Newport Tower, I called Bill Penhallow on December 12, 2007. He had a detailed scale model of Newport Town and a rod he used to illustrate the solar and lunar alignments during his lectures. I gave him the window, niche, and altitude data. After a few moments he said, "Very interesting. I hadn't considered that before." He paused a few more seconds, and then said, "I'll have to do some calculations."

I was pleased the Venus alignments I'd found were at least plausible to the one person who knew more about the subject than anyone else. With less than two weeks before the winter solstice (which fell on December 22nd in 2007), I called David Brody and asked if he wanted to spend a few days in Newport, Rhode Island, conducting some field research. He enthusiastically accepted. His novel, *Cabal of the Westford Knight: The Templars at the Newport Tower*, a mystery thriller, paralleled the research both he and I had been pursuing the previous two years. We discussed the possibility of Venus alignments in the Newport Tower and came to the conclusion that not only could they be there, but they *should* be there. As usual, there was only one way to find out.

Besides investigating the Venus alignments, I had another reason to travel to Newport. Jim Egan's slide of the illuminated keystone had intrigued me. Jim never offered an explanation why the builders incorporated the illumination at the winter solstice, but like everything else the Cistercians/Templars did, they had reasons. I had my own theory as to why and wanted to see the event for myself before voicing it.

With the likelihood of poor weather, we planned to stay for three days to increase the odds of a clear morning. I flew into Providence, Rhode Island, on December 19th. On the first morning (December 20th) we were up at 3:30 A.M. to go to Touro Park. David had parked his vehicle next to the Tower the previous evening, and we unloaded a sixteen-foot extension ladder and waited for a park employee to open the gate surrounding the stone structure. Shortly after 4:00 A.M., Charlie Ridolf arrived.

The forecast had predicted overcast skies, so we focused on things we could do regardless of weather. Once inside, we extending the ladder so I could climb up to inspect niche N-4. I turned my head to the southeast and looked up at window W-6 to see if there was even an opening for the light of Venus to come through. Sure enough, there was a small horizontal rectangle that could easily allow the light of Venus to shine through if the sky was clear.

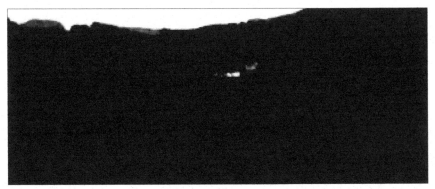

On December 20, 2007, David Brody and I investigated possible Venus alignments in the Newport Tower. After climbing a ladder to niche N-4, we saw a small rectangular opening in window W-6 confirming that an alignment with Venus was possible. Further research is necessary to confirm the alignment's existence. (Wolter, 2007)

The news was not as good for the alignment through W-7. After climbing up to check for an opening to allow for the light of Venus as an evening star, neither of us could see one. David then reminded me he had read where the top of the tower had been repaired in the past possibly, altering the shape of the window. Former Rhode Island Governor William C. Gibbs reportedly told historian Benson John Lossing, who was visiting Newport in 1848, ". . . roughly between 1775 and 1780, the British [occupying Newport] used the tower for an ammunition magazine. When they had to evacuate Newport, they tried to destroy the old building by igniting a keg of powder in it. The masonry did not collapse, however, and the only result was the loss of the roof and two or three feet of the upper stonework of the wall."[1] It is unclear if two or three feet were lost above the present height of the tower, or if the present top two to three feet was lost and then repaired. Without knowing where the repairs had been made we could only speculate.

The sky that morning didn't give us a glimpse of any stars, let alone Venus. We still examined all the windows, niches, and other interesting features we previously had been unable to reach. Charlie even chased down a twenty-four-foot ladder, which allowed us to reach the top of the twenty-six-foot structure. We were also able to get a close look at the cupules on the sill of window W-2 and the so-called runic inscription carved into a stone on the exterior of the tower.

There are four holes on the sill in the south window that formed an interesting pattern. The largest hole was roughly two inches across by an inch deep. Some speculated that a rod called a "plinth" could be inserted into this hole and used as a sundial for telling the time of day. The other three holes, roughly an inch across and about a half inch deep, were aligned in a northwest-southeast orientation. Some believed the marks were made as part of a method to document lunar eclipses and to calculate longitude. Documenting latitude was relatively easy at the beginning of the fifteenth century, but longitude was another matter. Determining longitude was an important aspect of navigation. For any group to be able to reach North America from Europe, it would be unwise to say they didn't understand how to figure it out. These shallow holes could be the evidence proving that the builders did know how to calculate longitude.

The other interesting features are man-made marks on a stone found on the exterior surface of the Newport Tower about twelve feet off

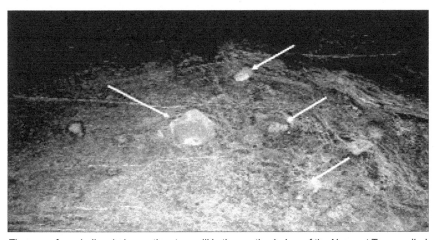

There are four shallow holes on the stone sill in the south window of the Newport Tower called cupules. The deepest hole (on the left), is thought to have had a rod inserted vertically to be used as a sundial. The three smaller holes (on the right), are believed to mark aspects of lunar eclipses for calculating longitude. (Wolter, 2007)

Many believe the marks inscribed on an exterior stone of the Newport Tower are a runic inscription carved during the "Viking" period. The marks do not look like runes to me and could be a mason's mark or simply modern scratches. (Wolter, 2007)

the ground. Many believe it is a Viking age runic inscription that dates the tower to around 1100 A.D. Although admittedly not a runic expert, I have personally examined and studied hundreds of runic inscriptions, and those marks didn't look like runes to me. The lines were definitely man-made in my opinion, and likely either mason's marks or more recent scratches made during the multiple tuck-pointing repairs conducted over the years.

The clouds continued to frustrate us the next two nights. We never saw Venus. After waiting three hours on Saturday morning (December 22nd), David and I walked back to our hotel. I decided to set my alarm for 8:00 A.M. for one last try. The 2007 winter solstice occurred at roughly 1:00 A.M., making Saturday morning when the sun would rise in the southern-most point in the eastern sky.

When my alarm went off, I quickly sat up, looked out the window and for the first time in three days I saw sunlight. Never was I more pleased to see that bight yellow orb we normally take for granted. I quickly headed off for the Tower. As I entered the gate and walked inside, I saw the vertical rectangular shaped box of sunlight partially filling the west window (W-3). Over the next forty-five minutes, the rising sun's rays passed though the southern window, and the glowing box of sunlight marched slowly downward toward the egg-shaped keystone. There was plenty of anxiety as the box of light faded in and out with each passing cloud. I feared a huge bank of clouds would block out the sun at the most inopportune moment. Finally, I caught some luck. At 9:00 A.M. the clouds cleared, and the sunlight burst through the south window, creating a glowing box of light to illuminate the egg-shaped keystone.

It was an incredible sight to witness what was clearly an intentionally designed feature incorporated into the Newport Tower by the original builders. My interpretation of this event is that the egg-shaped keystone on the inside was constructed to represent the "Orphic" egg inside the womb. When the sunlight, considered a male deity, struck the egg on the winter solstice, it was allegorically inseminated. The symbolically fertilized embryo inside the womb then underwent gestation until it hatched with the "birth" of the new ideology (Goddess worship), along with new life (spring), in the New Jerusalem (North America).

The keystone illumination was the highlight of the trip, but confirming the existence of the opening in window W-6 was also very encouraging. I am confident that future research into Venus alignments by qualified researchers will provide a better understanding and perhaps independent confirmation of their existence. If validated, my guess is that not only will they be present, but Venus will likely provide the primary alignments incorporated into the structure's architecture.

The winter solstice of 2008 provided another opportunity to witness the keystone illumination and record it for the Hooked X documentary film that History Channel bought and titled, *Holy Grail in America*. As fate would have it, a huge winter storm moved in on December 19th and for the next four days blanketed Newport with both clouds and nearly a foot of snow. The bad weather killed visibility. On Tuesday morning of the 23rd, the sun finally rose to clear skies and cinematographer Bo Hakala was ready with his camera to record the solar events.

Bo was joined that morning by researcher Vance Tiede, who had recently become interested in the Venus alignments and keystone illumination at the Newport Tower. Earlier in the summer, Vance had given us a tour of the Gungywamp site with numerous stone chambers and walls near Groton, Connecticut, that he believes could be an early Irish Christian site.

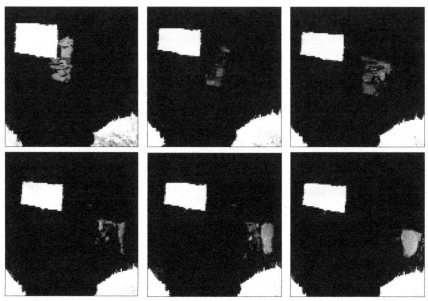

Beginning at 8:15 a.m. on December 22, 2007, a rectangle of sunlight passing through window W-2, moved progressively with the rising sun, downward and north along the west-northwest inner wall of the Newport Tower. At roughly 9:00 A.M. I was able to photograph the path, beginning in the upper left photo moving right and down, the rising sun's rays illuminating the egg-shaped keystone on the west-northwest archway. (Wolter, 2007)

"What time did the illumination happen last year?" Vance asked.

"Just about 9:00 A.M.," I said.

Vance quickly responded, "That's an important time of religious prayer. That was when Christ was nailed to the Cross."

His words sent my mind racing. I had never heard this before and was even more surprised when he explained how the hours of 6:00 A.M. (Ortus or sunrise), 9:00 A.M. (Trece or three hours after sunrise), 12:00 P.M. (Sextus or six hours after sunrise), 3:00 P.M. (Nones or nine hours after sunrise), and 6:00 P.M. (Vespers or sunset), were important medieval solar monastic hours of prayer.

Vance continued, "Christ expired at 3:00 P.M., and I wouldn't be surprised if something happens with your light box at the time. I'll stick around and let you know what it is."

209

On December 23, 2008, after illumination of the egg-shaped keystone at 9:00 A.M. in the archway between columns 7 and 8, the light-box created by sunlight passing through the west window of the Newport Tower illuminated the smaller keystone in the archway of columns 1 and 2 at 3:00 P.M. Both illumination events occur on the winter solstice at important monastic prayer times. (Wolter, 2008)

I spoke to him later that day. "Well, what happened?" I said.

Vance said, "The light box created by the west window, illuminated another keystone at the top of the archway between columns 1 and 2, right at 3:00 P.M." He then said, "It appears the Newport Tower is in synch with the daily monastic prayer cycle for the Rule of Benedict" (circa 530 to 543 and is contemporaneous with the time of St. Brendan.)

I pondered the significance of Vance's discovery in light of my own discovery and Jim Egan's photograph of the keystone. In a little over a year, the sharing of research appeared to have uncovered another important line of evidence incorporated into the Newport Tower by the builders. These important religious and Masonic aspects were consistent with a medieval Templar/Cistercian origin. This new evidence certainly needed careful review and independent validation. However, in my mind, there was no longer any doubt that the Knights Templar were heavily involved in building the Newport Tower in about the year 1400 A.D.

Note

[1]Means, 1942, p. 23.

36

The New Jerusalem

The question that had plagued me from the moment I realized the Kensington Rune Stone was genuine, was why was it placed here in Minnesota? I've researched the Spirit Pond and Narragansett Rune stones, which are undeniably linked to each other and the Kensington Rune Stone by the Hooked X. The evidence suggests that all five North American rune stones were carved by Cistercian monks who embraced an ideology of a dual god with the "X" representing both male and female, and heaven and earth. The hook appears to represent the continuation both as a tangible bloodline and a religious ideology that can be traced back to the megalithic people from over 5000 years B.C.

What appears to be unfolding is a historical religious conflict of ideology that continues to the present day. These people worshiped the heavenly bodies with an emphasis on the brightest planet in the sky: Venus. They tracked its movements and meticulously documented its cycles over days, months, years, and even centuries. Over the millennia, the divine worship of Venus evolved into important symbolism represented by a female deity or goddess.

The reverence of the female and the matriarchal line, or worship of the "Sacred Feminine," was certainly embraced by the Egyptians and later by the medieval Cistercian monks, Knights Templar, and the Teutonic Knights. There is evidence consistent with this reverence of the sacred feminine on the Kensington Rune Stone. The Cistercians built and worshiped in churches and cathedrals whose naves were designed with a 2:1 ratio to symbolize the woman's womb.[1] They believed the congregation praying within the nave of the church was analogous to

211

being nurtured in the womb of God, like a fetus inside its mother. They also believed building with stone was a sacred spiritual act of utmost importance. Based on this, I don't believe the carver accidentally made the final dimensions of the Kensington Rune Stone into a 2:1 ratio.

I also don't believe it any accident that church, cathedral, and abbey doorways were designed after the female genitalia. To the Cistercians, this representation of the entrance into the womb was symbolic of the source of life. To me, and no doubt to the Cistercians, this architecture is a beautiful representation of a faith that reflects how the real world works. I often laugh at the irony of how the male medieval mind was no different than today. The difference is that medieval monks didn't have the distractions of the modern world and found an elegant and beautiful way to embrace the "sacred feminine" through architecture.

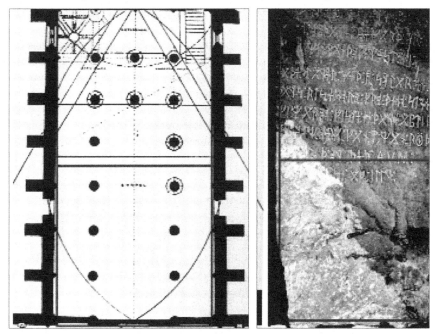

The nave of Rosslyn Chapel in Scotland, as well as the nave of medieval Cistercian monasteries and cathedrals in Europe and Scandinavia have dimension in a 2:1 ratio. The Kensington Rune Stone was intentionally broken to the same approximate 2:1 ratio before the inscription was carved and appears to represent the symbolism of the female womb. (Wolter, 2000)

The doorways into the medieval Cistercian monasteries, churches and cathedrals were designed after the female genitalia representing the entrance into the womb of God where life originates. The doorway on the left is at Lye Church on Gotland. This same feminine architecture is beautifully represented by exquisite, three-dimensional carvings throughout the Lady Chapel at Ely Cathedral in England. (Wolter, 2005; Wolter, 2008)

The feminine architecture on the exterior of many churches and cathedrals goes beyond just the doorways. The west facing facade of many churches exhibits incredible architecture that is distinctly female. Ernest L. Martin, Ph.D., wrote the following in his 1998 paper, "The Anatomy of a Church – Part 2,": "If a woman lies on her back in such a posture as Vitruvius mentioned, and then lifts her knees to be perpendicular to her body, her legs will obviously be elevated above her body as two projections. The genitalia will be given full view. Transferring this posture to an architectural application in regard to building a sacred temple, as Vitruvius would use it, the temple of the illustration would reveal two elevated towers with an entrance to a temple between the towers at their base. . . . Such a scene is not unlike prime Gothic cathedrals having two spires on each side of an entrance leading into the sacred precincts."

Perhaps this architecture was an allegorical representation for the birth of a new ideology "far to the west" in North America.

213

The architectural symbolism of these majestic and beautiful structures goes beyond the feminine aspects. If the Hooked X is a symbol of the union and duality of male and female with the hook representing a child or the offspring, it is logical to assume this symbolism is represented elsewhere. The Hooked X might indeed represent evidence in the belief that Jesus and Mary Magdalene were married and had a daughter named Sarah.

It is entirely possible that the churches themselves represent the same allegorical union and duality. When the rays of the sun, which in most cultural mythology is symbolic of the male, passes through the ornate rose window of a church, which is symbolic of Mary Magdalene, the sacred feminine or the Goddess, the light penetrates into the womb represented by the nave, completing this sacred union. The very essence of these structures appears to be an allegorical representation of the builders' true faith.

Knight and Lomas refer to this same symbolism in relation to the Grooved Ware People and their stone chambers such as Newgrange in Ireland, from around 3500 B.C.E. In *The Book of Hiram* they wrote, "Could the shaft of light [of Venus on the winter solstice] entering the uppermost part of the double entrance have been viewed as god's phallus penetrating this spectacular pudenda of the Earth, the life-bringing seed of heaven spilling down into this womb-chamber and all within it?"

The west-facing façade of many cathedrals built by the Cistercian and Templar stone masons incorporated feminine architecture representing a woman lying on her back with knees aligned vertically exposing her genitals as in the birthing position. This architecture could be an allegory for the birth of the "goddess" ideology in North America. (Reims, Notre Dame and Washington National cathedrals, Photo by bodoklecksel, posted on Wikipedia; Photo by Sanchezn, posted on Wikipedia; Wolter, 2007)

Some might suggest the symbolism within sacred Christian religious houses of worship couldn't possibly be so sexually suggestive. As if to drive the point of the male/female union to the extreme, medieval stonemasons also produced graphic depictions to the inside and outside of many of the incredible cathedrals, churches, abbeys, and castles they constructed. Sheela-na-gigs are graphic, often grotesque, publicly displayed erotic female stone sculptures.[2] Many of the carvings were "cleaned up" or destroyed in the 1800s, yet hundreds still survive in France, Spain, Britain and Ireland.

These carvings typically depict naked females (male figures are common as well) with enlarged genitals graphically exposed. Some scholars suggest the grotesque carvings were prominently displayed to discourage the monks from their natural sexual urgings. I don't agree with this opinion and, although I don't fully understand the motive for the financers to pay for the stonemasons to create such graphic and public carvings, they likely were intended to serve more than one purpose. Anthony Weir and James Jerman suggest the carvings could also represent the ancient pre-Christian "fertility" religion still followed by many in these regions during medieval times. The idea that the carvings were created as fertility symbols makes sense given the likelihood of how many people at that time likely embraced this ancient ideology.

The carvings that caught my attention the most were those depicting copulating couples with their legs intertwined into the shape of an "X." Authors Weir and Jerman describe these carvings

Another example of the "anatomy" of a medieval Gothic church was the large rose window, representing the goddess, that allows the light from the sun, the male deity in the heavens, to penetrate into the nave (womb) in a symbolic union of male and female. (Washington National Cathedral, Wolter, 2007)

215

as being in the "X-position." Perhaps the Hooked X represents not only an allegorical union, but the actual union of male and female as well.

As I've thought about the symbolism of these amazing structures and the ideology of the people who built them, I began to understand the conflict that eventually led these people to seek refuge on a different continent. There is no doubt in my mind that the Church in Rome had no tolerance for this matriarchal version of Christianity and its successful proliferation by the Cistercians across Europe and Scandinavia by the beginning of the fourteenth century. Starting with the first abbey at Cîteaux in France, founded by Saint Robert of Molesme, in 1098,[3] the number of Cistercian abbeys would swell to 750 throughout Europe, Scandinavia and into the Mediterranean region by the early 1300s.[4] One could argue that the attack by the Church was carefully crafted and started with the strategic elimination of the most serious and logical threat: the Knights Templar. Historians argue their demise was primarily about money, which no doubt played a significant role. However, there was much more at stake and once the military threat was removed in 1307, it was no coincidence the Cistercians and the ideology they embraced also began to decline.

Sexually explicit stone carvings are found on medieval churches, abbeys and castles throughout France, Spain, Britain and Ireland. "Sheela-na-gigs" are graphic and obscene female figures such as this detailed depiction of a female exposing her genitals with her hands (in a birthing position?) at Sainte-Radegonde, Poitiers Church in France (left). At Fuentiduena Church, in Ireland, a copulating couple with genitals fully exposed is found carved into an exterior corbel (right). (Photos used with permission from Anthony Weir)

216

The timing of the events leading up to 1362 was perfect for what history tells us and for what it doesn't. If many of the fugitive Templars and their fleet escaped to Scotland, as many historians believe, it would have been a logical move that fit nicely with the history that followed. King Robert the Bruce defeated the English at the Battle of Bannockburn in 1314 and became the greatest hero in the history of Scotland. Both he and the Templars were common enemies of the English and their French ally. Bruce's death mask carved in stone within Rosslyn Chapel provides evidence that he too was likely a Templar who welcomed his fugitive brothers to fortify his army.

The timing of the Inquisition coincides with these events and adds another intriguing motive for the Church that went looking for heretics with an emphasis on those who skillfully carried a sword motivated by a different version of Christianity. I believe the evidence suggests that the Church knew all about the secret bloodline of Jesus Christ and sought to eliminate the threat to their power and the patriarchal ideology the pope and his disciples were preaching. Their ideology of a male deity in the heavens was diametrically opposed to the reverence of the sacred feminine many called "Mother Earth." The hostile environ-

The legs of an intertwined couple form an "X" inspiring the term "X-position" for copulating couples often found carved on the exterior corbels of medieval European churches such as this one at LaBrede Church in Ireland. Notice the Templar style cross carved into the wall to the left of the corbel. (Photo used with permission from Anthony Weir)

217

On the lintel over a round arched exterior doorway at Whittlesford Church, Cambridgeshire, England, is a carving of male and female figures with genitals exposed in a scene suggesting copulation is about to commence. (Photos used with permission from Anthony Weir)

ment and hurricane of negative historic events provided the perfect motivation to implement a plan for escape. The middle of the fourteenth century was the perfect time to make their exodus to a place the Cistercians and Templars called the "New Jerusalem."

The tipping point that fits perfectly with the unfolding events of the 1300s was the plague that ravaged Europe and Scandinavia beginning in 1348. This scourge of the medieval world likely played a major role in the ambitious undertaking of bringing their heretical ideology in the eyes of the Church to the New World. In some areas of Europe and Scandinavia, up to two thirds of the population died, putting a huge financial strain on the already depleted coffers of the kings, nobles, and the Church. The parties who made the incursions into Minnesota in 1362 and the East Coast around 1400 A.D. had to have been well-financed. Mounting an expedition across the Atlantic in multiple ships with a crew of up to thirty men took money. The Cistercians still had money accumulated from many decades of simply outworking everyone else and selling the products of their labor. It could be argued that the monastic plans of economic and spiritual self-sufficiency through hard work and rapid expansion put into action by early Cistercian leaders like Bernard of Clairvaux in the early 1100s, paid important unforeseen dividends two centuries later.

There are a number of reasons why it makes sense that the mission of the Kensington party was to claim land near the center of the continent. If I've learned anything through this experience it's that these people never had just one goal in mind. There were always multiple motives with the religious angle playing an important, if not the dominant role. The area around Kensington, Minnesota, is a rich trove of natural resources that would have been very attractive economically to these industrious people. Beaver was a prized fur at that time and arguably the best pelts in the world, then and now, are found in that part of North America. Another reason for claiming this land may have been strategic. The headwaters to three major watersheds, the Red River Valley/Hudson Bay, the Great Lakes/St. Lawrence Seaway and the Missouri/Mississippi River to the Gulf of Mexico were the highways of that time. To control the headwaters to these important waterways would have been an important strategic advantage. The Cistercians were renowned for planning far into the future. They no doubt had grand long-range plans in North America.

There is another important point to consider when thinking about any party traversing a continent with indigenous people of varied religious beliefs. What virtually all Native people of North America share is a deep respect for the "Great provider all things." They respected the land, the water, the animals, the sun, the moon, the stars, and especially Venus. The Cistercians/Templars and Natives would likely have gotten along very well, considering they shared essentially the same ideology. They inherently respected both the sacred feminine of Mother Earth and the male deities of the heavens, including the stars, the moon, and the sun. One thing is certain in my opinion, the Kensington Rune Stone party didn't fight their way to Kensington; they traveled with the Natives.

I've already discussed the "business" part of the Kensington Rune Stone inscription and its function as a land claim document. However, the inscription also includes something else. The "Grail" prayer likely serves as a memorial to the ten dead men. One thing that has bothered me for a long time is why people assume that the ten dead men were "scalped by

Indians." The inscription doesn't say that. For that matter, the men who were killed may not have been from the Kensington party. That party may have come across the aftermath of a battle between two warring Native tribes. Another possibility is, because the plague was a world-wide phenomenon the "ten men red with blood and death" could have been suffering from plague symptoms.[5] Regardless, a Cistercian monk would certainly have carved a prayer for his Native brothers as well as his own people whatever they died from. The point is to be very careful about interpreting the inscription literally. When an argument is built upon a shaky foundation, the subsequent argument is vulnerable to collapse. This has happened numerous times in the history of this artifact.

Along with all the practical reasons, perhaps the most important reason for claiming land in the center of the continent was a religious one. This is also the most difficult reason to figure out. However, there appears to be a clue that can be gleaned from the writings of a relatively obscure figure in early American history. Samuel Sewall was one of the judges who presided over the Salem witch trials of 1692 that sent nineteen innocent people to their deaths at the gallows (one man was sandwiched between wooden boards with large stones piled on until his body was crushed). In 1721, Sewall wrote for the humane treatment of Indians, which was not a popular viewpoint in the early days of East Coast settlement. With an apparent attitude consistent with Cistercian/Templar ideology, Sewall wrote the following in 1697, "New England might be the seat of the New Jerusalem."[6]

It is unknown if Sewall became a Freemason or what else may have triggered his prophetic statement.

Notes

[1]Martin, 1998, p. 2.
[2]Weir and Jerman, 1986, p. 11.
[3]Kindler, 2002, p. 32.
[4]Könemann, 2006, p. 96.
[5]Reiersgord, 2001, p. 8.
[6]Yazawa, 1998, p. 161.

37

Keystones Alignment to Kensington

We returned to the Newport Tower on April 4, 2007. On a previous trip, something had caught my eye in one of the eight archways. Sitting near the middle of the west/northwest exterior archway was a keystone with a distinctly different shape than all the others. The tan-colored granite glacial boulder had been intentionally made into the symbolic shape of Freemasonry's Mark Master Mason's keystone. It is a tradition within stone mason guilds going back to at least medieval times, when the final archway in an important structure is completed a ceremonial final keystone is cut. The keystone is cut into the symbolic shape by the master mason, who usually inscribes his personal mason's mark on the keystone. Apparently no one had noticed this symbolically shaped keystone or the orb-shaped red granite boulder capstone directly above it.

One possible reason for this oversight is found in the best reference for Newport Tower scholars: Phillip Ainsworth Mean's 1942 book entitled, *Newport Tower*. His otherwise very thorough and well-reasoned analysis missed the mark when he said, "Moreover, the height of the arches vary somewhat, and they all lack a true keystone."

On this trip, I made a point to look at all the archways on both the interior and exterior of the Newport Tower. There were no other keystones with that same diagnostic Masonic shape. However, there was another tan-colored keystone that stood out for a different reason on the inside of the structure. The builders had placed a large egg-shaped, granite keystone in the same west facing archway, the same keystone illuminated from the sun's rays on the winter solstice. In fact, the two keystones were constructed back to back slightly south of the center of the archway.

221

The keystone on the outer side of the west-facing arch of the Newport Tower (left) was intentionally cut into the shape symbolic to both medieval stone masons and modern Freemasons. Directly above is a red-colored granite boulder that likely was considered an orb by the builders. The same symbolically shaped keystone of Freemasonry is the symbol for the State of Pennsylvania (right) where the Declaration of Independence was signed. (Left: Wolter, 2007; Right: Millar, 2005, page 218)

After examining the archways and the exterior keystone, I found myself wondering what was going on with it, what it was pointing to. After considering the significance of the curious placement, I turned and looked off to the west at roughly the same angle the keystone was facing. Suddenly, it hit me. All at once it seemed ridiculous, incredible, and obvious. The keystone was pointing in the direction of Kensington, Minnesota.

Later, I pulled out an atlas, drew a line from Newport, Rhode Island, to Kensington, and then did some rough calculations. I had long ago stopped being surprised and almost expected the results. Both the angle of the line to Kensington on the atlas and the angle of the line extending north of due west through the keystones in the Newport Tower were seventeen degrees.

With the idea of the coinciding angles between Kensington and Newport, I thought about the possibilities if this incredible connection was intentional. Depending on when it was built, the keystones were apparently

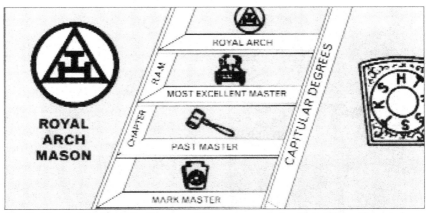

The first level of the Capitular Degrees of Freemasonry is the Mark Master Mason whose symbol is the stone mason's keystone. The fact that a similar-shaped granite keystone is in one of the arches suggests important intentional Masonic symbolism used by the builders of the Newport Tower. (Harwood, 2006, page 69)

placed indicating something about to happen, or acknowledging what had already occurred. If the Kensington Rune Stone was placed after the construction of the Newport Tower, then the keystones and the granite orb represented the likely starting point where the Kensington Rune Stone party began their trek. Using their astronomical skills which obviously included Venus, and technology such as the magnetic compass and the astrolabe, they could have made their way into the mid-continent area. The party probably traveled with Native guides, primarily following waterways and marked their route with triangular holes carved in rock, stone cairns, and other markers. These landmarks served as a breadcrumb trail for their return and for any future returning party. Upon reaching their destination at the north-south continental divide where the headwaters of the Red River and the Mississippi/Missouri river watersheds and very close to the headwaters of three major watersheds, the third being the Great Lakes/St. Lawrence River watershed, the Kensington Rune Stone was carved and then buried where it could be later relocated using the triangulation of the stone holes.

On the other hand, if the Kensington Rune Stone was placed before construction of the Newport Tower, then the keystones indicate that the builders already knew the location of the Kensington Rune

In addition to being associated with a religious astronomical alignment, the egg-shaped keystone on the inside of the west facing archway could also represent important symbolism, such as the Orphic Egg, to the medieval builders of the Newport Tower. Perhaps the egg inside the "womb" was placed in the west arch to represent the "Birth of the Goddess ideology in the New Jerusalem.," (Left: Wolter, 2007, right: Hall, 1909)

Stone land claim stone. The keystones and the orb represented a starting point and the direction to follow for a returning party. By traveling in the general direction indicated by the keystones (approximately seventeen degrees north of due west), and following Venus as an evening star, represented by the granite orb (and likely using other heavenly bodies to navigate by), they would eventually arrive in the Midwest. At this point, they would then pick up the bread-crumb trail of the already cut stone holes and make their way to Kensington. Upon reaching the area of the Ohman farm, they could then easily locate their land claim.

Relocating previously placed land claim documents, such as lead plates or inscribed stones was apparently a common practice in France where the Templars and Cistercians trace their very beginnings. Author John Fiske wrote the following passage in his 1902 book, *New France and New England*, "At this point of their route on the 29th of July [1749] they

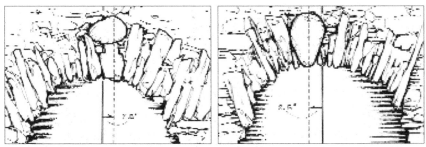

The egg-shaped keystone on the interior, and the symbolic Master Mason shaped keystone on the exterior are back-to-back in the west-northwest archway of the Newport Tower. Both keystones appear to have been intentionally placed by the builders approximately 2.5 degrees south of the center of the archway. (Sketches by Dan Wiemer, 2008)

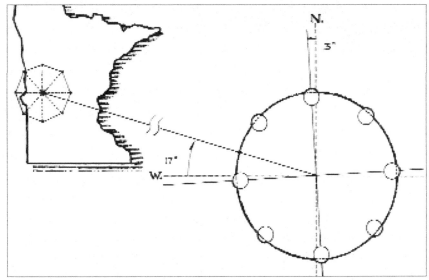

The Newport Tower was constructed with the north column aligned three degrees counter clock-wise of geographic north (magnetic north circa 1400?). When a line is drawn from the center of the tower through the symbolic keystones in the west-northwest archway, the angle is seventeen degrees north of due west. When extended westward, that line passes right through Kensington, Minnesota. Were the builders of the tower aware of the buried land claim stone and used the key-stones to mark the direction of its location? The round, red granite boulder sitting directly over the exterior keystone is important. A returning party could follow the planet Venus as a beacon to lead them into the hexagonal shaped "target" likely marked with stone holes and cairns. Once in the vicinity, the stone holes at Rune Stone Hill on the Ohman farm would enable a returning party to locate the land claim stone. (Sketch by Dan Wiemer, 2009)

took possession of the country in the name of King Louis XV. This act of taking possession was performed as follows: The royal arms of France stamped upon a tin plate were nailed to a tree. At the foot of the tree a plate of lead was buried, upon which was an inscription stating that Monsieur Céloron had buried this plate 'as a token of renewal of possession heretofore taken of the aforesaid river Ohio, of all streams that fall into it, and all lands on both sides to the source of aforesaid streams, as the preceding kings of France have enjoyed or ought to have enjoyed it, and which they have upheld by force of arms and by treaties, notably by those of Ryswick, Utrecht, and Aix-la-Chapelle.' It will be observed that this is the usual style which France has maintained for some centuries."[1]

If the Newport Tower was built by Cistercian/Templar stonemasons, the two symbolic keystones could very well provide additional evidence. The architecture and astronomical alignments alone comprise a compelling case for a medieval origin, but there appears to be much more. After taking the time to learn as much as I could about the esoteric side of these medieval orders, I started to look at the structure differently. The guidance I received from the modern-day Knights Templar and other Freemasons helped open my eyes to the importance of symbolism. If indeed the Newport Tower is a Cistercian/Templar structure built with their ideals, it no doubt served multiple purposes. In addition to the likelihood of being the "prime meridian" filled with astronomical alignments for numerous practical uses, there had to be more going on.

One of the other purposes was certainly religious with the structure serving as a place of worship. The similarity of the Templar-inspired architecture of the Newport Tower with the altar at the Church of the Holy Sepulcher is undeniable. The octagonal footprint exhibits the Cistercian concept of heaven being represented by the eight-fold. This suggests that the top of the tower could have had a spire, like all Cistercian churches, to help obtain the inspiration of the Holy Spirit, i.e., the Goddess.

If the builders believed the center of the continent was an important place, perhaps where they believed the messiah would someday return, eventually they would get there. The red granite orb may represent how they were able to do it. The planet Venus was certainly important to the Cistercians and the Templars. With their mastery of mathematics, geometry, and astronomy, and by marking their route with triangular holes cut into stone, they could easily have navigated by the glowing red orb as either a morning or evening star.

One other curious feature of the Newport Tower that prompted interesting speculation with regard to possible long-range alignments, are the high-white quartz cobbles scattered throughout the second-story cylinder. The largest white quartz cobble is found roughly halfway up the circular second story in the southwest side of the tower. In November of 2008, Steve St. Clair performed laser measurements of the angles of lines projected from the center of the tower, through the quartz cobbles and beyond. David Brody and I assisted Steve with his work, and we were all surprised to learn that when projected onto a map, the line going through the largest white quartz cobble extended through the area at the mouth of the Mississippi River in the Gulf of Mexico.

If, upon independent validation by surveyors, the lines do extend to Kensington and the mouth of the Mississippi, then some interesting possibilities arise. Assuming the keystones and the quartz cobble were intention-

ally positioned, the builders had to have prior knowledge of both locations from earlier exploration. This would suggest the likelihood of several expeditions in the past that apparently navigated the entire Mississippi waterway. Logic says if this was true, then there should be evidence found within the Mississippi watershed consistent with earlier Norse expeditions.

In fact, several runic inscriptions are found not far off the Arkansas River, which is a major tributary of the Mississippi, in Oklahoma. The Heavener Rune Stone is an inscription comprised of eight runes that date to the period 800-850 A.D. Several other runic inscriptions are found in the Heavener area that skeptics claim to be

An image of the Goddess carved in sandstone looks quietly over the campus on the exterior of Pillsbury Hall at the University of Minnesota, in Minneapolis, Minnesota. (Wolter, 2007)

hoaxes. I have personally examined the Heavener Rune Stone and five other runic inscriptions in the area, and, although I cannot vouch for their authenticity, what I can say is there is no factual evidence that is consistent with several scholars' negative opinions. The only reasonable position to take regarding the numerous unknown artifacts and sites found in North America, by both amateurs and academics, is that they need to be preserved and properly studied.

I realize that my theory about these medieval people and their motives behind creating the rune stones, and the Newport Tower, falls firmly in the realm of speculation. However, my ideas are based upon sound historical facts that resonate with consistency every step of the way. Logic says there must be an explanation for who these people were, where they came from, and why they came here. Whatever that explanation is, it must hang together if it is correct. The story of the medieval Cistercians and Knights Templar coming to North America that has unfolded over the course of the last seven years is logical, consistent, and hangs together beautifully.

Note
[1]John Fisk, *New France and New England*, pp. 265-266.

 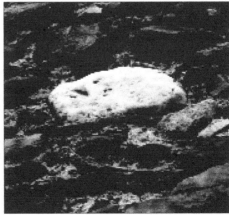

In the southwest corner, roughly halfway up the round second story of the Newport Tower, is a high-white quartz cobble that stands out from the rest of the stones used in its construction (directly above the column and to the right of the west window in this picture). When a line is extended from the center of the tower, through the quartz cobble and beyond, the lines passes through the Mississippi River delta area. (Wolter, 2008/2007)

Part VIII

The Goddess
Ideology

38

Statue of Liberty

One could also make the case that the people of the United States owe their successful democracy to the Cistercians and Knights Templar. The Kensington Rune Stone could metaphorically be compared to the Declaration of Independence as a much earlier document written by people who embraced a similar ideology, and sought out a new land (paradise) to pursue liberty and religious freedom. That ideology to the Cistercians/Templars in the fourteenth century was apparently symbolized by the Hooked X. To the Freemasons who founded our country, the Goddess appears to have been central to their ideologies and thoughts. The strongest evidence of this is found in what is arguably the most visible symbol to the world of the United States that stands tall in New York Harbor, the Statue of Liberty!

The top of the tablet Lady Liberty holds in her left arm is dated July 4, 1776, and has the notches of the Mark Master mason keystone. That tablet could symbolically represent the book of documents that outline the laws, principles, and ideals our found-

The Goddess ideology first brought to North America in 1362 still thrives in the United States and is blatantly symbolized on two recently issued state quarters. The Statue of Liberty is arguably the most visible icon of America, and the statue "Commonwealth" appears on the Pennsylvania State quarter along with the Masonic symbol of the keystone that is also present in the Newport Tower. The "Keystone" state of Pennsylvania is where our founding fathers, most of them Freemasons, signed the Declaration of Independence and wrote the Constitution and the Bill of Rights. These documents could be considered the critical element, or keystone, that helped hold our union together at the outset of our country's initial construction. (Wolter, 2007)

ing fathers instilled for the New Republic. One of those ideals of freedom is the separation of church and state that were based likely on the lessons learned by their persecuted medieval Knights Templar ancestors.

Most scholars have dismissed these artifacts and the history they represent. They continue to offer negative opinions with little or no factual support. Different religious ideologies also might dismiss the evidence and conclusions I have put forth. But my experience in material forensics has shown that evidence always wins.

39

Alan Butler

I n less than a year I had made five trips to the East Coast, and each
time David Brody and I made new discoveries. Our research and
reading was ongoing. Each book we read added something new,
but a watershed moment occurred in the spring of 2007. I found an
author from whom I learned more practical knowledge about the
Cistercians than in everything I'd read previously.

The Knights Templar Revealed is a misleading title because it was
really about the truth behind the ideology of the medieval Templars
and the Cistercian monks who created them. Much of what I had speculated as being behind the motivation of the people who carved the
North American rune stones and who built the Newport Tower was
validated in the book. Authors Alan Butler and Stephen Dafoe presented a highly controversial, yet plausible, theory strongly supported by
historical facts. A quick online search of Alan Butler led to a satisfying
discovery. He had written several recent books with tantalizing titles,
*The Goddess, the Grail and the Lodge, The Virgin and the Pentacle: The
Freemasonic Plot to Destroy the Church, Rosslyn Revealed: A Library in
Stone*, and *Sheep*.

I was convinced of the main points of his arguments and gained
a better understanding of the proper historical context in Europe leading
up to the pivotal year of 1362 A.D. I knew I had to contact him. I gave
him a brief synopsis of my work on the rune stones and the Newport

Tower.

The next day I received two lengthy emails from Alan. He was unaware of Dick's and my research on the Kensington Rune Stone and had no idea there was factual evidence that the Cistercians had come to North America, though he had no problem with that idea. I sent him my papers on the Spirit Pond Rune Stones and the Hooked X. Alan's response left little doubt that he believed we were on the right path, offering the following passage, "The hooked cross (X) is indeed both significant and fascinating. It may indeed carry the message you suggest and it is all the more interesting when it is realized that Columbus used it—bearing in mind his own background and that of his father-in-law as an ex-grand master of the Knights of Christ."

On June 20, 2007, I called Alan in England. When the Newport Tower came up, I tried to further stimulate his interest in studying the Venus alignments that appeared to be there. I told him that, if he wished to inspect the Tower personally, I would be glad to meet him there.

I finished Alan's *The Goddess, the Grail and the Lodge*, focusing on Alan's explanation of the symbolism as, ". . . the horn is yet another representation of the womb as it was also a drinking vessel. The reverse aspect of the horn, i.e. its external features, was closely associated with the phallus."

The horn and knife rocks next to the flowing spring in the Whetstone Valley of South Dakota instantly took on renewed interest. The advanced weathering of both incredible carvings could easily date back to medieval times, providing another possible link to the presence of the Cistercians and Knight Templar.

After finishing Butler's books, I felt as if I finally had the proper understanding of the historical context behind the ideology whose influence spans at least five thousand years of history right up to the present day. I have also come to realize that the discovery of the Hooked X represents an important previously unknown medieval thread of the people Alan coined "The Troyes Fraternity" or "Star Families," who sought to establish its "Goddess" ideology in North America. I asked Alan if I could use the summary of his research and discovery of the ideology and force behind what he collectively calls "The Golden Thread" and he graciously agreed:

> A group of nobles springing from the Merovingian bloodline (called "Star Families"), and ultimately megalithic origin, began to find their ancient religious beliefs threatened by the strangle-hold of feudalism and an ever more repressive Christian Church. Elaborate plans were laid to alter both state and Church, in order to allow religious practices held sacred for thousands of years to continue. This involved ensuring that Jerusalem would be captured and that a representative of the Troyes Fraternity would be placed on the throne there.
>
> Meanwhile, a new and revolutionary monastic order was created, which gradually subverted the very basis of the feudal economy. It was designed to grow rapidly and in order to ensure that it followed the appointed course, a young man born of a significant Troyes Fraternity family, Bernard of Clairvaux, was put in charge.
>
> With Jerusalem secure and in sympathetic hands, the Troyes Fraternity then embarked upon the next stage of its plan—to build the largest and most powerful standing army the West had ever known. But this institution would be much more, and the reality of its fighting acumen merely masked its economic intentions. Champagne was made the economic heart of Europe, and at the center of Champagne was Troyes, also the home base of the Templars. None of these situations can be divorced from each other, and it is impossible to see these events as being a coincidence. At the back of them stands the form of the ancient Goddess. The form of the Goddess remains central to all that was taking place. In her new persona, as the Virgin Mary, every Cistercian abbey was named for her, and hers was the name the Templars cried as they went into battle.
>
> The greatest wonder of all is that every one of these plans and strategies was put into place with the absolute approval of the established Roman Catholic Church, which was outmaneuvered at every turn, for over two centuries. The same is true of the dictatorial monarchs of the region, whose power base was gradually eroded as international trade broke local monopolies and encouraged free enterprise.
>
> However, not every churchman or king was stupid, and there came a time when the great heresy was recognized for what it truly was. The destruction of the Templars and the gradual demise of the

Cistercian Order could have put paid to the influence of the Golden Thread forever. It is fortunate for the freedoms most of us still hold dear today that over three thousand years of experience and knowledge was not so easily swept aside.

Alan Butler has presented a compelling case that includes how the Goddess has survived, and in fact thrived in the Republic known as the United States of America. What my research appears to have discovered with the Kensington Rune Stone is tangible evidence of the initial claim to establish the "New Jerusalem" by the Cistercian and Knights Templar orders. The people who carved and buried the Kensington Rune Stone

This sixteen century (1506 to 1509 A.D.) painting on wood (left) and wood engraving (right) circa 1491 A.D., each depict Our Lady (The Goddess) protecting the Order of Cîteaux with two angels holding up her voluminous cloak. Beneath her are the white monks led by St. Bernard holding his crozier on her right and a community of nuns headed by Ysabel de Maléfiance. (Left: France, 1998, page 186 [Painting attributed to Jean Bellegambe Inv., No. 408, Prov. Flines (Nord), France—Douai, Musée de la Chartreuse]; Right: France, 1998, page 125 [Wood engraving in Peter Meflinger, Collecta Privilegiorum ordinis Cistercians Prov. Dijon (Côte d'Or), France-Dijon, Bibliothèque Municipale])

in 1362 were followed only a few decades later by another party who embraced the same ideology symbolized by the Hooked X. That party carved and buried the Spirit Pond Rune Stones along the coast of Maine, where there is clear evidence of a pre-colonial habitation site.

The Spirit Pond Rune Stones could very likely be connected to Prince Henry Sinclair's voyage of circa 1400 A.D. The Spirit Pond Map Stone clearly points out the location of Vinland that apparently was two days sail south of Popham Beach, Maine. If Prince Henry indeed sailed two days south, he would have ended up in the Cape Cod/Narragansett Bay area where the Hooked X again shows up on the Narragansett Rune Stone. Across the bay to the east we find the Newport Tower built with indigenous stone using the unmistakable architecture and symbolism of the Cistercians and Knights Templar. The astronomical and Venus alignments, which have yet to be fully studied, are consistent with a construction date contemporaneous with Prince Henry's voyage. The keystones in the Newport Tower are definitely Templar and likely indicate that the builders already knew the location of the Kensington Rune Stone land claim that had already been, or was soon to be carved and buried.

In 1362, thirty men sailed to the New World and then carved and buried a land claim now known as the Kensington Rune Stone. Among those men was at least one Swedish-educated Cistercian monk capable of writing runes. No doubt many other Cistercian monks traveled by ship to the continent they called the New Jerusalem. In this miniature from 1409, Cistercian monk Odo of Châteauroux served as the Papal Legate and traveled with the Royal Fleet to Dalmietta in 1249. (France, 1998, p. 188)

40

The Goddess

On December 1, 2007, Janet and I attended a Christmas party hosted by Rich and Ann Cammick, who asked if I would be willing to give my presentation on the Kensington Rune Stone. Afterward, there were many questions about the Kensington Rune Stone and the Goddess ideology that definitely had people's minds racing.

The next morning, Janet woke me to say, "I think I know what the 'big secret' is." She then explained how we'd been tip-toeing around the Goddess question without realizing we were already there.

Ancient cultures expressed their Goddess ideology using the common symbol of the triangle. The triangle represented the pubic triangle of the female, symbolic of where life originated. The triangle was a common symbol of Freemasonry that represented the feminine regardless if the point was up or down. Realizing that the orientation of the point was irrelevant, my mind drifted back to the triangle above the altar in the Church of Maria Magdalena in Stockholm, Sweden. That triangle, often referred to as the Delta of Enoch, appeared to be a symbol of reverence for the sacred feminine. It could also be what the all-seeing eye meant within the triangle above the pyramid on the dollar bill.

Janet later said, "That eye in the triangle looks vaguely familiar." The eye reminded her of Leonardo Da Vinci's painting of the Mona Lisa. "That painting is somehow connected to all this. I'm sure of it," she said.

Janet's eyes suddenly widened as the conversation triggered another realization, "The Nile Delta! The Egyptians have always looked upon that area where the river meets the Mediterranean Sea, as a haven for life within the desert. It's shaped like the pubic triangle of a female. In this case, the life-giving triangle of the Goddess."

Later, after checking, sure enough, the lush green triangle of the Nile Delta stands out like a beacon when viewed from above. It's probably not a coincidence that the Egyptians built the pyramids at the point where the Nile River first enters the delta.

The discussion between us continued over the course of the next couple of weeks with frequent calls to Westford, Massachusetts, to seek input from our friends David and Kim Brody. His Jewish upbringing and contacts proved invaluable whenever we needed help with the Hebrew culture or language. Then, on January 18, 2008, David made an important discovery. "In Hebrew, like in Spanish and French, words are either masculine or feminine. I knew this. But what I didn't know and just learned (and should not have been surprised by!) is that words that end in "hey" are *always* feminine. Remember our unpronounceable word for God, called the tetragrammaton, found inside the Delta of Enoch? In English it is pronounced Yahweh. In Hebrew it is written "Yud" "Hey" "Vuv" "Hey." It ends in "hey"—it is a feminine word! In ancient Judaism, God is feminine!"

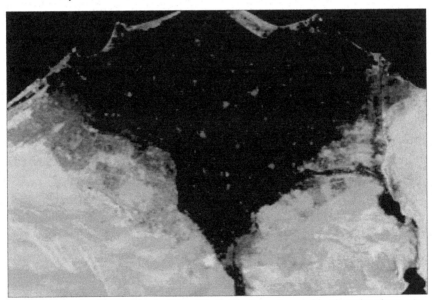

This www.virtualearth.com image of the Nile Delta shows its roughly triangular shape produced by green foliage. The Great Pyramids were built where the "life-giving" waters of the Nile enters the pubic triangle of the Goddess.

239

David's discovery also served to validate the triangle symbol being feminine regardless whether the point is up or down, since we had seen the ancient Hebrew word for God in both. The other possibility is that when the point of the triangle is up, it symbolizes the male aspects of the creator thereby reinforcing the concept of duality.

Almost a year to the day after David made his discovery of the "Hey" being a feminine word in Hebrew, we happened upon a completely different example of the Delta of Enoch being feminine that was discovered independently by another researcher in Montréal, Canada. Canadian researcher Francine Bernier wrote in her 2001 book, *The Templar's Legacy in Montréal, the New Jerusalem*, that while researching the history of the founding of Montréal and the likely existence of an esoteric religion based on the Essene tradition among the original founders, she made a startling discovery in the Notre-Dame Basilica originally constructed in 1672. Above the pulpit just above a descending dove of the Holy Spirit is a golden Tetragrammatron with the ineffable name of God in Hebrew letters. Only this golden triangle should be called "Tri-grammatron" because it contains only three Hebrew letters, "Hey" "Vuv" "Hey." Bernier goes on to explain the three letters in Latin spell, E-V-E, Eve, the Mother of All Living.[1]

Our discussion of the symbolically important triangle brought to mind the triangle-shaped keystone in the archway in the nave of the church at Eynhallow in Orkney, Scotland. I wondered if Abbot Lawrence and his Cistercian brothers may have incorporated a keystone illu-

The Delta of Enoch triangle in Freemasonry is a feminine symbol regardless if the point is up or down. The unpronounceable ancient Hebrew word of God inside both triangles, read right to left, ends in "Hey" making it a feminine word. The font at right at St. Michael's Church in Garway, England, has triangles pointing up and down that could be referencing the Sacred Feminine. (Internet; Internet; Brighton, 2006, page 205)

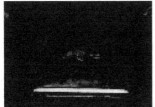

This highly unusual example of the Delta of Enoch is found above the pulpit in Notre-Dame Basilica in Montreal, Ontario, Canada. This example is missing the typical Hebrew "Yod" and has only the "Hey" "Vuv" "Hey" which in Latin spells E-V-E or Eve, the Mother (Goddess) of all Living. (Photograph courtesy of Tim Suess)

mination event on the winter solstice, analogous to the Newport Tower. Though in ruins today, there may still be evidence present at Eynhallow if the site is properly investigated.

The realization of the symbolism behind the sacred feminine led to a discussion about the alternate possibilities for the allegorical meaning of several other interesting symbols of Christianity and Freemasonry.

The Vesica Pises is a common symbol of sacred geometry produced by two intersecting circles that form a vertical almond shape. Usually, a sacred figure, such as Jesus, is found surrounded by the shape.[2] In Christianity, the symbol is used to represent Christ's ascension to heaven.[3] In contrast, this symbolism could be interpreted as the sacred feminine (Goddess) giving birth to Jesus, and other important religious figures through the allegorical birth canal.

It also occurred to me that the length to width ratio of the visica pises is 2:1, the same ratio of the nave of the churches and the final dimensions of the Kensington Rune Stone. Apparently, this ratio is sacred because it is symbolic of the regenerative powers of the Goddess.

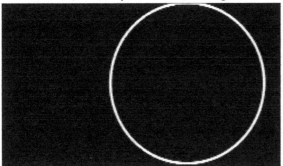

The Vesica Pises is a common symbol of sacred geometry produced by two intersecting circles. This symbolism could be interpreted as the sacred feminine (Goddess) giving birth to Jesus, and other important religious figures, through the allegorical birth canal. This example is found at the Washington National Cathedral in Washington, D.C. (Wolter, 2007)

The obelisk is a common symbol of ancient Egypt and Freemasonry. The obelisk at left is of Thutmosis I at the Temple of Amon-Re (1500 B.C.) in Egypt. At right, the Washington Monument in Washington, D.C., in September of 2006. (Photo courtesy of Wikipedia, Wolter, 2006)

The obelisk was a common symbol of ancient Egypt. It is also found in most cities in the United States. In Minneapolis, we have the Foshay Tower (Wilbur Foshay was a known Freemason), and in Washington, D.C., the Washington Monument towers over the nation's capitol. The obelisk is a phallic symbol that represents male generative power, fertility, regeneration, and is a stabilizing force.[4] Founding father Benjamin Franklin would certainly have been aware of the symbolic energy generation of the obelisk as a prominent Freemason. He would also have been acutely aware of the actual draw of energy—lightning—by the towering pointed structure. The obelisk is essentially a lightning rod.

Janet and I wondered if the prominent location of the Washington Monument in the center of the National Mall was an allegorical symbol to the sacred feminine. Could the towering phallic have been erected as a beacon to the Goddess above to release her divine powers to the Earth?

It made sense to the point where it appeared obvious. One longtime Freemason said, "It was always the Goddess, until Christianity turned it around." The historical evidence suggests this is true. However, as we've discovered, in spite of patriarchal religions' attempts to put down the Goddess ideology, it has survived and indeed flourished. This is certainly true in the United States. Our forefathers, most of whom were Freemasons, learned the lessons of their persecuted ancestors of the fourteenth century (the Knights Templar) and established a democracy that insisted on the sep-

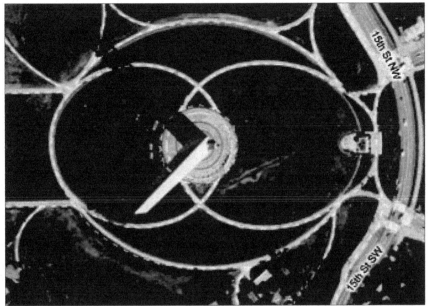

Satellite view of the Washington Monument in the National Mall in Washington, D.C., reveals sacred geometry that can only be seen when viewed from above. Two intersecting circles within a larger circle create the Vesica Pises from which the white marble obelisk rises in what is the unmistakable Masonic symbolism of the allegorical union of male and female analogous to the Hooked X. (www.virtualearth.com)

aration of church and state. At the same time, our Constitution allows for the freedom to embrace whatever religion one chooses.

Perhaps the most convincing example that our fore fathers embraced Goddess ideology is found in the layout of three of the most important structures in Washington, D.C.: The White House, the Capitol Building, and the Washington Monument. These three icons form what is commonly known as the federal triangle. The Capitol Building stands in full view from the Washington Monument as one looks due east down the National Mall. From the Capitol Building, Pennsylvania Avenue extends to the White House, which had a clear sightline when originally laid out. The north-south line from the White House to the Washington Monument completes a right triangle and is called the Jefferson Meridian. If one follows the Jefferson Meridian (Sixteenth Street NW) north beyond the White House, there are several notable places along the street including Lafayette Park, the National Geographic Society, the Scottish Rite Temple, and Meridian Hill Park.

In April of 2008, my family and I met David Brody and his wife, Kim, in the nation's capitol for a four-day weekend. After a tour of the Scottish Rite Temple, we wandered through Meridian Hill Park several blocks farther north. We found Masonic symbolism that included decorative concrete obelisks along with a surprising stone sculpture quietly nestled within the landscaping. Staring serenely to the west was the Goddess "Serenity" carved in pure white marble.

After scouting the park, we all looked south down Sixteenth Street and saw the Jefferson Memorial was clearly visible, directly in line with the White House. To our surprise, the Washington Monument was not in line with the meridian. It was several hundred feet east. The mystery of the Washington Monument offset puzzled us for the next few months, until Janet found the answer in a book written by David Ovason, entitled, *The Secret Architecture of Our Nation's Capitol: The Masons and the Building of Washington, D.C.*

Every year on August 10th, three prominent stars appear over the capitol, after sunset, that form what appears to be a perfect right triangle that mirrors the Federal triangle: Regulus, Arcturus, and Spica. However, the ninety-degree angle represented by the Washington Monument is not perfect. It turns out Spica is slightly off. This fact was not lost on the original architects who correctly placed the Washington Monument to reflect accurately the positions of these important stars. What made this stellar triangle so important? Within that triangle in the heavens, the constellation of Virgo (the Goddess) is found. It seems our founding fathers paid the ultimate respect to the great Goddess through a symbolic reflection using three of our nation's most important buildings. This astronomical sacred geometry is perhaps the most impressive example illustrating the ancient phrase: "As above, so below."

If one elevates the Goddess, then many things suddenly begin to fall into place. Saint Bernard of Clairvaux selected the beehive as his personal symbol and modeled the numerous communities of monks under his leadership after the silent communal effort of thousands of bees working for the greater good. Was the queen bee, who ruled over the hive, yet another, and perhaps even the primary inspiration for his selection, of this metaphorically powerful symbol? Chess is a game the Knights Templar learned from the Arabs. Is it an accident that the most powerful piece in the game is the queen?

As Janet and I kept coming up with more examples of the dominant role of the Goddess, another likely example occurred to me. In Rosslyn Chapel I had carefully scanned the ornately carved stone columns and beams of the interior. I remembered a lone inscription carved in Latin into the beam in the southeast corner over the stairs that descend into the crypt. The inscription read, "Wine is Strong, a King is Stronger, Women are Stronger Still, but the Truth Conquers All."

Perhaps the "V" in the Hooked X is on the top for a very good reason. Maybe the cultures who have embraced the ideology of the sacred feminine in the distant past up through today, believed the

Sitting quietly within the landscaping of Meridian Hill Park in Washington, D.C., is a sculpture carved in high-white marble of the Goddess "Serenity." (Wolter, 2008)

The only inscription carved into Rosslyn Chapel appears to confirm the belief that the supreme deity is the Goddess after all. Translated from Latin it reads, "Wine is Strong, a King is Stronger, Women are Stronger Still, but the Truth Conquers All." (Photo by Scott F. Wolter with permission of the Rosslyn Chapel Trust, 2006)

Goddess, actually was God? After all, women do have the ability to give life. Could that be why the Mona Lisa is smiling?

Having said all this about the Goddess being at the core of the conflict between the Church and the Cistercians and the Knights Templar, I need to add that my analysis of the historical context of events that ultimately led the Templars to North America is still a work in progress. However, the evidence presented here indicates that something motivated them to venture beyond Europe. I strongly believe that religious conflict was the root cause.

What appears to have happened is the Cistercian/Templar emphasis on the feminine aspects of the Godhead was an attempt to tip the scales back to a balance, or duality of the male and female aspects that the Church had tipped too far to the masculine side. In case I haven't stated it clearly enough, the Hooked X symbolizes the pursuit of that religious balance.

I am not a Freemason. No doubt I've made some mistakes in my interpretation of certain points. However, the message I have received from Freemasons who have helped to guide me, is the craft is mainly about an individuals own pursuit of knowledge, self-improvement and ultimately passing through the "seventh gate," via whatever religion one chooses, into the eight-fold of heaven. From my perspective, the most important part about Masonry isn't necessarily that one reaches a destination, it is the journey.

Notes

[1]Bernier, 2001, p. 186.
[2]Cooper, p. 185.
[3]Bruce-Mitford, p. 105.
[4]Cooper, p. 121.

41

The Holy Trinity

In March of 2008, I flew to Scotland and England with a three-man crew from Committee Films on the first of several trips for a documentary film about the research I'd done. As the primary consultant, I made sure to contact Alan Butler about an interview. He graciously agreed to participate. I was eager to meet the man who had masterfully researched and cogently written several books that explained his controversial theory of the "Star Families" successful plan (in my view) to restore the feminine component to the Godhead. Not only had he thoroughly and convincingly presented the case I had independently begun to explore, but Alan had demonstrated great courage by boldly sharing his work with the world. Catholics especially would find many of his theories offensive. However, the historical

The three magnificently carved pillars in the altar at Rosslyn Chapel could also represent the Holy Trinity of the Father, the Son and the Holy Spirit (Mother Goddess). The layout of the text of the inscription on the Kensington Rune Stone with three groups of three lines on the face side and three lines on the split side likely is another example of this sacred symbolic numerology. (Photograph by Scott F. Wolter with kind permission of the Rosslyn Chapel Trust, 2006)

evidence is undeniably consistent with Alan's conclusions. Instead of outrage and criticism, I hoped people would try to learn from both his and my work.

In Alan's third book, *The Virgin and Pentacle*, he made an excellent point concerning what Christians call "The Holy Trinity." Since reading his analysis, both Janet and I have asked several of our Christian friends this interesting question: "If the Holy Trinity represents the Father, the Son and the Holy Spirit. What, or more appropriately, who is the Holy Spirit?" Most people pause, don a quizzical look and then say, "The spirit of Jesus?"

Alan presents an interesting perspective by asking a simple question, "If you have the Father, and the Son (the child), who's missing?" The answer is obvious. To complete the Holy Trinity you have to have the Mother. To the medieval Cistercian and Templar brothers, the Holy Spirit no doubt was symbolic of the Mother Goddess.

We also agreed that the Hooked X symbol represents the Holy Trinity so important to the Cistercians and their military brethren. Their obsession with geometry and numbers was reflected in virtually everything they did, both spiritually and literally. The most literal expression of these concepts was in their architecture where multiples of three are dominant. In Norse mythology, the God Odin, who hung from a tree and was wounded with a spear, similar to the crucifixion of Jesus, has a symbol that reflects important symbology and numerology. The symbol of Odin is called the Valknot or the Knot of the Slain and incorporates three triangles and the apparent sacred equation of three times three.[1]

We also see this important numerical expression reflected in the

The symbol for the Norse God Odin is three interlocking triangles reflecting the sacred numerology of three times three.

inscription of the Kensington Rune Stone. The runic text itself was laid out by the carver in three groups of three lines on the face side, followed by three more lines on the split side. It is reasonable to assume that the dating code and the Grail Prayer were coded within this inscription so as not to disrupt the apparently important numerical layout and preserving the Holy Trinity within this sacred text.

Note

[1]Montgomery, 2006, p. 134.

42

The Tironensians

This book would be lacking if I didn't mention a mysterious group of monks very likely tightly connected to the Cistercians. The Tironensians were established in 1109 by a reformed Benedictine monk named Bernard de Tiron (1050 to 1118).[1] The "gray monks" were master builders and like the Cistercians, were highly respected by nobility in France, England, and Scotland, and experienced rapid expansion. By 1200, Tironensians owned twelve abbeys, twenty-eight priories, and twenty-two parishes. Although parallels exist between the orders, such as their origins in central France (the Cistercians at Cîteaux, and the Tironensians in the forests of Tiron, near Chartres), superior craftsmanship and stonemason skills, and a return to strict asceticism and humility of the early Benedictines, there apparently were notable differences.

Canadian researcher, Francine Bernier, has studied the Tironensians and theorized that the two orders had major cultural and spiritual differences. She argued how the Tironensians clashed with the Roman Catholic Church, ". . . when Bernard (of Tiron) left Saint-Cyprien in 1101, he was rebelling against Cluny and the supremacy of the Roman clergy." Bernier continued, "The Cistercians, under Bernard di Cîteaux, quickly became the most powerful arm of the Roman Catholic Church in France and England."

Bernier discussed another important difference between the orders in their tonsures, or religious haircuts. The Tironensians embraced the Celtic, or Pagan religion, as evidenced by a Celtic tonsure with their hair shaved in the front following a line tracing ear to ear over the top of the head, keeping the hair in the back long. The Cistercian tonsure consisted of a bald top of the head with a band of hair encircling their head symbolizing the "crown of thorns" worn on Christ's head during his crucifixion.

Bernier's analysis is logical given the generally accepted interpretation of these orders by modern historians. However, in light of my and Alan Butler's research, the Tironensians and the Cistercian leadership might, in fact, have been more alike than previously thought. Outwardly, there appeared to be stark differences in the orders' relationships with the Catholic Church. However, they could have been secretly aligned with common goals and objectives. What they appeared to share were fundamentally the same ideological religious beliefs (Goddess Ideology). Indeed, it appears the Tironensians were openly defiant whereas the Cistercians pursued a two-hundred-year plan of subterfuge against the Church, only to be struck down in 1307. One could argue the Church in Rome, and the king of France, teamed up to take down the "muscle behind the machine." Not coincidentally, the put-down of the Templars coincided with the decline of the Cistercians.

Specific information about how the decline of the Templars impacted the Tironensians is not clear. Relatively little information is known about them. However, the Tironensians are credited with establishing Kilwinning Abbey, in Scotland, between 1140 and 1162. To build Kilwinning, the finest Tironensian stone masons were sent from France, and used their superior skills on "free stone," limestone or sandstone uniform enough to be carved and worked in any direction. Kilwinning is where modern Freemasonry traces its origin to the medieval term "freestone mason." It seems consistent that the Tironensians at Kilwinning gave rise to the ideals of Freemasonry through superior stone mason skills, and an open, free-thinking religious ideology. The Cistercians and Knights Templar appear to have embraced the same religious ideology choosing long-range, subversive tactics to undermine the power structure within the Roman Catholic Church. In the opinion of this author, that effort was successful.

Note

[1]Bernier, 2005.

43

Findings, Interpretations, and Conclusions

The following is a summary of the factual and historical evidence that have led to what I believe represents the most plausible explanation for the North American artifacts and sites under discussion. This will be followed by a list of interpretations and conclusion. I have carefully considered all the known facts and feel confident that the basic premise of what these artifacts represent is correct. It is my hope that this book will inspire both amateur and academic scholars from relevant disciplines to continue serious research that no doubt will yield more important and exciting new facts about the pre-Columbian history of North America.

Kensington Rune Stone Facts

1. After analysis of Olof Ohman's book collection, written notes, photographs, interviews, and over sixty letters written in his own hand, there are no indications of his involvement in the creation of the Kensington Rune Stone inscription. Interpretation: Olof Ohman was a serious, honest, and trustworthy man and was likely telling the truth regarding the circumstances surrounding the discovery of the Kensington Rune Stone.

2. The root leaching pattern on the back of the Kensington Rune Stone is consistent with the written affidavits of twelve first-hand witnesses who saw the flattened roots around the stone. This evidence is also consistent with the discovery story told by Olof Ohman and his sons Olof, Jr., and Edward. Interpretation: The Kensington Rune Stone

was found under the twenty-five- to thirty-year-old aspen tree as reported by Olof Ohman and his two sons in September of 1898.

3. The first four scholars of Scandinavian runes and languages all dismissed the inscription as a hoax in 1899 after examining a written copy and without ever examining the actual artifact. Interpretation: These early runic scholars did not make a serious effort to study the actual artifact and reached their conclusion on erroneous data.

4. Olof Ohman scratched out the inscription with a nail. Interpretation: The fresh appearance of the inscription created confusion and bias on the part of past investigators.

5. The side of the Kensington Rune Stone containing the last three lines of the inscription has numerous impact fractures along the perimeter as well as a different color, texture and weathering profile than the rest of the stone. Interpretation: Prior to carving the inscription, the carver intentionally broke the previously larger glacial erratic stone slab into its present shape.

6. The intentionally dressed final dimension of the Kensington Rune Stone is approximately a 2:1 ratio. Interpretation: This shape held important religious significance to the carver.

7. Pyrite crystals exposed within the unscratched grooves the day the original Kensington Rune Stone inscription was carved have completely weathered away. Pyrite crystals of the same size in the grooves of a modern inscription carved by pranksters in June of 1985 near the Kensington Rune Stone discovery site are still actively weathering. Interpretation: As of June 2008, the Kensington Rune Stone inscription is at least twenty-three years old, which means Olof Ohman could not have been involved in creation of the Kensington Rune Stone inscription since he immigrated to the United States nineteen years before the Kensington Rune Stone was found.

8. Biotite minerals have completely weathered away from the surfaces of the original inscription of the Kensington Rune Stone. Biotite minerals of the same grain size and exposed to similar weathering conditions as the Kensington Rune Stone, on slate tombstones in Maine, began to weather away after about 200 years. Interpretation: The Kensington Rune Stone inscription is older than 200

years from the date it was discovered in 1898 because it hasn't been in a weathering environment since it was discovered.

9. The geological investigation of Professor Newton H. Winchell in December of 1909 concluded that the Kensington Rune Stone was genuine. Interpretation: My geologic work has replicated and confirmed Professor Winchell's work.

10. All the words on the Kensington Rune Stone have been found to be Old Swedish. Interpretation: The Kensington Rune Stone inscription is Old Swedish.

11. Numerous linguistic, runic, grammatical and dialectic traits found in the Kensington Rune Stone inscription are also found in medieval runic inscriptions on Gotland. Interpretation: The carver of the Kensington Rune Stone inscription was likely educated in these aspects of the Old Swedish language on the island of Gotland.

12. The rare medieval rune called the dotted R was not known to modern scholars until 1935, yet is found on the Kensington Rune Stone found in 1898. Interpretation: The presence of the dotted R indicates the Kensington Rune Stone inscription could only have been carved during medieval times.

Conclusion: The factual evidence from multiple disciplines, such as history (at the time of the discovery and in medieval times), geology, language and runes, are consistent with the Kensington Rune Stone being a genuine medieval artifact.

New Kensington Rune Stone Facts
Since my first Kensington Rune Stone Book

1. In a previously unknown letter written by Olof Ohman to Hans Voigt on May 19, 1910, that came to light on September 16, 2006, Ohman wrote, "I could not make the Stone nor could any other emigrant have had enough knowledge to do it." Interpretation: This letter further confirms Ohman's honesty and integrity.

2. Several hand-cut, highly weathered, triangular-shaped holes in glacial boulders were found in proximity of the Ohman Farm. When plotted on a satellite map, lines drawn connecting the stone holes intersect at

the exact location where the Kensington Rune Stone was discovered. Interpretation: The stone holes were likely made by the party responsible for carving the Kensington Rune Stone, who then buried it and left the holes as directional markers so it could be re-located at a later date.

3. The location of the piece(s) of the Kensington Rune Stone that were intentionally split off by the carver is unknown. Interpretation: The possibility exists that another inscription is buried somewhere else.

4. The carver had two areas of rock spall off on the first two lines of the inscription. The first was in the upper loop of the dotted R in the word "NorRmen" on line one and the second was the entire first word "(ten)o" on line two. Interpretation: A stone carver from Gotland, used to carving in relatively soft rock types (limestone and sandstone), had difficulty carving in rock as dense, hard and brittle as the Kensington Rune Stone metagreywacke.

5. Kensington Rune Stone researcher and plant physiologist Professor Rodney Beecher Harvey observed the root leaching and photographed each rune on the Kensington Rune Stone in the 1930s. Interpretation: My documentation of the root leaching and generation of the photo-library of the Kensington Rune Stone inscription has replicated and confirmed Professor Harvey's work.

6. When two runes and the pentadic number eight that were apparently singled out by the carver are plotted on the medieval Easter Table, used extensively on Gotland, it gives the year 1362. Interpretation: The carver of the Kensington Rune Stone intentionally placed a coded date within the inscription to confirm the same date of 1362 carved in pentadic numbers in Arabic placement.

7. Several punch marks and short strokes occur within numerous characters in the Kensington Rune Stone inscription. Interpretation: These characters were intentionally singled out by the carver and appear to spell out in sequence a prayer for the ten dead men, "Grail these [10 men have] wisdom [the 10 men are with the] Holy Spirit."

8. The Kensington Rune Stone was found buried in the ground and has a runic inscription that includes information related to who the party was, where their location was, when they were there and why.

The location of the Stone appears to be marked using a triangulation of hand-cut holes cut into glacial boulders in the general proximity of the artifact so it could be re-located at some future date. Interpretation: The Kensington Rune Stone is a land claim.

Conclusions: Previously unknown documents and past research confirm and reinforce known research and conclusions that are consistent with the Kensington Rune Stone being a genuine medieval artifact. The hand-cut stone holes at the Ohman Farm were made to relocate the Kensington Rune Stone after it had been carved and buried as a land claim. By using "sacred geometry" with other stone holes, locating a second runic inscription land claim stone may be possible. Numerous characters singled out by the carver (who likely was a Cistercian monk) reveal a second encoded date of 1362 within the inscription using the medieval Easter Table dating practice that was also used extensively on Gotland to protect the known pentadic date from alteration. The carver also encoded a prayer with the word "Grail" presumably for the ten dead men.

Gotland Facts

1. The language, runes, dialect, grammar, and dating features of the Kensington Rune Stone are found in the Swedish literature. They were then confirmed on numerous runic inscriptions found primarily on grave slabs mortared into the floors inside the ninety-two medieval churches on the island. Interpretation: The Kensington Rune Stone inscription is consistent with the runic and language practice of medieval Gotland.

2. The only known people educated enough to compose such an inscription were Cistercian because they were the only monks present on Gotland in the middle of the fourteenth century. Interpretation: The Kensington Rune Stone inscription was carved by a Cistercian monk in 1362.

3. Numerous crusader "Templar" crosses are found carved into medieval grave slabs and painted on the walls of churches. Interpretation: The Knights Templar and/or their brothers in the Baltic region, the Teutonic Knights, were present on Gotland at that time.

Conclusions: The previously unknown anomalies in the Kensington Rune Stone inscription are found on Gotland and indicate the carver was a Cistercian monk. The Templar crosses on Gotland indicate the presence of military monks (most likely the Teutonic Knights) closely associated with the Cistercians who were present on Gotland during the fourteenth century.

Cistercian and Knights Templar Facts

1. The Cistercians were established in 1098 and took strict vows of chastity, poverty, prayer and work.
2. The Cistercians experienced incredible growth in the number of abbeys founded and built across Europe, Scandinavia, and into the Holy Land. Beginning with a single abbey at Cîteaux, France, in 1100, the order eventually grew to over 750 abbeys by 1350. Interpretation: The Cistercians had a highly successful strategy for expanding their numbers, territory and influence on Christianity across Europe.
3. Each Cistercian abbey generated vast income through agriculture, sheep farming, and manufacturing. The Templars handled the finances and transported the Cistercian-made goods using their large fleet of ships. Interpretation: Working together in an apparently very carefully crafted way the Cistercians and Templars became extremely wealthy and influential.
4. St. Bernard of Clairvaux led the meteoric rise of the Cistercians from 1115 until his death in 1153. Interpretation: Bernard was a very charismatic, intelligent, persuasive and influential man who was successful in crafting the course of history in medieval Europe.
5. New Cistercian abbeys were established when twelve "brothers" ventured into the wilderness, or what they metaphorically called the "desert," to established a new abbey, or "paradise." The abbeys were founded in forests, mountains, prairies, and swamps, always incorporating rivers or streams to allow for the use of fresh water. Interpretation: The Cistercians had a well-organized plan for expansion away from population centers where they could acquire vast tracts of land more easily.
6. St. Bernard wrote the charter for the Knights Templar in 1128, and argued successfully to Pope Innocent II that a new order of monastic

knights was necessary to fight the infidel and protect pilgrims traveling to the Holy Land in Jerusalem. Interpretation: By establishing a military order closely aligned to the Cistercians it gave them flexibility and power to pursue their religious and financial objectives.

7. Cistercian and Templar stone masons incorporated the use of geometry, mathematics, and astronomy, which they considered a higher order of knowledge called "Sacred Geometry." They used this knowledge to build hundreds of abbeys, churches, and cathedrals across Europe and Scandinavia using both Romanesque and Gothic architecture. Interpretation: These massive and beautiful structures demonstrated their superior building skills during this era.

8. The Cistercian and Knights Templar revered the Virgin Mary and named each abbey in her honor. Interpretation: The Cistercians and Templars likely revered the Virgin Mary as a metaphor for the ancient belief in the reverence of the "sacred feminine," also called "Goddess worship."

9. Goddess worship traces back thousands of years through many cultures and is believed to originate from ancient cultures worshiping the planet Venus and the various cycles it traces in the sky. Interpretation: The planet Venus and its association with Goddess worship has been around for a long time.

10. Allegorical representations of the sacred feminine were considered sacred to the Cistercians and Knights Templar and were incorporated into the churches and cathedrals they constructed. Examples include the nave and rose windows representing the womb, and the peaked doorways representing the female genitilia symbolic of the allegorical birth canal. Interpretation: Sacred feminine architecture should be considered when evaluating structures as a potential clue toward identifying the builders.

Conclusions: The financial success and Goddess ideology of the Cistercian and Knights Templar orders were perceived as a threat to both the King of France and the Church who moved against the "muscle behind the machine" by putting down the Templars in 1307. The combination of religious persecution by the Church, war, famine and the plague beginning in 1348, all combined to turn the attention of the Cistercians and Templars to the "New World" of North America.

Venus and Astronomical Alignments Facts

1. The planet Venus has been revered for thousands of years in many cultures as a symbol of love, sex, reproduction, and restored life.

2. Venus and its periodic cycles are believed to be associated with the "Goddess" ideology of the Grooved Ware People, Minoans, Egyptians, Cistercians, Knights Templar, and Freemasons. Interpretation: Observance and reverence of Venus by ancient civilizations has been practiced for thousands of years.

3. Retired Professor of Astronomy and Physics at the University of Rhode Island William Penhallow has documented numerous solar and lunar alignments within the Newport Tower. The three largest windows (W-1, 2, and 3) were constructed to allow both moonlight and sunlight to pass through during important celestial events such as equinoxes, solstices, and eclipses. Penhallow proposes that by capturing lunar eclipses, the builders could determine longitude. Interpretation: The Newport Tower is a sophisticated structure built for highly practical purposes such as a calendar, a clock and for determining longitude.

4. There are two windows in the southeast (W-6) and west (W-7) sides and within roughly one foot of the top of the Newport Tower. Two niches (N-4 and N-2) are built into the inner walls on the opposite sides of the two upper windows. The altitude of both lines connecting W-6 to N-4 and W-7 to N-2 is approximately 22 degrees. The planet Venus is located in the southeastern sky as a morning star and appears in the western sky as an evening star. Interpretation: The 22 degree angle of both alignments appears consistent with the builders incorporating Venus alignments into the Tower for apparent religious reasons.

5. Astronomical alignments of the sun, moon, and Venus are captured within many structures across time and include the early stone chambers and standing stone sites, grave mounds, Solomon's Temple, and the great Gothic Cathedrals across Europe and Scandinavia. Interpretation: Astronomical alignments were considered important for religious and practical reasons such as determin-

ing time, configuring the annual calendar, and studying solar and lunar eclipses for calculating longitude.

Conclusions: Astronomical alignments are an important clue to the culture and ideology of the builders of structures that capture them. There are solar and lunar alignments, and apparently Venus alignments built into the Newport Tower. These alignments are consistent with Cistercian/Templar construction of religious structures.

Spirit Pond Rune Stones Facts

1. All three Spirit Pond Rune Stone inscriptions contain the Hooked X. Interpretation: The Spirit Pond carvers are likely related to the carver of the Kensington Rune Stone.

2. All three Spirit Pond Rune Stone inscriptions are carved in runes using medieval Old Swedish. Interpretation: Another clue that the carvers are linked to the Kensington Rune Stone carver.

3. The Spirit Pond Inscription Stone is dated to 1401 (once) and 1402 (twice) using the medieval Easter Table dating practice. Interpretation: Yet another link to the Kensington Rune Stone carver.

4. The Spirit Pond Inscription Stone has seven barred runes that correspond to six of the dotted runes on the Ukna slab (Sm 145) from Småland, Sweden, circa 1325. Interpretation: These extremely rare runes are consistent with a medieval origin and highly unlikely to be known by a modern forger.

5. The Spirit Pond Map Stone is dated to 1402 using the medieval Easter Table dating practice. Interpretation: The date was important to the carver of the Map Stone and provides another link to the Kensington Rune Stone carver.

6. The Spirit Pond Map Stone has the same arced X symbol (X̄) that appears on only one known medieval French astrolabe (# 191) that is dated circa 1350 to 1400. Interpretation: This symbol fingerprints both the arced X and the Spirit Pond Map Stone to medieval times. The possibility of a modern forger being aware of and understanding this virtually unknown symbol is untenable.

7. The arced X symbol (X̄) on the various latitude plates of astrolabe #191 was used for the number 40 and appears to be a combination of the Roman number ten (X) and the Hindu-Arabic number four

(ᚷ). Interpretation: This unique symbol is ingenious and serves as an indicator of the high intelligence of the creators of the symbol.

8. The pentadic number 44, in a different type than the Kensington Rune Stone, Spirit Pond Inscription Stone and Map side of the Spirit Pond Map Stone, appears on the symbol side of the Spirit Pond Map Stone. Interpretation: The carver understood different types of pentadic numbers.

9. The Spirit Pond Rune Stones were discovered near Popham Beach, Maine, which is very near latitude 44 degrees north. Interpretation: The carver knew the latitude of Popham Beach, Maine, and appears to have been indicating with the carved effigies on the Symbol side of the Spirit Pond Map Stone what was at that location.

10. The floorboard piece of wood collected from an archaeological site near the Spirit Pond Rune Stones discovery site was dated to about 1405. Interpretation: The archaeological site at Spirit Pond is likely connected to the rune stones and should be further investigated.

11. Astrolabe #191 has twelve plates that correspond to the latitudes of 38, 41, 42, 45, 46, 47, 48, 49, 50, 55, 57, and 58 degrees north. Interpretation: These plates could have been used to sail from Europe and Scandinavia to Iceland, Greenland, Newfoundland, Nova Scotia, Maine, and Narragansett Bay and then back again.

12. The Spirit Pond Map Stone says that Vinland is two days sail south from the Popham Beach, Maine, area. Interpretation: The carver likely had already been to the area then known as Vinland.

13. The area around Cape Cod and Martha's Vineyard, Massachusetts, and Narragansett Bay, Rhode Island, is roughly two days sail south from Popham Beach, Maine. Interpretation: This area along the East Coast of North America is Vinland.

Conclusions: The factual evidence such as the barred runes, numerous linguistic features, the medieval Easter Table dating, the arced X on astrolabe #191, and the Hooked X are consistent with all three Spirit Pond Rune Stones being genuine medieval artifacts since they were all found together. The arced X and the pentadic number 44 on the Map Stone, and the arced

X on astrolabe #191, indicate the Map Stone is referring to the location of 44 degrees latitude north where the Spirit Pond Rune Stones were found.

The Narragansett Rune Stone

1. The Hooked X appears within the nine-character inscription. Interpretation: The Narragansett stone carver is likely connected to the carvers of the Kensington and Spirit Pond rune stones.
2. Only three of the nine characters (ᚻ, ✳ and X) in the inscription are found on either the Kensington or Spirit Pond Rune Stones. Interpretation: The inscription is a unique North American runic inscription and was not copied from any of the other runic inscriptions.
3. The glacial boulder the inscription is carved into is a sedimentary rock called a graywacke that contains a relatively high quartz content. Interpretation: The rock type is relatively stable allowing the inscription to weather very slowly thereby increasing the likelihood it could be centuries old.
4. The inscription is currently only visible for approximately twenty minutes a day. Interpretation: The likelihood of a hoaxer carving an inscription on a boulder with such scant visibility is highly problematic and unlikely.

Conclusions: The Narragansett runic inscription was not copied from the Kensington Rune Stone or Spirit Pond Rune Stones. The high quartz content makes the inscription more resistant to weathering in the relatively harsh environment in the waters of Narragansett Bay. The presence of the Hooked X indicates a likely medieval origin and a connection to the Cistercians and Knights Templar.

Prince Henry Sinclair

1. Prince Henry Sinclair is believed by many scholars to have been a member of the Knights Templar. The charter of the Scottish Rite Freemasons appoints the head of the Sinclair Clan as the hereditary Grand Master.
2. Prince Henry and his Sinclair ancestors had Norse heritage dating

back to into the Viking period (prior to 1000 A.D.). Interpretation: These familial contacts made it highly likely he had knowledge of the New World prior to 1398.

3. Prince Henry Sinclair reportedly sailed from Scotland to North America in 1398. Interpretation: Since clergy routinely traveled on voyages such as this and with the Cistercians so closely linked to the Templars, a Cistercian monk would very likely have traveled on a Templar ship such as Prince Henry Sinclair's. This could explain a connection to the Spirit Pond and Narragansett Rune Stones, and the Newport Tower.

4. Rosslyn Chapel in Scotland was constructed by Prince Henry's grandson, William Sinclair in 1446, in part to honor his grandfather's trip to the New World. Interpretation: This is consistent with many scholars' research and many of the carvings within the structure.

5. Aloe leaves and maize (corn) were carved into a beam and above a window in Rosslyn Chapel prior to Columbus' voyage to the New World. Interpretation: The most plausible way this information could have been acquired is if Prince Henry had been to North America and interacted with the Natives, and several members of his party returned to Scotland.

6. King Robert the Bruce of Scotland fought alongside Prince Henry's grandfather, Sir William Sinclair; his great-grandfather, Sir Henry St. Clair; and his great-granduncle, William St. Clair at Bannockburn in 1314. Bruce's death mask carved in stone is in Rosslyn Chapel. Interpretation: Both William Sinclair and Robert the Bruce were Templars. Many of the fugitive Templars who fled France after the arrest order in 1307 went to Scotland and joined Robert the Bruce to fight their common enemy in the British.

Conclusions: Prince Henry Sinclair was a Templar Knight and likely sailed secretly to the New World around 1398. Prince Henry was likely in Popham Beach in the time period of 1401-1402. A Cistercian monk of Scandinavian background and capable of carving the Spirit Pond Rune Stones was likely on that trip. Prince Henry probably sailed two days south into the Cape Cod/Narragansett Bay around 1400.

Newport Tower

1. The architecture of the Newport Tower is similar to the two-story altar at Tomar, Portugal, which is a replication of the Church of the Holy Sepulcher in Jerusalem. Interpretation: Both were built as religious structures consistent with Templar architecture and religious beliefs.
2. The Newport Tower was built using architecture that is not consistent with pre-Colonial construction practices before the first known recording in Benedict Arnold's will in 1677. Interpretation: The Newport Tower is pre-Colonial.
3. Based on Jørgen Siemonsen's 1997 photogrametric data the standard unit of measurement used to construct the Tower was 0.4666 meters. This is the same unit of measurement used to construct the round Templar churches Østerlars and Nylars, on the island of Bornholm in Denmark in the twelfth century as demonstrated by Erling Haagensen in his 1993 book, *Bornholm Mysterium*. Interpretation: Since the standard unit of measurement used in construction throughout New England in the seventeenth century was the English foot, the Newport Tower was not built by the seventeenth century colonists.
4. After studying a 1997 Danish report on Carbon-14 dating of mortar from the Newport Tower Professor Andre J. Bethune wrote "Thus the Carbon-14 analysis of these three 2 fractions of gas gives us an indication that Newport Tower was standing in the years 1440-1480." Interpretation: Construction of the Newport Tower could date to 1400.
5. Numerous solar and lunar alignments were documented in the Tower by Professor Emeritus William Penhallow. Interpretation: The builders of the Tower considered astronomical alignments to be important.
6. The remains of two wooden posts spaced equidistant from two columns were found during a salvage archaeological dig in June of 2008. Interpretation: The posts are consistent with the previous presence of an ambulatory around the tower.

7. A shell fragment with mortar attached was collected during the June 2008 archaeological dig and was carbon-dated to 1450 A.D., plus or minus thirty years. Interpretation: The 1450 date likely represents the original construction of the tower, or when the tower was subsequently repaired.

8. The keystones in the west-northwest facing archway of the Tower are egg-shaped (on the interior) and have the symbolic fluted wedge-shape (on the exterior) consistent with the medieval practice of stone masons associated with secret orders or guilds. Interpretation: Both keystones were made by medieval stonemasons and are symbolically important to medieval Templars and modern Freemasons.

9. On the winter solstice a rectangular box of sunlight from the rising sun passes through the south window of the Tower and illuminates the egg-shaped keystone in the west-northwest archway. Interpretation: This event was intentionally built into the Tower and likely represents important religious symbolism to the builders.

10. A large, round, red-colored granite boulder sits directly above the symbolic fluted wedge-shaped keystone on the exterior of the Tower. Interpretation: The red orb was symbolically important to the builders and likely represents either the sun or the planet Venus, as a directional indicator.

11. The angle of a line drawn from the center of the round Tower through the symbolic keystones, which are not centered in the west-northwest facing archway, is seventeen degrees. Interpretation: The placement of the keystones in this specific archway was intentional.

12. The angle of a line extending from Newport, Rhode Island, to Kensington, Minnesota, from a line running due west from Newport, Rhode Island, is seventeen degrees. Interpretation: The symbolic keystones intentionally point in the direction of the Kensington Rune Stone indicating the builders likely knew of its existence and indicates the Tower was built after 1362.

Conclusions: The architecture and astronomical alignments in the

Newport Tower suggest a construction date of around 1400 A.D. The ability to calculate longitude by use of alignments could explain the purpose of the Tower as the prime meridian for Templar settlers in the New World. The likelihood that Prince Henry Sinclair sailed south into the Narragansett Bay area, as suggested on the Spirit Pond Map Stone, makes him the most likely historical candidate as the builder of the Newport Tower. The symbolic keystones pointing to Kensington suggests the Tower was probably built *after* the Kensington Rune Stone was carved and buried. The red granite orb above the exterior keystone likely indicates that a returning party to the center of the continent (Minnesota) likely followed the planet Venus as an evening star in the west. Once in the vicinity of the Kensington Rune Stone, the stone holes would pin point the location of the land claim stone.

The Hooked X

1. The Hooked X appears in five runic inscriptions found in North America in Minnesota, Maine, and Rhode Island. Interpretation: These inscriptions were likely carved by Cistercian monks educated in the Baltic region of Scandinavia.
2. The Hooked X appears on dated inscriptions from two exploration parties during a forty-year period (1362 to 1402 A.D). Interpretation: At least two secret missions came to North America with at least one Cistercian monk and Templar Knights aboard on each trip.
3. The Hooked X appears in Christopher Columbus' sigla after he returned from his trips to the New World. Interpretation: Columbus was a Templar (Knight of Christ).
4. The Hooked X appears in the Larsson Rune Rows as the symbol for "a" and "ä" in 1883 and 1885. Interpretation: The original source of the Larsson Rune Rows was likely a nineteenth century Freemason or Knight Templar.
5. The Swedish text above the rune row in which the Hooked X appears in the Larsson Papers was referred to as ". . . the Secret Style." Interpretation: The alphabet was known within a secret organization such as the Freemasons or Knights Templar.

6. Edward Larsson was a tailor and is believed to have copied the rune rows from a document that belonged to a Swedish Freemason. Interpretation: Either Edward Larsson was himself a Freemason, or he copied the rune rows from a document he may have found in a customer's costume who was a Freemason.

7. The first known medieval "X for a" symbol was found being used as a code in a fifteenth-century Cistercian document of German provenance in a 2001 publication. Interpretation: Both the "X for a" and the Hooked X used in runic inscriptions in North America and Scandinavia are medieval.

8. The Hooked X symbol is found at Rosslyn Chapel used as a mason's mark. Interpretation: At least one stone mason who worked at Rosslyn chapel in the fifteenth century likely understood the symbolism of this unique character.

Conclusions: The Hooked X is an important coded runic symbol likely created by Cistercian monks. The "X" is symbolic of the allegorical representation of the duality, equality and balance of man and woman, and heaven and earth. The hook in the "X" is symbolic of the child or offspring, representative of the continuation and perpetuation of the "Goddess" ideology through common bloodlines and thought. The Hooked X could also be a reference to the belief that Jesus and Mary Magdalene were married and had a child many believe was named Sarah.

Final Conclusion

Based on the geological, astronomical, runological, linguistic, architectural, and historical evidence, the Cistercians and Templars (Teutonic Knights and/or the Knights of Christ) in the late 14th/early 15th centuries are the only logical candidates to explain the origin of the five North American rune stones, the Newport Tower and the Hooked X.

The Goddess

While it would seem that many ancient cultures, and many Freemasons, believe that God is a female deity, it doesn't mean that it is true. No one knows for sure who or what God is. The answer to those questions can only be answered on an individual basis.

References

Bellec, François, *Unknown Lands: The Log Books of the Great Explorers,* The Overland Press, Peter Mayer Publishers, Woodstock and New York, New York, 2000.

Bernard of Clairvaux, *In Praise of the New Knighthood: A Treatise on the Knights Templar and the Holy Places of Jerusalem*, Translated by M. Conrad Greenia, Cistercian Publications, Kalamazoo, Michigan, 1963, Introduction by Malcolm Barber, 2000.

Bernier, Francine, *The Great Architects of Tiron,* The Steps of Zion-ULT, Arizona, 2005.

Bernier, Francine, *The Templars Legacy in Montreal*, Frontier Publishing, the Netherlands, 2001.

Brighton, Simon, *In Search of the Knights Templar: A Guide to the Sites in Britain,* Weidenfeld & Nicolson, The Orion Publishing Group, 2006.

Brown, Ian F., *Born on the Bottom Rung,* The Glasgow and West of Scotland Family Historical Society, Glasgow, Scotland, 2006.

Brown, Ian F., *The Drummonds of Madeira & Christopher Columbus,* The Glasgow and West of Scotland Family Historical Society, Glasgow, Spring 1993 Newsletter.

Bruce-Mitford, Miranda, *The Illustrated Book of Signs and Symbols,* Dorling Kindersley Limited, London, England, 1996.

Butler, Alan and Dafoe, Stephen, *The Knights Templar Revealed,* Barnes & Noble Publishing Inc., 1999.

Butler, Alan and Ritchie, John, *Rosslyn Revealed*, O Books, United Kingdom, 2006.

Butler, Alan, *The Virgin and the Pentacle: The Freemasonic Plot to Destroy the Church,* O Books, United Kingdom, 2005.

Butler, Alan, *Sheep: The Remarkable Story of the Humble Animal that Built the Modern World,* O Books, United Kingdom, 2006.

Butler, Alan, *The Goddess, the Grail, and the Lodge,* O Books, United Kingdom, 2006.

Cartocci, Alice and Rosati, Gloria, *Egyptian Art*, Barnes & Noble, New York, 2007.

Carlson, Suzanne and Dranchak, John, *The Newport Tower: Arnold to Zeno,* NEARA Publications, Edgecomb, Massachusetts, 2006.

Chapman, Paul H., "Discovering Columbus," The Institute for the Study of American Cultures, Columbus, Georgia, 31902.

Cooper, J.C., *An Illustrated Encyclopedia of Traditional Symbols,* Thames & Hudson Ltd, London, England, 1978.

Cowie, Ashley, *The Rosslyn Matrix*, Wicker World Limited, East Kilbride, England, 2006.

Desroches-Noblecourt, Christine, *Tutankhamen: Life and Death of a Pharaoh,* New York Graphic Society, 1963.

Feather, Robert, *The Mystery of the Copper Scroll of Qumran: The Essene Record of the Treasure of Akhenaten*, Bear & Company, Rochester, Vermont, 2003.

Fiske, John, *New France and New England*, Houghton, Mifflin and Company, Boston, Massachusetts, 1902.

France, James, *Medieval Images of Saint Bernard of Clairvaux*, Cistercian Publications Inc., Kalamazoo, Michigan, 2007.

Francoise, Henry, *The Book of Kells: Reproductions from the Manuscript in Trinity College*, Dublin, Thames and Hudson, London, England, 1974.

Francoise, Henry, *The Cistercians in Scandinavia*, Cistercian Publications Inc., Kalamazoo, Michigan, 1992.

Folda, Jaroslav, *Crusader Art: The Art of the Crusaders in the Holy Land, 1099-1291*, Lund Humphries, Burlington, Vermont, 2008.

Gadon, Elinor, W., *The Once & Future Goddess: A Sweeping Chronicle of the Sacred Feminine and Her Reemergence in the Cultural Mythology of Our Time*, Harper San Francisco, 1989.

Gahlin, Lucia, *Egypt: Gods, Myths and Religion*, Lorenz Books, New York, 2001.

Gardner, Laurence, *Bloodline of the Holy Grail: The Hidden Lineage of Jesus Revealed*, Barnes & Noble Inc., 2001.

Graves, Robert, *The White Goddess: A Historical Grammar of Poetic Myth*, Farrar, Straus and Giroux, New York, New York, 1948.

Gunther, Robert, T., *Astrolabes of the World*, The Holland Press, London, 1932, Reprinted 1976.

Haagensen, Erling, and Lincoln, Henry, *The Templars' Secret Island: The Knights, the Priest, and the Treasure,* Barnes and Noble inc., 2002.

Hall, Manley, *The Secret Teachings of All Ages*, Penguin Group Inc., New York, N.Y., 1909, reprinted in 2003.

Harwood, Jeremy, *The Secret History of Freemasonry*, Anness Publishing Ltd, London, 2006.

Hodge, Susie, *The Knights Templar: Discovering the Myth and Reality of a Legendary Brotherhood*, Hermes House, London, England, 2006.

James, T.G.H., *Tutankhamun*, Friedman/Fairfax Publishers, Vercelli, Italy, 2000.

Kinder, Terryl, N, *Cistercian Europe: Architecture of Contemplation*, Cistercian Publications, Institute of Cistercian Studies, Western Michigan University, Kalamazoo, Michigan, 2002.

King, David A, *The Ciphers of the Monks*, Franz Stiener Verlag, Stuttgart, 2001.

King, Peter, *The Finances of the Cistercian Order in the Fourteenth Century*, Cistercian Publications, Kalamazoo, Michigan, 1985.

Knight, Christopher and Robert Lomas, *The Book of Hiram*, Barnes & Noble Publishing, Inc., New York, 2005.

Lawler, Robert, *Sacred Geometry: Philosophy & Practice*, The Crossroads Publishing Company, New York, New York, 1982.

Leroux-Dhuys, Jean-Francois, *Cistercian Abbeys: History and Architecture*, Könemann, Paris, France, 1998.

Lithberg, Nils, *Computus*, Nordiska Museets handlingar 29, Stockholm, 1953.

Lithberg, Nils, and Elias Wessén, *Den Gotländska runkalenderen 1328 [The Gotlandic Runic Calendar of 1328]*, Kungl, Vitterhets *Historie och Antikitets Akademien handlingar*, Item 45.2, Stockholm.

Martin, Ernest L., *Female Sex Signs in Churches*, http://askelm.com/doctrine/d981127.htm, November 27, 1998.

Means, Phillip Ainsworth, *Newport Tower*, Henry Holt and Company, New York, 1942.

Mitchell, John, *At the Center of the World: Polar Symbolism Discovered in Celtic, Norse and Other Ritualized Landscapes*, Thames and Hudson Ltd, London, England, 1994.

Millar, Angel, *Freemasonry: A History*, Thunder Bay Press, San Diego, California, 2005.

Monk, Michael A. and John Sheeban, *Early Medieval Munster: Archaeology, History and Society*, Cork University Press, Cork, Ireland, 1998.

Montgomery, Hugh, *The God-Kings of Europe: The Descendents of Jesus Traced through the Odonic and Davidic Dynasties*, The Book Tree, San Diego, California, 2006.

Montgomery, Hugh, *The God-Kings of England*, The Temple Publications, Wells, United Kingdom, 2007.

Morison, Samuel Eliot, *Christopher Columbus: The Voyage of Discovery 1492*, Brompton Books Corporation, 1991.

Nielsen, Richard, *An Old Norse Translation of the Spirit Pond Inscriptions of Maine*, Epigraphic Society of Occasional Papers, pp. 158-217, Volume 22, 1993.

Novaresio, Paolo, *The Explorers*, White Star Publishers, Vercelli, Italy, 2004.

Ovason, David, *The Secret Architecture of Our Nation's Capitol: The Masons and the Building of Washington, D.C.*, Century Books Limited, London, United Kingdom, 1999.

Peck, William H. and Ross, John G., *Egyptian Drawings*, E.P. Dutton, New York, 1978.

Pendergast, John, *Bend in the River*, Merrimac River Press, Massachusetts, 1992.

Pohl, Frederick J., *Prince Henry Sinclair: His Expedition to the New World in 1398*, Davis-Poynter Limited, London, England, 1974.

Robinson, John J., *Born in Blood: The Lost Secrets of Freemasonry*, M. Evans and Company, New York, New York, 1989.

Romer, John, *Valley of the Kings*, Castle Books, Edison, New Jersey, 2003/1981.

Rosslyn, Helen and Maggi, Angelo, *Rosslyn: Country of Painter and Poet*, National Gallery of Scotland, 2002.

Rozenberg, Silvia (Editor), *Knights of the Holy Land: The Crusader Kingdom of Jerusalem*, The Israel Museum, Jerusalem, 1999.

Schütz, Bernard, *Great Monasteries of Europe*, Abbeville Press Publishers, New York/London, 2004.

Schütz, Bernhard, *Great Cathedrals*, Harry N. Abrams, Inc., Publishers, New York, New York, 2002.

Seaver, Kirsten A., *The Frozen Echo: Greenland and the Exploration of North America ca A.D. 1000-1500*, Stanford University Press, Stanford, California, 1996.

Sinclair, Niven, *Beyond Any Shadow of Doubt*, 1998.

Toman, Rolf and Bednorz, Achim, *Romanesque: Architecture, Sculpture, Painting*, Könemann, Paris, France, 2004.

Urban, William, *The Teutonic Knights: A Military History*, MBI Publishing Company, St. Paul, Minnesota, 2003.

Wicca-Spirituality.com, *Wicca Goddess Symbols/Traditional Goddess Symbols*, 2006-2007.

Weir, Anthony, and Jerman, James, *Images of Lust: Sexual Carvings on Medieval Churches*, Batsford Academic and Educational, an imprint of B.T. Batsford, Ltd., London, England, 1986.

Wolter, Scott F., and Nielsen, Richard, *The Kensington Rune Stone: Compelling New Evidence*, Lake Superior Agate Publishing, Chanhassen, Minnesota, 2006.

Yazawa, Mel (Editor), *The Diary and Life of Samuel Sewall*, The Bedford Books in History and Culture, Boston, Massachusetts, 1998.

Young, Alan and Stead, Michael J., *In the Footsteps of Robert Bruce*, Sutton Publishing Limited, Glouchester, United Kingdom, 1999.

Index

216, 231, 234, 237, 243, 245, 246, 248, 259, 261, 265, 266.
Horn rock, 117.
Horns of Venus, 156, 198, 199.

Innocent II, 56, 256.
Institute of Dialectology, Onomastics and Folklore Research in Umeå (DAUM), 107-109.
Irish Ogham, vii, 66.
Iron oxide, 8.
Isis, 56, 92, 93, 95, 199.

J.V. Fletcher Library, 177, 178, 189.
Jefferson Meridian, 243.
Jerusalem, 38, 55, 82, 83, 128, 153, 154, 181-183, 185, 187, 190, 234, 256, 263.
Jesus Christ, 90, 217.
Johansson, Sven-Erik, 16.
Johnson, Captain John, 124, 125.
Johnson, Gunnar, 23, 24.
Junkel, Paul, 87.

Kåring, Göran, 46.
Kennebec River, 75, 80, 85.
Kensington alignment, 221, 222, 265.
Kensington, Minnesota, ix, x, 3, 4, 8, 9, 17, 18, 20, 23, 24, 40, 41, 88, 115, 159, 219, 222, 224, 225, 227, 264.
Kensington Rune Stone, viii, x-xii, 3-19, 22-28, 31-40, 43-46, 58-60, 63, 65, 66, 70, 73, 75, 77, 85-90, 92, 96, 98, 104, 106-108, 110-112, 115, 116, 123, 124, 129, 131-136, 140, 141, 147, 151, 159, 161, 163, 166, 169, 172, 211, 212, 219, 220, 223, 230, 234, 236-238, 240, 247, 248, 250, 252-255, 258, 260, 261, 264, 265.
Keystone illumination, 208, 240.
King, David, 77, 97, 99, 100, 102, 110, 112.
King "Phillip the Fair," 56, 57.
Kilwinning Abbey, Scotland, 250.
Kirkwall Cathedral, 191.
Knight, Christopher, 198, 200, 214.
Knights of Christ, 60, 89, 104-106, 186, 234, 265, 266.
Knights Templar, x, xi, 38, 54, 55, 57, 60, 87, 89, 91-94, 104, 105, 120, 121, 133-136, 146, 147, 154, 161, 176, 180, 181, 187, 192, 210, 211, 216, 225, 228, 231,

232, 234, 236, 237, 242, 245, 246, 250, 255-258, 261, 262, 265, 266.
Kolberg, Thomas, 16-18, 88, 89.
Kolberg-Streeter, Joanne, 16, 17.
Krueger, Ben, 152.
Kunze, Bruce, 41, 42.

L'Anse aux Meadows, 106.
LaBrede Church, 217.
Ladd, Seneca A., 154.
Lafayette Park, Washington, D.C., 244.
Lake Minnetonka, Minnesota, 124-127, 129.
Land claim, 12, 36, 37, 39-41, 44, 67, 117, 123, 131, 132, 219, 223-225, 255, 265.
Lane, Elizabeth, 124, 125, 127, 129.
Lärbro Church, Sweden, 14, 50-53.
Larson, Clarence, 19.
Larsson, Edward, 107, 110-112, 265.
Larsson Papers, viii, 90, 98, 107, 108, 110-112, 265.
Lawler, Robert, 111, 125.
Lawrence, Abbot, 240.
Lawrence, Dawn and Steve, 164.
Leduc, Gerard, xii.
Lenik, Edward, 188.
Lewis, Bob, 72.
Lieffort, Al, 41, 43.
Lincoln, Henry, 38, 41.
Lomas, Robert, 198, 200, 214.
Lossing, Benson John, 205.
Lumber Exchange Building, 128.
Lummelunda Church, Sweden, 48.
Lund Bone, 13.
Lye Church, Gotland, Sweden, 59, 61, 213.
Lynch, Rick, 169, 183, 190.

Magdalene, Mary, 38, 46, 90, 149, 156, 214, 266.
Maltese cross, 60.
Mann, William, xii, 91, 133, 138, 186.
Martin, Ernest L., 213.
Maulbronn Abbey, Germany, 182.
Means, Philip Ainsworth, 191.
Mellifont Abbey, Ireland, 203.
Melrose Abbey, Scotland, 183.
Meridian Hill Park, 244, 245.
Mi'kMaq Indians, 134, 135.
Michlovic, Michael, 67, 110.
Milbank, South Dakota, 116, 118.
Minnesota Historical Society, 19, 22, 23, 25.